AF569564

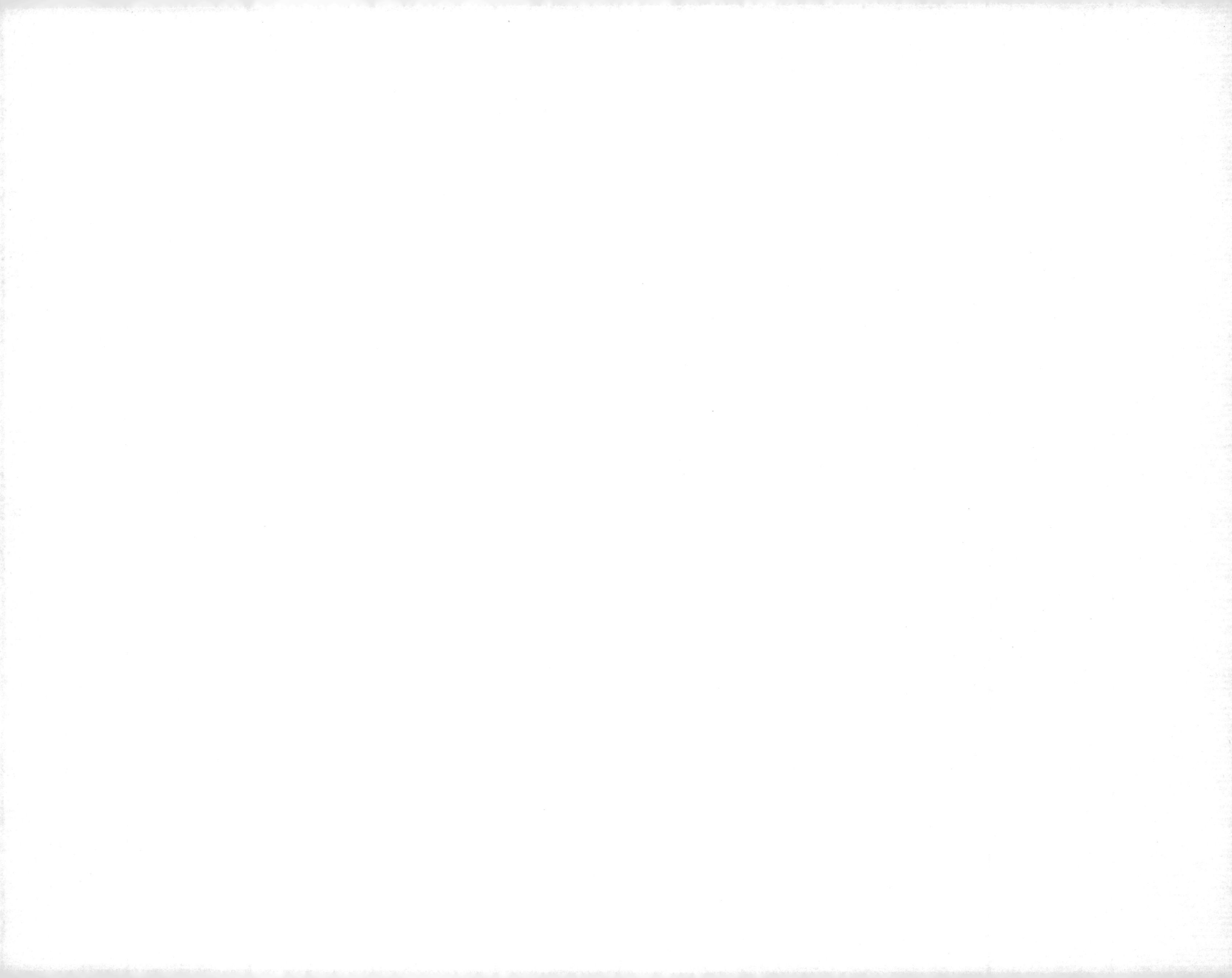

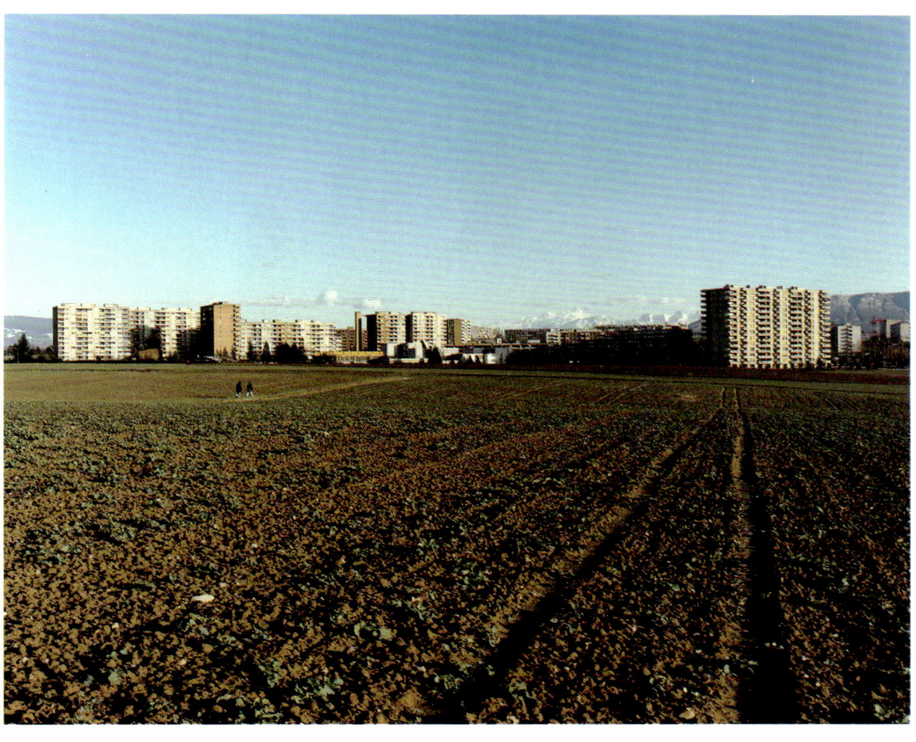

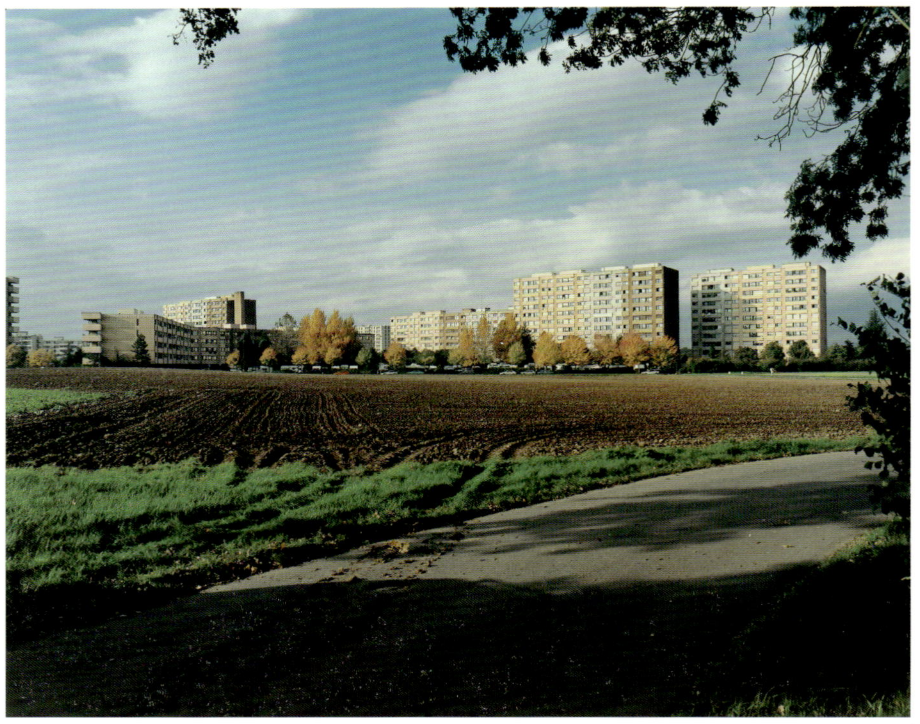

The Publisher wishes to thank the Commune de Meyrin whose generous support made this project come to life.

Citizens of the World — Meyrin | Photographs by Nicolas Faure, texts by André Klopmann

Translated from the French by Stephen Sartarelli | Design: Hans Werner Holzwarth, Design pur, Berlin | Production: Steidl, Göttingen

Distributed in North America by D.A.P., New York City, distributed in Europe and Asia by Thames and Hudson, London

 | First Scalo Edition, 1995 | ISBN 1-881616-52-5 | Printed in Germany

Photographs by Nicolas Faure

Citizens of the World—Meyrin

Texts by André Klopmann

Commune de Meyrin Scalo Zurich – Berlin – New York

I dedicate this book to my son Mathias—Nicolas Faure

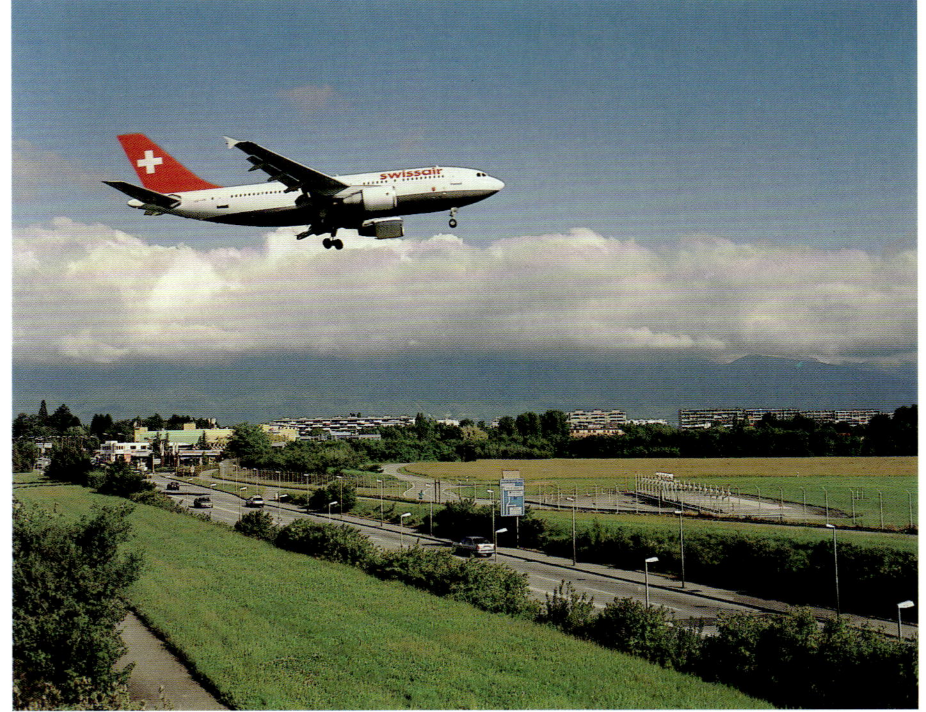

Meyrin, Citizens of the World: A Unique Experience, in All the World

This book is the culmination of a project born at the beginning of the 1990s. A photographer living in our city, Nicolas Faure—whose recent reputation I had yet to discover—came to see me and shared with me his surprise at a rare peculiarity in a city of twenty thousand souls: the presence of inhabitants from over one hundred different nations! Yes, this rather modest town—with a population perhaps the equivalent of a couple of apartment blocks in a large urban center—has become the permanent home of foreign nationals from the five continents.... At that moment, I became quickly convinced that the project proposed by our photographer—to make portraits of a certain number of these inhabitants in their family environments, "at home"—should be supported and promoted as much as possible. At this same time the municipal government was building a cultural center, the *Meyrin Forum,* which was to have, among other features, some rooms for art exhibition. It became clear that we had on our hands the very subject that would inaugurate those spaces at the opening of the whole complex in early September 1995.

A fine idea, an exhibition; but there was reason to fear that once it closed, the memory of it might fade just as quickly. It thus seemed desireable, to the various partners involved in this venture, to leave behind a record of it in the form of a publication. You are presently holding in your hands the object conceived to this end. It is one element of Meyrin's cultural patrimony that is thus secured, and for a long time.

Complementing the photographer's vision is the writing of one of the finest pens of Genevan journalism, that of André Klopmann, who while chiseling a few gems in these pages, has also proved a sensitive witness to the paths of suffering. But for this work to come to fruition, it was necessary for Walter Keller of *Scalo Publishers* to show a keen interest in it and involve the prestige of that house to this end. I take this opportunity to thank all these people, as well as the actors in this story, our citizens from abroad, for their enthusiastic support of to the project.

At a time when unfortunate divisions of ethnicity, race and religion are spilling blood in many different parts of the world, Meyrin, the "radiant city", we daresay, bears witness to the possiblility, and even success, of cohabitation among these ethnic groups, races and religions. Yes, the possibility of living together does exist.

May this experience attract the attention of other communities and countries, in Switzerland and elsewhere. May others draw inspiration from it when reflecting on their own existence. May *Citizens of the World—Meyrin* serve as an example for other original projects, that artistic vision may leave a lasting impression in our cities and consciences.

On behalf of the authorities:
Roger Portier,
Mayor

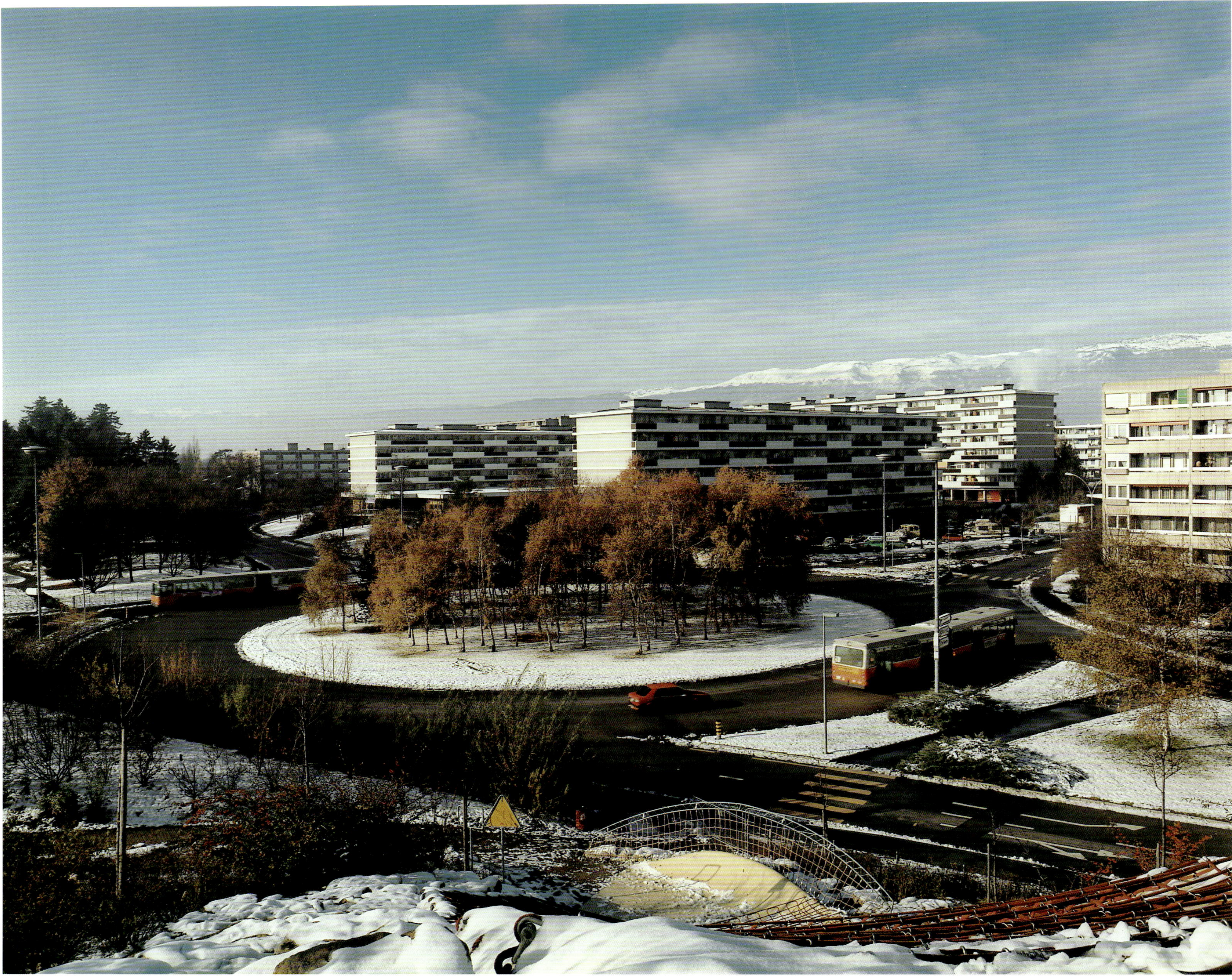

Introduction

In the 1960s, when politicians and urban planners huddled together to study the disturbing demographic statistics, they gravely predicted a minor apocalypse on the horizon. The cities were going to explode. We would no longer know where to put babies, industries, cemeteries. Unless we built the cities entirely upward, as Le Corbusier had already prescribed, agriculture would soon give way to concrete. Were we heading toward megalopoles, where work and leisure would be strictly linked, or toward the explosion of all sectors? Such were the stark alternatives, soon settled by visionaries more technocratic than learned. They decided that satellite cities would be built around the established cities, like so many moons around the earth, to unclog the saturated urban centers. Geneva would have the center, the industry, and the services; the satellite cities, residence and recreation. At the start and end of the day, the population would travel between the areas of economic activity, and the clustered residences that had to be built in the countryside. No sooner said than done. Meyrin suddenly appeared before the eyes of the Genevans like a mushroom after a rainstorm: the wide open spaces of a small village on the way to the French border would soon be covered with a new architecture. The city in the country—the optimists hailed the genius of the idea. The pessimists, disoriented, looking for the center, the movie-houses, the businesses and not finding them, were quick to point out the limitations of such a project and even invented a stinging term to describe it: the dormitory-city. At the same time, one took to reflecting on the very notion of collective recreation. In France, between two wisps of smoke, André Malraux glimpsed the Maisons des Jeunes et de la Culture (Youth and Culture Houses) he was to count on to channel the creative and even reconstructive passions of a youth in the throes of gloom. In Geneva, in rue du Prieuré, the police and groups of youths would clash around an "autonomous center" that already prefigured the great misunderstanding: the young people wanted spaces for themselves, not places authorized by adults. Twenty years later, on the banks of the Rhône, in the quarter of la Jonction (with l'Arve), l'Usine would confirm the feasibility of such a concept. As for the *Maison des Jeunes* in Geneva, it changed its name, putting an epoch to rest and taking on the name of the district in which it is located, Saint-Gervais. It was originally created to channel a revolt; today it is a cultural institution. In the interim, the satellite-cities have become real cities. Some would turn out badly, like those which the children of immigrants in France vandalized in the early 1980s because they were symbols of exclusion. Others became happy places, like Meyrin, which, thanks to good political management, was able to grow in a balanced, harmonious fashion.

I am one of these children of Geneva whose great passion for his city has led him to know everything about its history, but who knew nothing about this nearby Meyrin. Except for its bad reputation, which stuck to it tenaciously. A group of concrete boxes: such was the general image of it. We had no idea of the rich past of this outlying town, whose traces of human settlement stretched back to the iron age, and whose ancient burial sites were discovered during the construction of the airport; not a clue as to the effects that the successive administrations of the Dukes of Savoy, their Excellencies of Berne, the Barons of Gex, and the Emperor of France had had on the region before its final integration, in

Abbreviations

CHU—Centre hospitalo-universitaire; university hospital

IAEA—International Atomic Energy Agency

ICRC—International Committee of the Red Cross

ILO—International Labor Office

UNCTAD—United Nations Conference on Trade and Development

UNHCR—High Commisssioner for Refugees

WMO—World Meteorological Organization

WIPO—World Intellectual Property Organization

UBS—Union de banques suisses; Union Bank of Switzerland

1816, into the Swiss fold. We didn't even know that the seigneuries had controlled vast tracts of land there, leaving to the modern age a number of fortified manors as well as the communal coat-of-arms, adopted in 1922, an amalgam of the armorial bearings of the Families of Meyrins (with an s) and Livron; nor much more about the quarrels that Catholics and Protestants had engaged in there, as elsewhere. Aware of this collective lacuna, the Commune of Meyrin in 1991 published a large work containing everything: *The History of Meyrin*, an indispensable book realized by the historian Eugène-Louis Dumont. Upon reading it, one realizes how wrong one is to see Meyrin as nothing more than a group of "modern" buildings. And yet! If one looks really hard at them, those same buildings tell not the vertical story of the place, but indeed the horizontal story of the times. There the world unfolds its wounds, and Meyrin heals them. Suceeding its age-old past is the new era brought on by the construction of the modern city. It is a future movement, multicultural and bountiful.

Today, the sight of cows grazing near these same buildings moves me deeply. They speak to me, these cows. They tell me that everyone was wrong in the Sixties, the years when the baby-boomers came of age. First the urban planners who thought they were resolving all the problems by inventing de-centralized cities serving only as residential areas; then those puzzled people who, clinging to the idea of drab cities—drab because seen through prejudiced eyes—were decidedly wanting in curiosity; and lastly, those who pined for a Heimat free of immigrants and who at the time set Switzerland on the way to a heartbreaking isolationism. Today I see Meyrin through different eyes. Technically, its natural evolution has transformed the domitory-town into a veritable city with all the amenities of a metropolis: business, recreation, industry, transport. One can easily live in Meyrin without leaving the area. Socially, the new city, which a third generation is now starting to populate, has even given rise to a kind of local petite bourgeoisie. On the outskirts of the large complexes, some individual homes have sprung up. As one lands at Genève-Cointrin, one can count from the window all the little swimming pools in their little yards, so many signs of a new level of comfort. Philosophically, one could expatiate at great length on the exceptional, unique model today presented by this totally cosmopolitan city, half of whose inhabitants are foreigners. There are, depending on the years, between 100 and 110 different nationalities there. Might it be that the schools at Meyrin are considered among the most dynamic in the canton precisely because of this formidable meeting of cultures? Cultural diversity is not a myth, and the human enrichment it engenders is directly linked to the finest civic model imaginable.

In Geneva a group of people once founded the Red Cross. Others created the League of Nations, which would later become the United Nations. Its affiliated organizations serve science, mutual aid, international dialogue. Matters for bigwigs? Certainly. Geneva today entertains a highly fluctuating, quasi-marital relation with her international partners. In Meyrin, a mirror somewhat out of the range of the cameras, one finds the heart of the world. Diplomats and refugees. People from the north, people from the south. Laborers and intellectuals. Fondue and baklava. Natives and immigrants. Foreigners, some of whom take part in

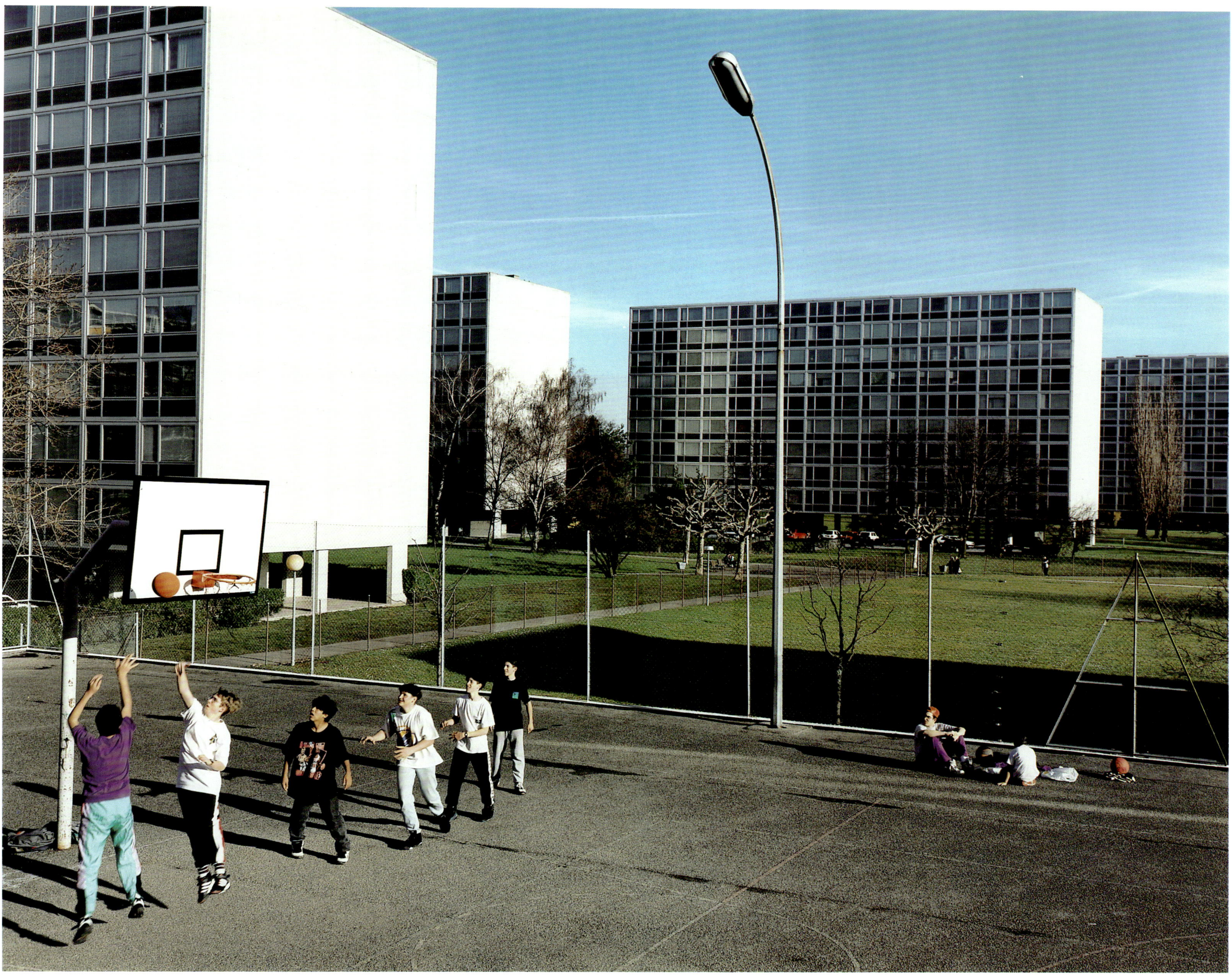

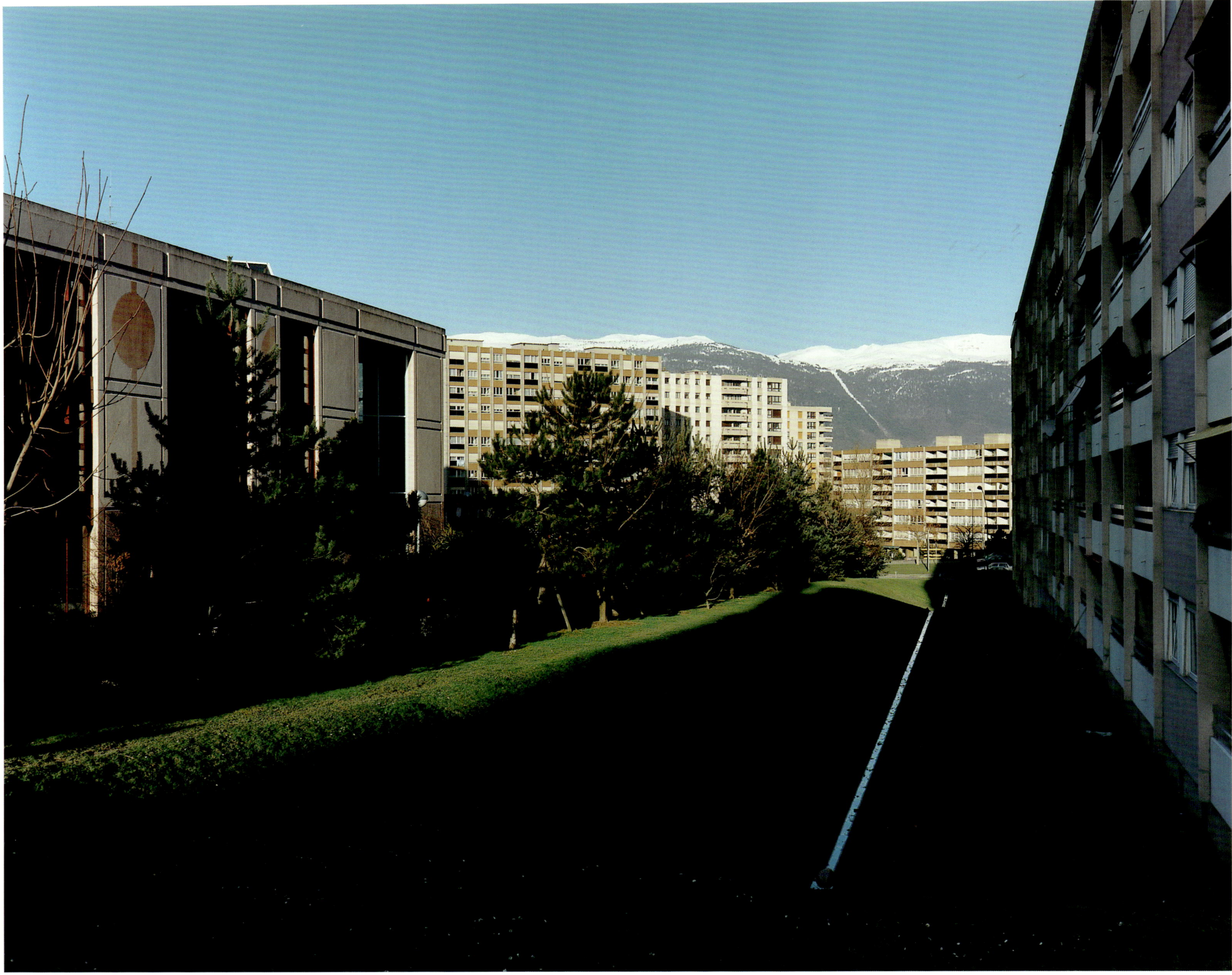

advisory committees; there is even a young people's parliament in Meyrin. A mosaic.

It was time to go out and meet this world. Behind each door there is a different story, and what is so special about these stories taken together is that they tell at once the story of the city, that circumscribed place within a small territory, and that of the vast world struggling to live. It certainly was a bold idea. Nicolas Faure, who conceived it, pleaded his case passionately with the authorities. We are indebted to Michel Aebischer, in charge of cultural affairs, and to the mayor at the time, Roger Portier, for having immediately perceived not the local but the universal character of such an experiment. Today, now that so many wish to exhibit this collection of images, we know that it has a potentially worldwide resonance. At the outset, however, the municipal council had just barely voted in favor of the necessary funding, after a bitter and conflict-filled debate. What's the good of it? asked the skeptics. May this work, in what is not said, furnish them with the answer to their question.

The authors worked for more than three years to put together these pages. It all began with reading lists of names, a rather cold and bureaucratic task, for the purpose of grouping the nationalities while favoring diversity. Then the photographer determined his work-method, which he purposely made uniform as a form of self-effacement in the face of his subjects. In the printing, Maurice Vouga respected this wish for unity by making sure the light was balanced. What matters here is not artistic expression, but the objective conveyance of a power peculiar to the subjects, who were all photographed at home in similar situations. Certain families chose to pose in dress proper to their nationalities, others chose not to. At times it was necessary to temper the garrulity of some, at other times, to reassure those who were more shy. Posing is not an easy thing for someone unaccustomed to it, but Nicolas Faure excels in the art of making people feel at ease. He always went to the families' homes alone; only later did I also visit them, usually alone, sometimes accompanied by one of my children. At that point I had to define my own approach, and I took the opposite way: I decided to vary the texts as much as possible. Like an exercise in style. In the face of the images, which are objective, it is the subjective option that intervenes by way of complement, like a kind of yin and yang. There is no way of knowing, before beginning to write, what the keyboard will yield. Thus the writing is spontaneous in a way, based on concrete notes and abstract emotions.

To those who doubt, to those who fear, to those who judge askance, and to those who break off dialogue in ignorance, this testimony of exemplary cohabitation, this vision of a special city, is dedicated as an appeal to humility.

André Klopmann

Citizens of the World—Meyrin

Angelos and Athanasie Agoritsas, Greece

When the Agoritsas moved to Meyrin, it was little more than a few apartment buildings, the mere sketch of a city with neither business center nor cultural center—and barely an administration.

But thirty-five years later, the Agoritsas are here to stay. Even leaving the Champ-Fréchet sector would be hard for them to bear.

The love-affair with Meyrin began when one of Angelos's brothers got married. He traveled from Macedonia to the wedding in Geneva. And since the IAEA was hiring, he took a look around there to see if they might not need a technician....

A doctor in chemistry, Athanasie chose to devote herself to her children, Elisabeth and Thomas, who now amuse themselves by mixing languages to create their home dialect—that is, on the rare occasions when they aren't playing their beloved piano.

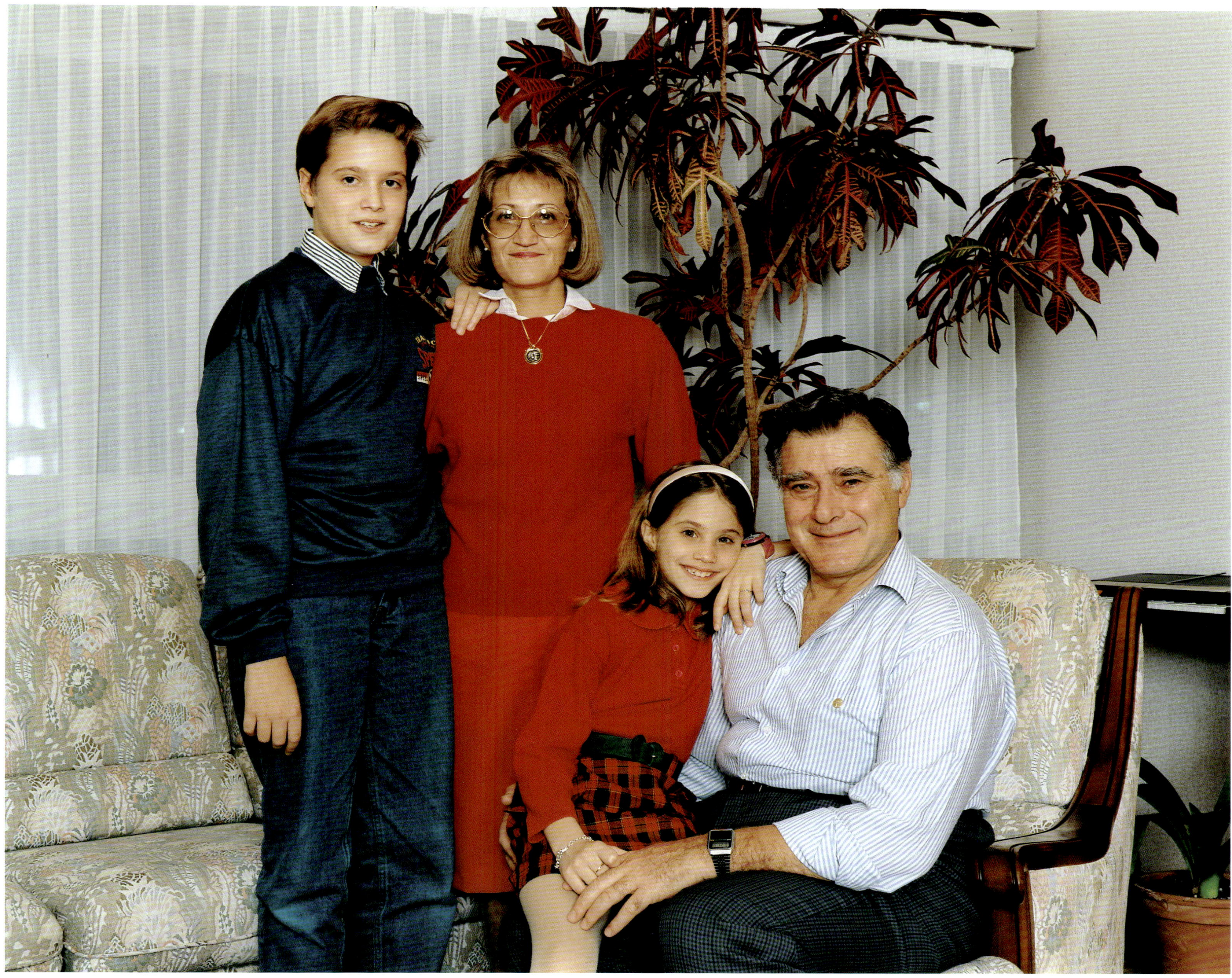

Finola Marras and Mats Ahnlund, Ireland—Sweden

There was a young woman from Meyrin,
Whose language was terrible wearing,
She spoke many tongues,
Though we didn't know which ones,
But her world is the one we'll soon share in.

Make what you will of this limerick. I stuck my nose in *The Penguin Book of Limericks* to try and understand the structure of these cheeky verses from the fringes of the English literary tradition: five lines, with lines 1, 2, and 5 rhyming (and with nine monosyllabic sounds in each), and different rhymes in lines 3 and 4, which are only six syllables long. A whole world.

When I arrived in this green garden dominated at the far end by a renovated farm, I didn't know what a limerick was. Each time I come, I learn something new. Limerick is also the name of a town in western Ireland with about 70,000 inhabitants, minus Finola, who discovered Switzerland while in training at an Ecole Hôtelière. She married an Italian from Meyrin, the father of Flavia and Sebastiano, and never went back.

Mats spent forty-two years in Södertalje, a large town about four times the size of Meyrin, where he was alderman in charge of immigration records. His first daughter, Anna, was born in Sweden. Having moved to Geneva less than three years ago, he works in an enormous non-governmental organization, the International Cooperative Alliance. This organization boasts seven hundred million members—as many Catholics as there are on earth—many of whom are not aware of being so. Take me, for example: thanks to a couple of miserable actions for Coop-Suisse, I too am a member. As I said, each time I come, I learn something new.

The couple met at the Alliance. Nice symbolism. They lived for a while in Sweden before returning to Geneva. Clare is the fruit of their union: that makes four children who, either with their mother or father, or with both, live in a maelstrom of languages. The three oldest are mastering English, French, Swedish and Italian. The youngest speaks only three languages—minus the Italian—but that's not bad for a four-year-old. One might say she's arming herself for the future. Effortlessly, of course, like all children, who are true parrots in the jungle of idioms.

For adults, it's obviously more difficult. As an adolescent, Mats had learned some of the rudiments of French, but it was only on coming to Geneva that he really applied himself. At his school in Sweden, the girls usually chose to study French, considered more romantic, while the boys opted for German, which they thought more technical.... For chasing after girls, then, it was better to take French. Good excuse. They can arouse feelings seldom piqued by the mere play of syntax, except, perhaps, when composing a limerick.

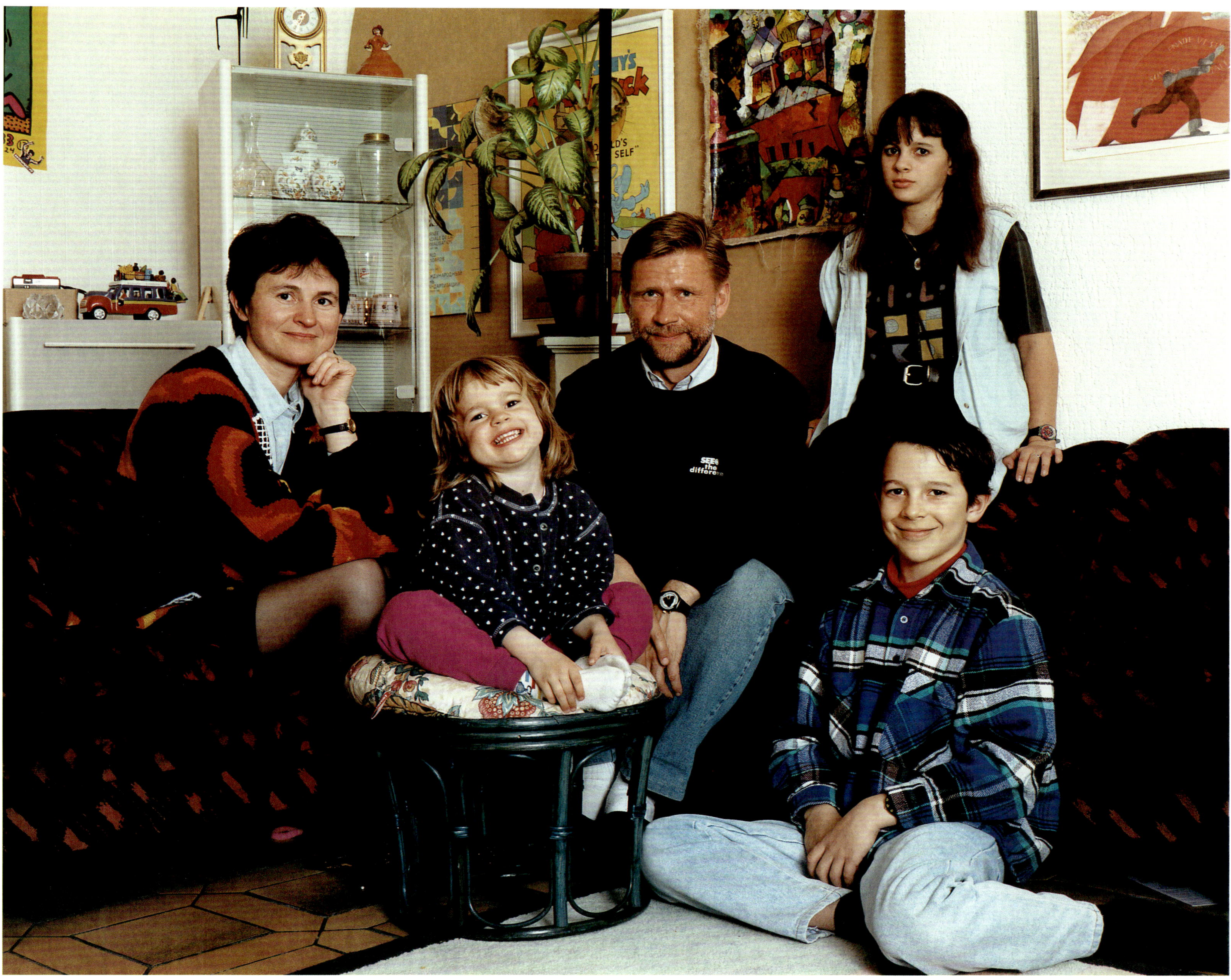

Ibrahim and Suad Al-Atwi, Jordan

Contrary to the widespread misconception, the Middle-Eastern woman enjoys unquestionable power. And it was seeing Ibrahim and Suad together that convinced me of this.

At first, we spoke about identity. If Ibrahim Al-Atwi is Jordanian today, it is because he left his native village in British-held Palestine in 1948, during the war for Israeli independence. Under attack, the new state designed by the United Nations seized lands that had not been granted it before the conflict, and Ibrahim's village burned down, driving his family into exile. There are Al-Atwis all over the world now. But Ibrahim, having no money or personal effects, crossed the River Jordan and took refuge in Jordan like so many other Palestinians, where he continued his studies in science. He told me about those years. Sipping Turkish coffee strongly scented with cardamom, I also listened to a family friend, who pleasantly joined in the conversation. He is from Jericho, a Palestinian. Identity comes before passports. Some day they will both be on equal footing. I also listened to the children swirling about: they have six bright and lively boys and girls (the eldest is married and lives in Amman) who in three years' time have achieved an elegant mastery of the French language. Their father ranks education with the higher, fundamental vaules.

When this meteorologist moved to Geneva to work with the World Meteorological Organization, he had first to lay the groundwork; only later did the rest of the family join him. I asked Suad:

"Wasn't that difficult for you? With the father deciding the fate of the whole family?"

"You know, in our culture it's the man who assumes the responsibilities," Ibrahim replied. "He makes the decisions."

But as he was saying this, Suad, a distant cousin and close wife, tenderly slid her arm around her husband's neck as if to say, "Yes, my lord, but under supervision...." And it's quite clear, that's the case.

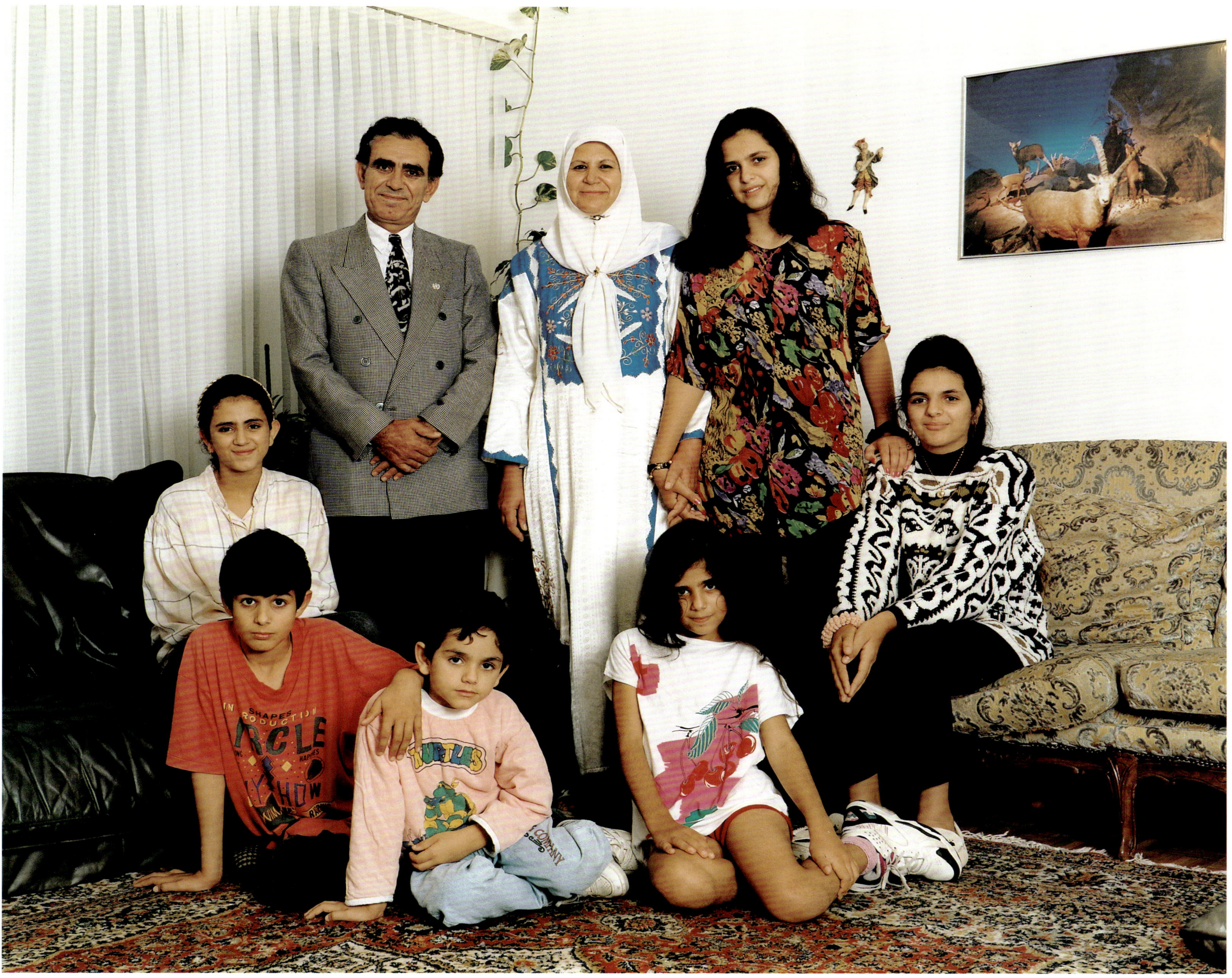

Mussaid Al-Eshaiwi and Alya Al-Abdulghani, Saudi Arabia

On the large television screen, the referee is about to signal the start of the Oman : Kuwait match of the Inter-Emirate Soccer Championships. Behind the television, the green and yellow Meyrin countryside stands out in perfect contrast. It is a splendid autumn. From his box, a prince salutes the teams. The whistle is blown, the game begins. Football is obviously much appreciated in Saudi Arabia. What was the name of that formidable player who, during the '94 World Cup in the United States, crossed the entire field alone, against a paralysed Belgian defense, before scoring a splendid goal? I know nothing about soccer, but this great sporting feat had caught the eye of more than a few Swiss who, like the Saudis, were rooting for their team during these world championships. Indeed both figured among the lesser teams that surprised observers with their achievements on the same field as the great ones.

Inside the sober but luxurious home of the Saudi Arabian representative at GATT all is light and space. On the walls and the consoles are scenes from Islamic life and calligraphies. In the middle, on the table, a yellow-hued coffee strongly redolent of cardamom stands among Oriental figs and Favarger chocolate: a speciality of your land, a speciality of mine.

The second-born of a family of eleven children educated in the finest schools—their father had a high position in the government—Mussaid continued his studies in Arkansas after studying economics at the university of Ryad. Education is one of the family's top priorities. Before following her husband to Switzerland, Alya ran a finishing school for girls. Today she is raising Sarah, Selwan and Yasser who, when they reach school age, will attend the international school as long as their father is stationed in Switzerland. They also take courses at the Geneva Mosque, which offers both a religious and lay education.

Mussaid speaks readily and asks questions even more readily. The epitome of Oriental hospitality, he prompts his visitor to express himself at great length and listens attentively. The football match is no longer of any importance. Each learns from the other—it's one definition of life—and the exchange, which language difficulties made initially improbable, soon takes on a magnificent resonance.

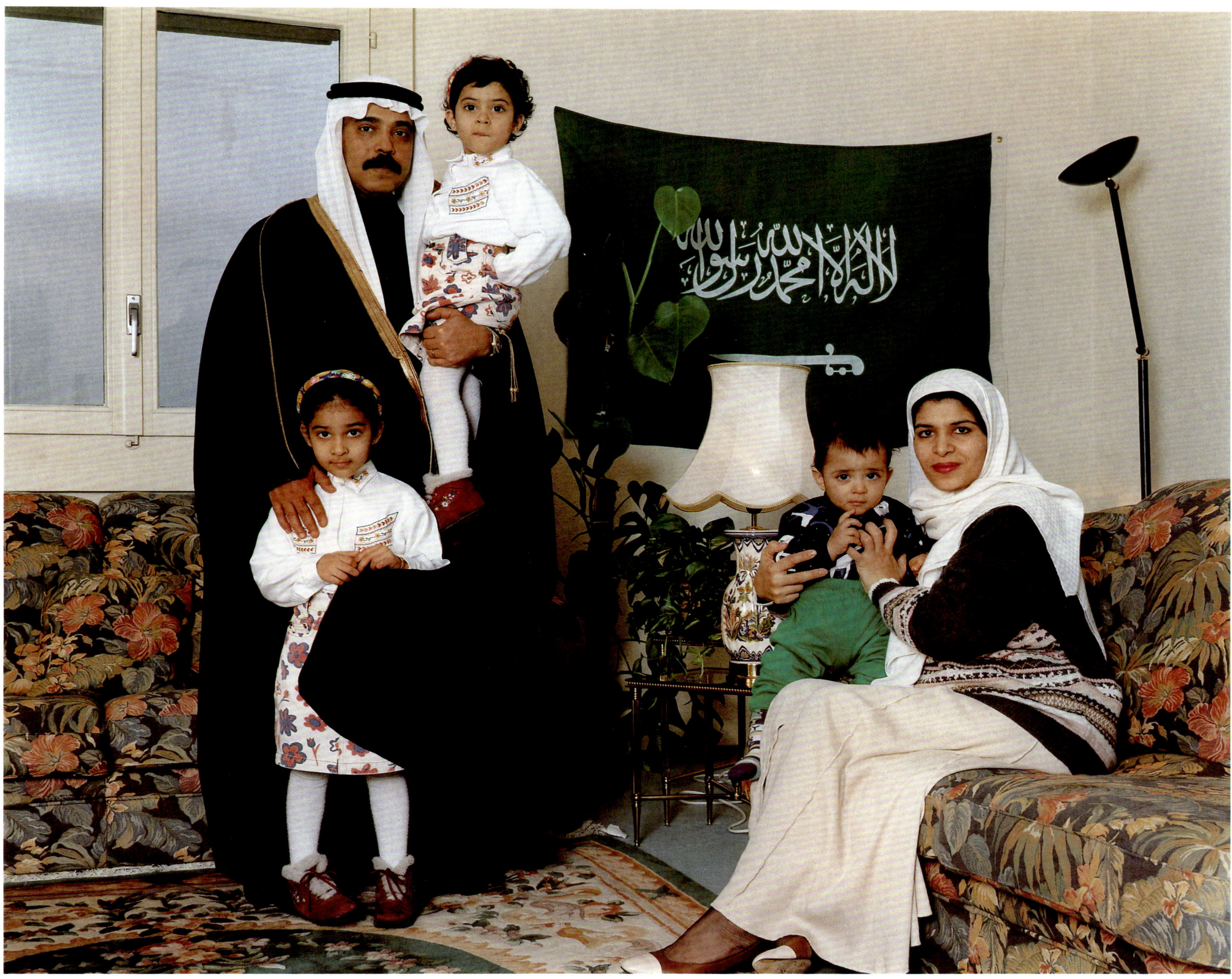
لا إله إلا الله محمد رسول الله

Geneviève and Frédérick Bordry, France

Often Genevans will do everything they can to move to nearby France, where the cost of living is lower. Here we have the opposite: a couple as French as can be who, when they came to the region, deliberately chose to live in Switzerland. Among IAEA employees, it's quite a rare thing.

The Bordrys navigate a bit like salmon, against the current. In their personal history, the very notion of emigration takes on a particular cast. Though they haven't encountered the difficulties of integration involved in learning a new language in Meyrin, they have certainly had this experience elsewhere. Formerly residents of Brazil, they had to immerse themselves in a universe fundamentally different from their own, to understand the society, and master the language in record time. They know all about uprootedness, isolation, administrative run-arounds, the blues.

And so the path of these salmon passed through Brazil. An interesting story: with a university degree, a Ph. D., and the title of Lecturer, Frédérick wanted to trade his twelve months of obligatory military service for eighteen months of civil service, a period he actually chose to extend. A French development worker dropped into southern Brazil, he was to conduct university courses there while his wife, whom he met at Toulouse when she was becoming an adviser in social and family economics, rolled up her sleeves and went to work in the shantytowns. During his holidays he would join her, getting involved on the ground as well, reparing a meter here, a cable there—in short, putting his knowledge of electrical engineering to work for the untrained populations. It was then that Sébastien, their adopted son, was born. Natasha would follow later, in Meyrin.

Back in Europe, Frédérick agreed to head a post-doctoral scholarship program for two years at the IAEA. What followed is typical: he never left! Today owners of an apartment in Meyrin, they are both deeply involved in community life, particularly with the students' parents association and the recreation center. In Geneva, Geneviève works at the Information Center for women and families; at first a beneficiary, then a volunteer, she is now a salaried employee of this institution. No more navigation for these salmon who have now settled along the banks of the rue de la Prulay.

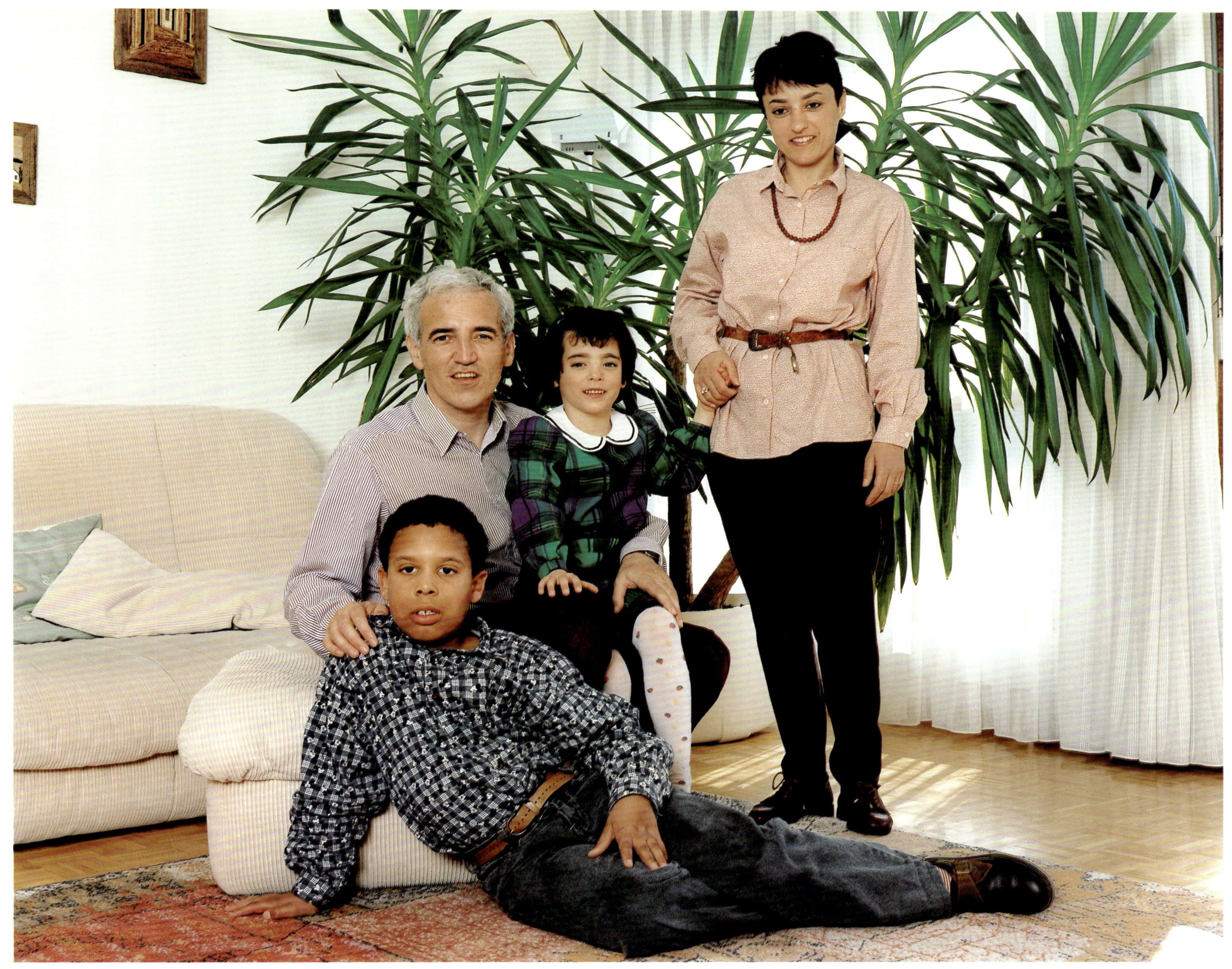

Marie-José and André Boulmier, Switzerland—Haiti

They are passionate talkers who will readily talk about themselves and artfully ask questions, but they cultivate discretion.

"Please, nothing about us!" All right. Just some indications, almost in alphabetical order.

Arcadia—Thirst for wide open spaces and discoveries: he, as a young man, decides to embark for Canada.

Nuns—She, Haitian by birth, was educated at a boarding school outside the country run by nuns. An intellectual's fate.

Canada—They met there during her student days. They weren't that strict after all, the Clarisses.

Didier—Their third son, born in 1966. Professional race-car driver, former champion of Europe (see under Model Cars).

Escape—André did not wait to retire from the IAEA. Too many things to do. And friends.

Flute—The sounds of the Queen of the Night float out of the stereo. Spellbinding.

Galvanoplasty—The specialty of André Boulmier, an expert in the treatment of metallurgical surfaces.

Haiti—A beautiful, run down country. Marie-José Boulmier's brothers and sisters have all moved abroad.

Engineer—The profession of their eldest son, Patrick, who specializes in computers.

Garden—A splendid rose bush that one sees from the bright living room, rustled by a light wind on a well sheltered terrace.

Kerosene—When the wind is bad, the airport seems closer. The planes aren't the only things moving.

Legacy—André Boulmier is an old native of Meyrin. He had his house built on family land.

Model Cars—On a scale of 1 : 8.... The kind, remote-controlled, that Didier drives and produces by profession.

Nepeta—Pleasant scents, at the entrance to the villa. A lot of lavender.

Optics—André practices photography. Marie-José plays the piano. This house breathes the pleasures of the five senses.

Physical Therapy—The profession of the second son, Claude. A chance to have the entire family in the photo.

Quarks—Who ever dreamed that, behind the heads of the IAEA, there are the tutors without whom they can do nothing?

Tour (de la)—Name of the private hospital of Meyrin. A nurse, Marie-José has worked there since it opened in 1977.

Urban Planning—Opposite their home, the beautiful wheat field may disappear. A parcelling plan has been submitted.

Village—The unappreciated part of Meyrin. A bell-tower, old half-timbered houses, the countryside: their neighborhood.

Wyandotte—A footrace for chickens, which are still raised, together with cows, in this Meyrin not made of concrete.

Xenophobia—During the "Schwarzenbach years" one had to put up with insults in silence. But things have calmed down.

Yucca—No trace, in their living room, of the ornamental plant of city apartments. Normal.... (see Garden).

Zest—The delicious welcome given by the Boulmiers. An exotic scent, like a lingering flavor of the Caribbean.

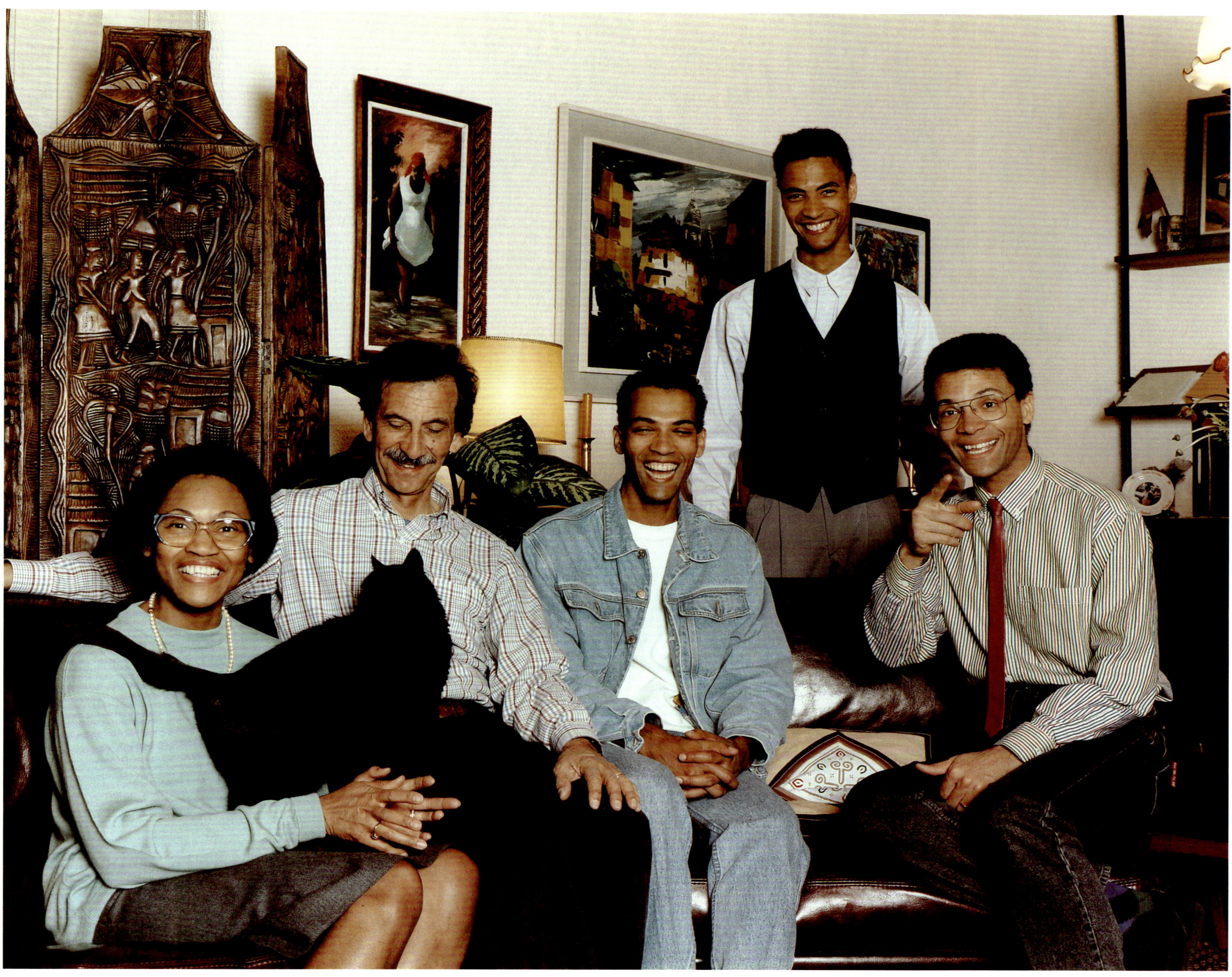

France and Olivier Broccard, Switzerland—Vietnam

Grandmother sleeps upstairs
Taking siesta in pairs
Paris
Madame
Comes from Vietnam
Dreams of the time
The flowers
The fields
Back then
Before
Uncle Hô
And exile

In France
Got stuck
Children
Of Paradise
Is that what
Paradise is like?
The worries
Begin
The new life
Too
That economizing
Brings in

Prosperity
Achieved
The frugal life
Is not in style
He'll be a doctor
A proctor
Dialysis
He'll learn
He'll love
And find
Beacons
In the wind

In training
Twitter
Plumage
Broccard
Man of art
Traveller
A glimmer
Marriage
Meyrin
Serene
La Tour
Amour

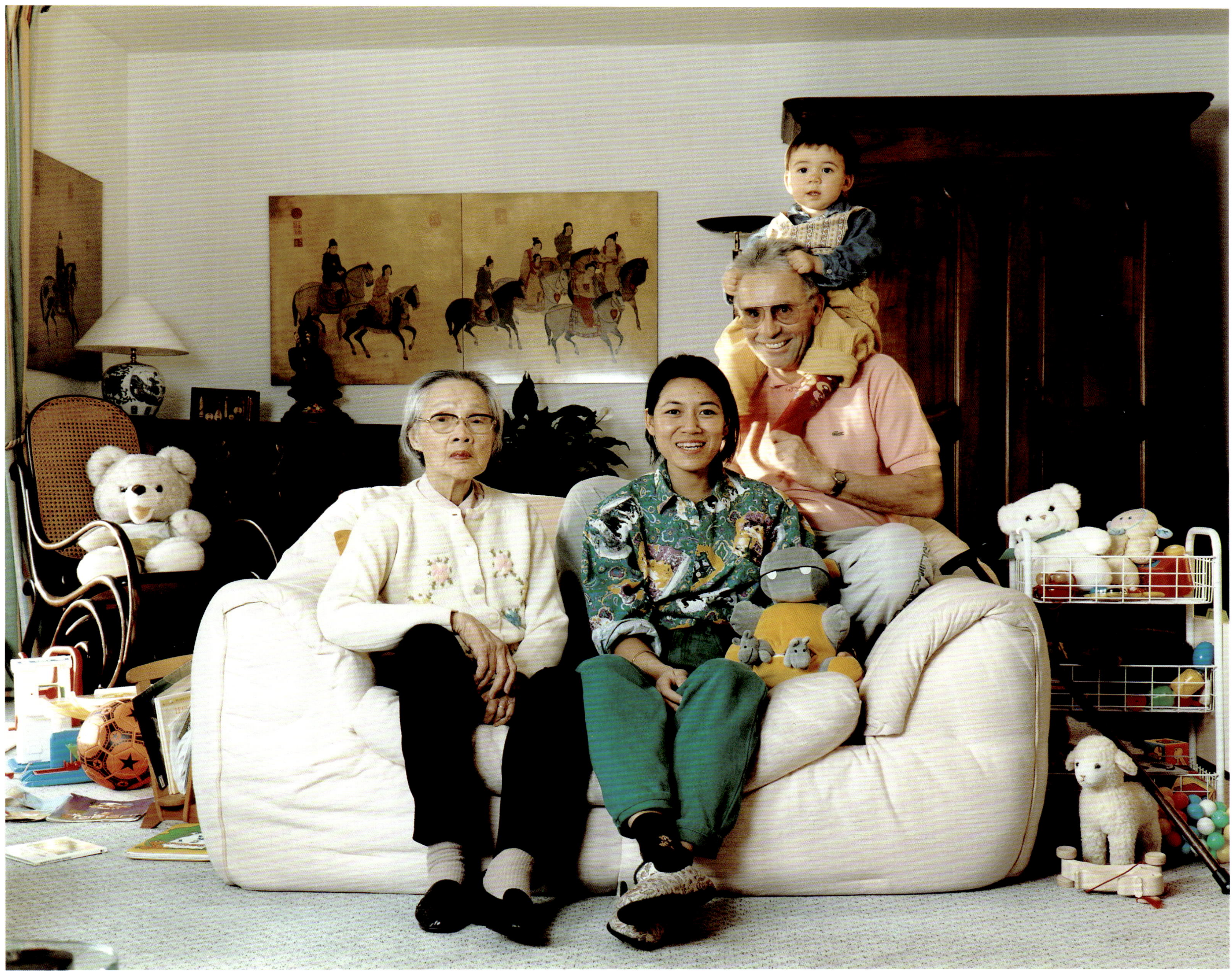

Bertil and Margaret Byskov, Denmark—Great Britain

The people of the North have the reputation of centering their existence around children and their education. So Bertil's speaks highly of the school at Livron: the commitment of its teachers, the refinement of the instruction they provide to so many children from so many different countries of origin, and the quality of the courses they give are, he says, remarkable, even exceptional. Anna agrees. The remark is all the more valid as it is based on a comparison: Majbritt, her elder sister, attended the school of Léman, which hardly has a reputation for producing dunces. For Bertil this discovery was a key. As of that moment he began to truly love Meyrin. At first, still attached to his smart little villa in Copenhagen, he had no desire at all to move to the Swiss town, of which Margaret was, however, rather fond. Settlement.

He is Danish, she is English. But Great Britain lies outside the family's culture. It's even a little odd: except for a few old history books, there is nothing, in the Byskov house, to remind one of the country where Margaret, after all, grew up and lived for twenty-two years. She's covered her tracks. She herself is astonished by it. She married a Viking. And the beautiful long-ship of carved rush adorning the library seems to sail in one direction only: toward Denmark, where the family goes each year. They very rarely go to England. The couple, moreover, who met in France when she was a secretary and he an economics student, chose to live in Copenhagen for six years. The four of them now speak Danish as perfectly as English, French and... oh yes, Spanish! The souvenir of another long sojourn: Anna was born in Ecuador. At school, Majbritt was a rare specimen: a blonde! Every advantage was assured this certainly gifted but not very studious angel; one could write a whole book on the effect the color of her hair and eyes had on the reception of good grades. Psychology.

Contrary to a notion all too widespread, the artistic sense and the flair for economics can get on very well together. Majbritt sings, dances, and performs with an amateur theatre group in English; like her father, however, her sights are aimed at advanced studies in economics. Her mother plays the clarinet in a local group. *Moderato con brio.* She also teaches English as a volunteer at the Université Populaire of Geneva. Opening.

These, then, are the Byskovs. Contrary to what their name suggests even to the highly organized prospectors of the Jehovah's Witnesses, who speak Russian when they show up at their door, the family is not Russian: the name comes from the contraction of the Danish words for city and forest. Symbiosis.

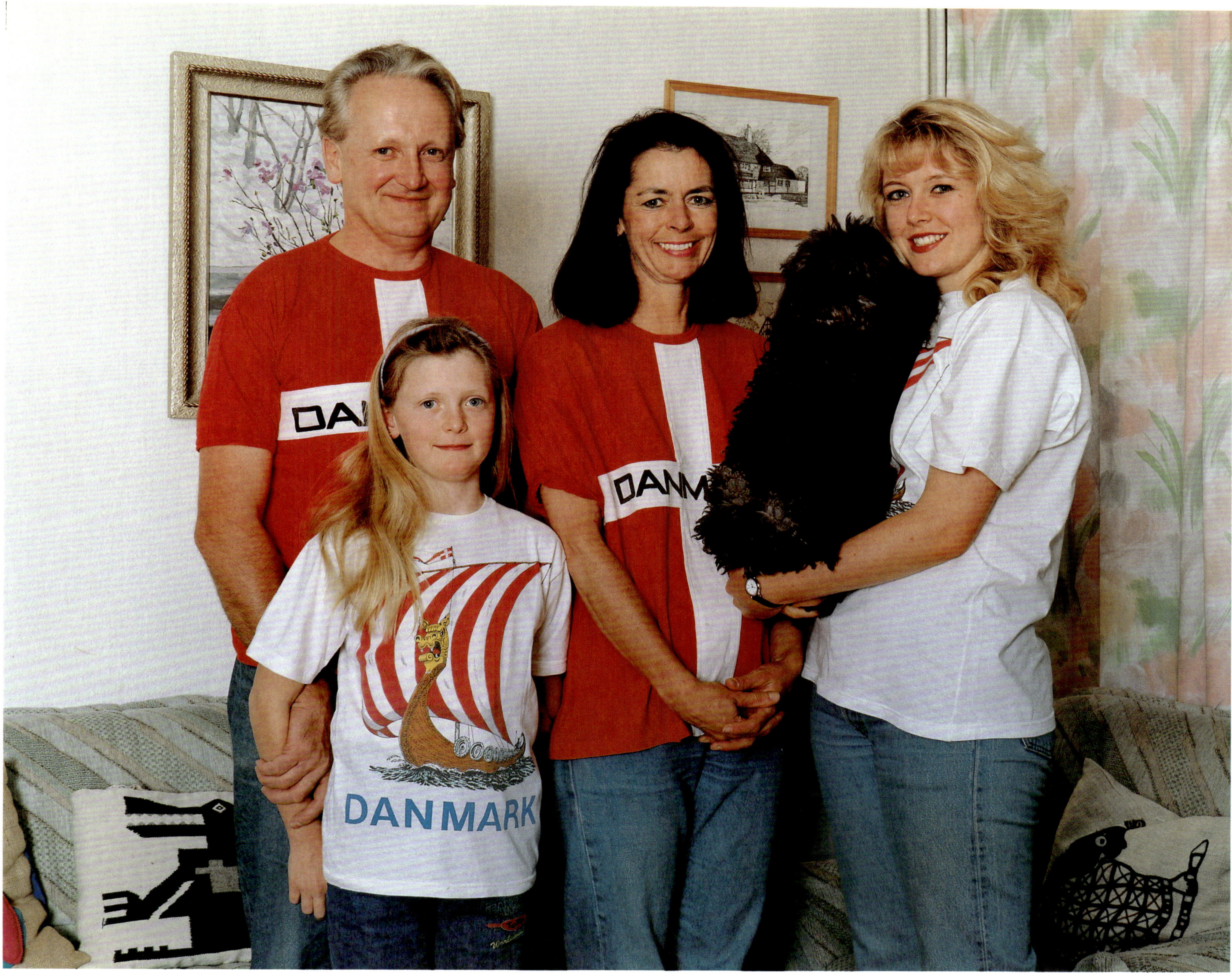
DANMARK

Aurora and Romeo Cacdac, Philippines

First, a sister. Then another. Then a third. There were nine children, a few being girls. Leaving the Philippines, three reached Geneva: one, the trail-blazer, lives in the Lignon; and the others in Meyrin. Together. Two apartments in the same building.

The sense of family is strong in the Philippines. Christmas lasts a good week during which, when you invite someone, he arrives with a crowd. It's normal, commonplace, and even desired. You multiply the number of dishes and share the cassava cake.

In this oblong living-room which resembles a camper, large cardboard boxes announce an upcoming dispatch of various parcels. A massive one. To the family, of course. Electronic materials, European merchandise sometimes second-hand but always useful back home.

It was Aurora who blazed the trail. The first one to move here, and an employee of the WHO, she had Romeo come join her. Their son Rommel bears a name born of a contraction: Romeo + Aurora Linda = Rommel. It's as simple as that. In the Philippines, the Registry Office is a cool place.

Maïté, the youngest, makes no end of cutting things out. Mostly from magazines. She designs for fashion, which is her great passion, but not the only one. Daughter of a security agent, she also feels drawn to criminology. She dreams of being a forensic pathologist. Clippings.

The youngest is Evangelo. Which is shortened to Yvan. A basketball player. His brother prefers football. They love literature in this family, but also sports. When the parents retire to their homeland, the children have no plans to join them. They know so little about it. They're Swiss.

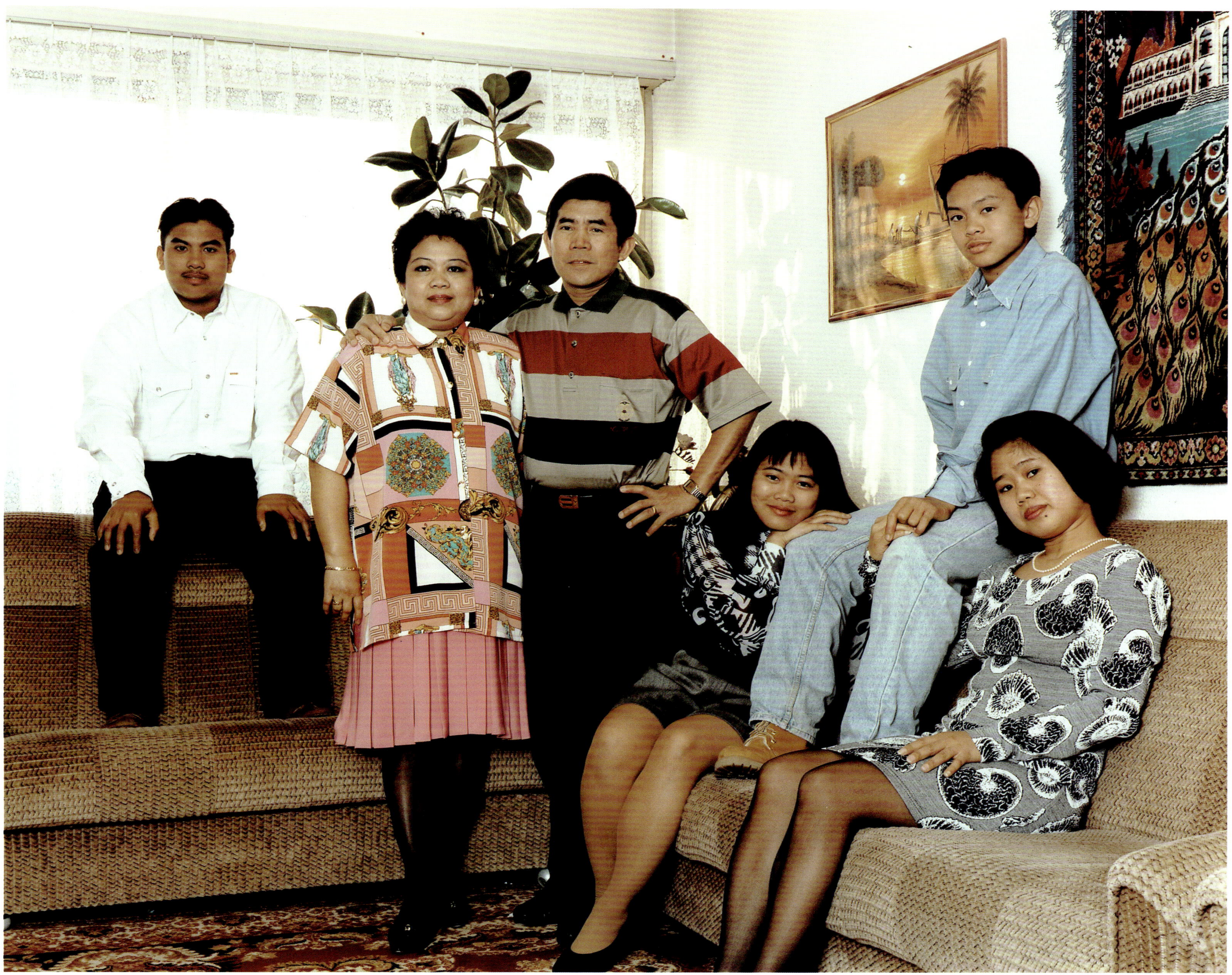

Martin and Claudia Carnino Ilutovitch, Argentina

Emigrations
Stability, movement. Or is it the other way around? Family emigration in installments: from Italy in search of fortune, from Moldavia probably to escape pogroms, and finally from Argentina, two generations later.

Dictatorship
Argentina during the dark years. Having come from the middle classes of Buenos Aires, Claudia and Martin became politically active and spent time in prison. Arbitrary detention which they could only come out of to leave the country.

Luck
Many of their friends died during the fascist period. Others have disappeared without trace. There are others still who committed suicide in exile, apparently a frequent occurrence. The two know how lucky they've been.

Hesitations
In fact, there were two departures. First in 1978 and then in 1986, after an attempt at moving back to their homeland. A failure—since, in the interim, the couple had already undergone training in Switzerland....

Continuity
Always attentive to others; a certain social concern. Initially active in politics, the two now express their ideas in the professional sphere: she is a psychologist, he an educator.

Males
Claudia has some experience of female survival in a male environment. She had three brothers. Her first son is Pedro, her second, Manuel.... Then came Pablo and Gabriel, the twins.

Royalty
There are a dozen Argentine families living in Meyrin. Several other come from neighboring countries formerly united in a vice-royalty (Spanish), and it is under this name that some of them meet each week.

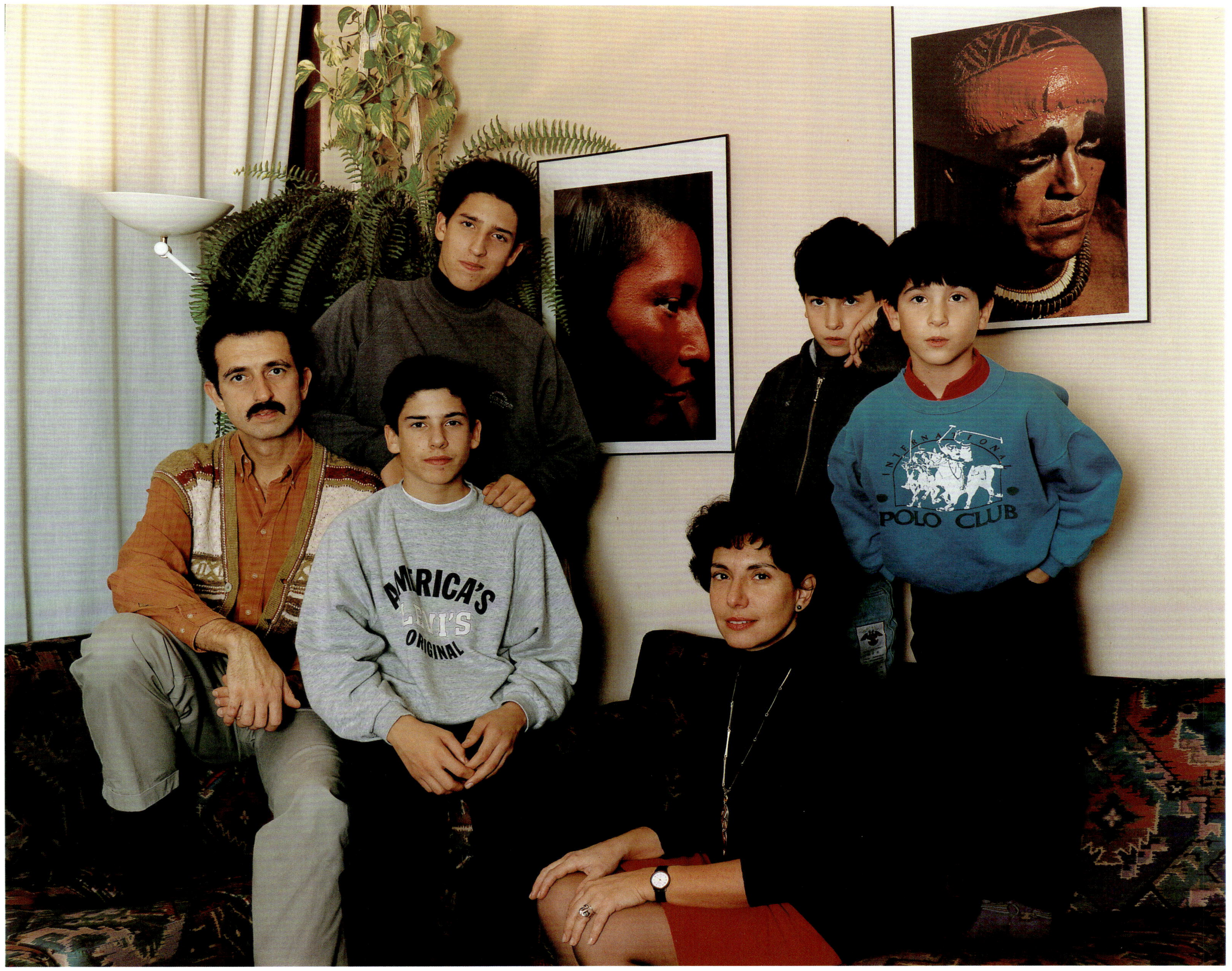
INTERNATIONAL
POLO CLUB
ORIGINAL

Mawunu Chapman Nyaho, Ghana

I. *When she is in good spirits*

■ I don't like interviews. Would you like some water? I like water, myself. I would kill for water and the color blue. Make yourself at home, please. Here, have some biscuits; I made them myself. I'd forgot about our appointment, that's funny, that's not like me at all. I had even written it down. Anyway.... Water or grape juice? Take a napkin. What would you like to know?

I knew Geneva because my family lived there from 1963 to 1966. I'm from Ghana and I work in a specialized agency of the WIPO.

Evenings, I'm trying to take up music again. Piano. I have trouble reading music. I'm also taking voice lessons. Please have another biscuit. Yes, I do have a lot of energy, don't I. Especially in the morning! It's evening now. Ah look! The storm... I have the impression that the climate here affects people a little. Where I come from they're more pleasant. But I'm happy anywhere. And I'm sure anyone can be happy anywhere. You can't take things very seriously if you want to get ahead....

That photo there? That's my maternal grandfather. He was a traditional chief. I never knew him. He was wise and respected. All his children adored him. My children? I've got two. Nana Kow and Kwesi, the firstborn. I've been lucky: they're angels. They're grown up now. Over twenty. One day maybe I'll go back home. In Ghana, when someone says "Have a nice day," they really mean it.

II. *When she's not in good spirits*

■ I have nothing to say. I don't like interviews.

III. *Synthesis*

■ Come see me with your text.

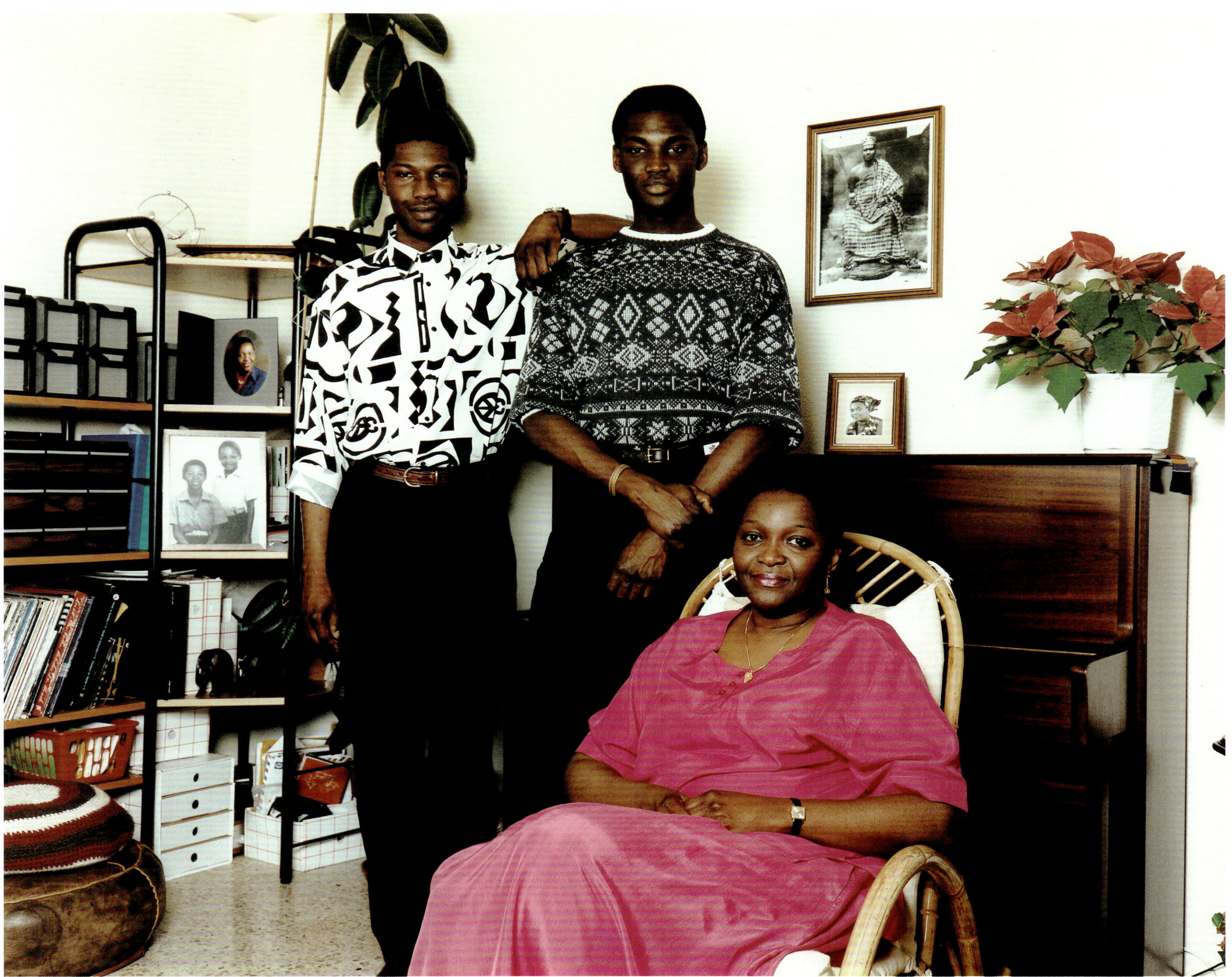

Yun-Ang Chung and Ro-Sa Koh, South Korea

In Korea, as in other Asian countries, a married woman keeps her own name. It's more elegant. In Switzerland, on the other hand, we had to fight a very long time to get to that point. And still the two names are stuck together. One might say that in essence, from the Asian point of view, marital status concerns only those who have chosen it.... Thus Ro-Sa and Yun-Ang, devout Christians who every Sunday frequent one of the two Korean churches of Geneva, were married in the first place before God. He knows how to recognize his own.

Today the Chungs have returned to their country. A meteorologist, Yun-Ang had come to Geneva for two years, to attend a program at the World Meteorological Organization (WMO). He has since gone back to Seoul to his five brothers, his friends and the Korean meteorological headquarters. A former student at the school of Plan-les-Ouates, In-Kyo now attends a new school, while her mother Ro-Sa tends her new home. Meyrin will remain a parenthesis in their itinerary, the memory of a formative step.

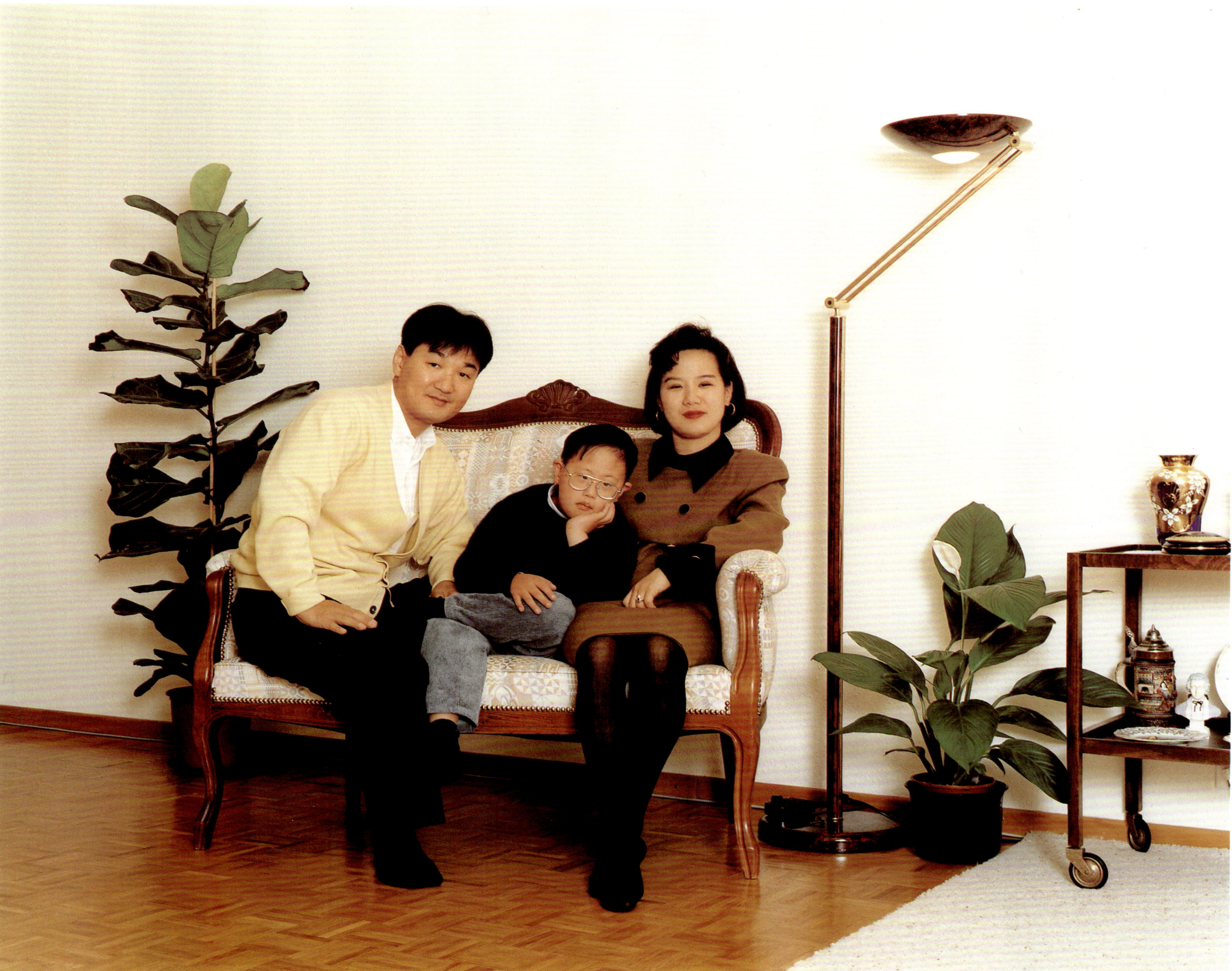

Ernest and Marie-Anne Daragus Kolosy, Hungary

The finest example of integration—her greatest professional success, in short, since she worked at the UBS—is to have set up, at this same bank, in a few days, a fifty-year-old refugee from Transylvania, Ernest Daragus.

The finest love story of this book might well be that of this marriage, when in 1972 Marie-Anne Kolosy said "yes" to this same Daragus, who was her beau in 1939 at the Youth Ball of Budapest, thirty-three years earlier.

Their story is a fireworks display.

She owned Roumanian, Hungarian, Austrian and Belgian passports before obtaining Swiss citizenship in 1987. She speaks all those languages too, plus English and Spanish.

He is a doctor of law, and experienced the Russian front, prison, and the snows of the Carpathian mountains, grave of half of the 120 officers who, like him, tried to save their skins in 1944.

She divorced her first husband, father of her daughter "with the very Swiss name" of Lioba, actually the surname of an Irish saint of the 13th century.

He was a widow when he came to Switzerland carrying a few postcards of Hungary and his diploma, decorated in the old-fashioned way, with a majestic wooden seal.

She met in Brussels a Mgr Bouvier, head of Caritas in Switzerland, an institution for which she would work for thirty years in Switzerland, until her seventieth birthday.

He survived typhoid fever. His parents, built like castles, lived very long lives in perfect health. His father sold the family house at the age of ninety-five, without being taken to the cleaners.

She knows her wines. When the two visit Burgundy, they go at it like *bon-vivants:* two wine-cellars, one church, and so on. Indeed her mother's maiden name was Bordeaux. Her French ancestors moved to Transylvania after the Revolution to produce a local champagne there.

Them: There is a glamorous side to the nobility of this couple. He's a lawyer and financial auditor, she is a social worker educated at Brussels and the Sorbonne. Their apartment is a museum. They have never left it, and, as if to confirm their attachment to Meyrin, they have hung on their wall, amidst all the images, armorial bearings, cards, books, photos and souvenirs, the original of the map of Meirin (with an i), drafted in 1829 by the surveyor Jean-Robert Mayer. The gift of another immigrant, a Pole.

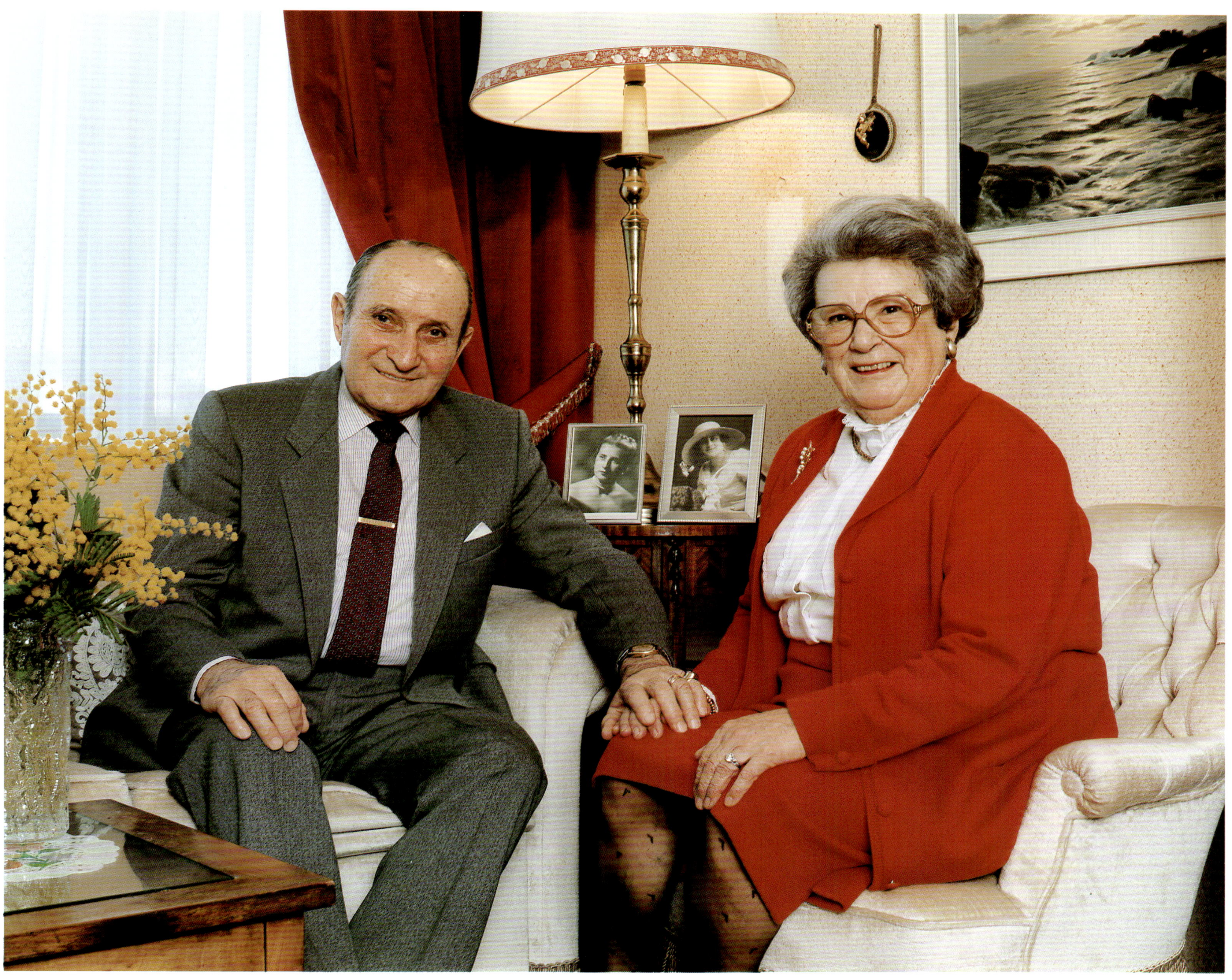

Bassan and Lamia Dib, Lebanon

Beirut
  childhood
  apprenticeship
  as confectioner

Kuwait
  work
  savings
  plans

Beirut
  return
  building
  one's life

Geneva
  family
  cousin
  fifteen years

  chocolates
  exporting
  machines

Beirut
  cousin
  marriage
  moving in

  war
  factory
  destroyed

Geneva
  return
  school
  resumption

  perseverance
  federal
  certificate

Meyrin
  no
  question
  of emigrating

  faithful
  grateful
  worker

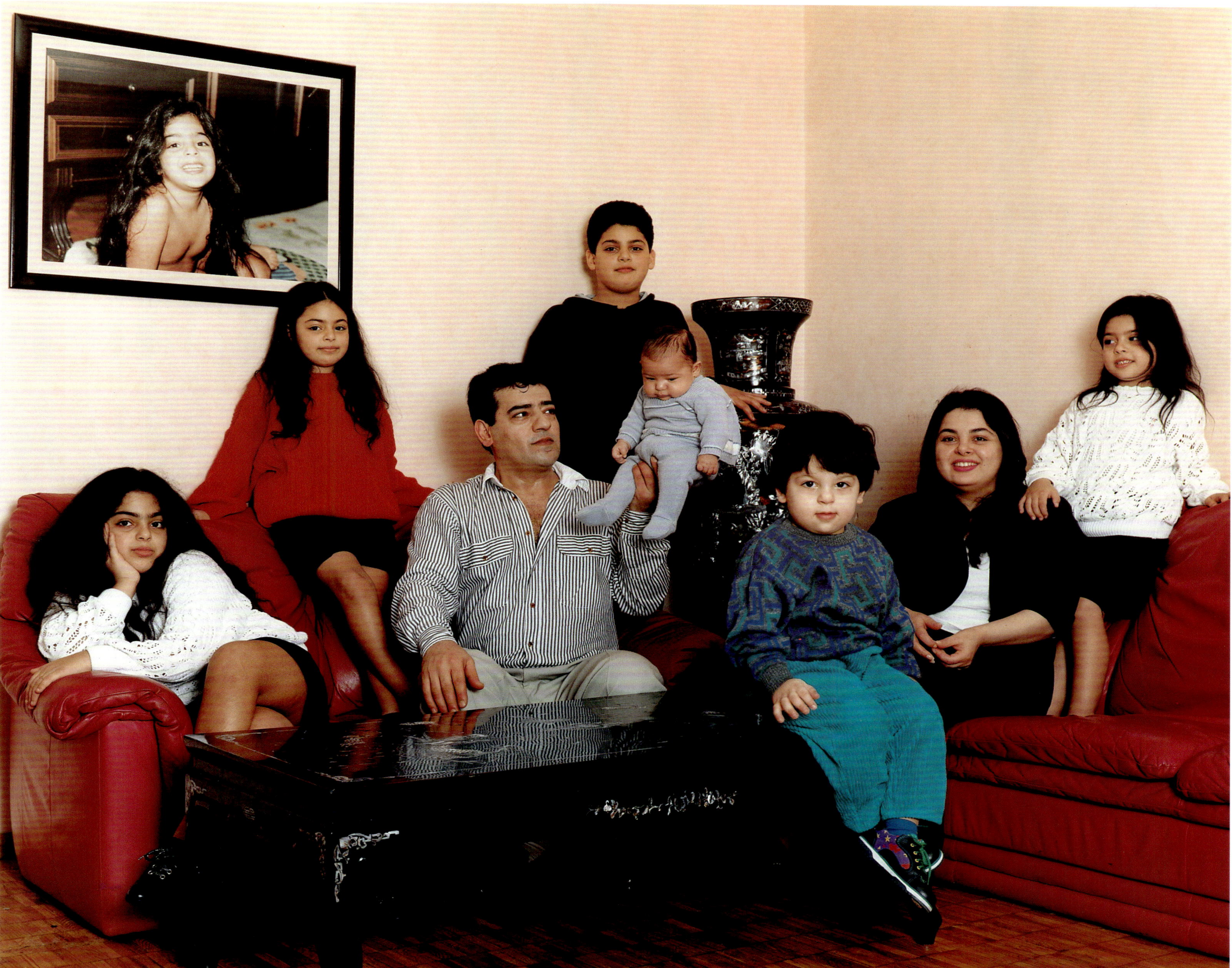

Mohsen and Naïma Djebbi, Tunisia

In the village, which numbered only about twenty families, people worked the land and grew grapes for the White Fathers who made wine from it. Naïma, educated in Tunis, ran the corner pharmacy. By turns a nurse, a home-care assistant, family planning teacher, and, why not, a midwife, she lived in perfect harmony with the Catholic missionaries, as did all the Muslims of the village. At Thibar, during this period, a nun from Valais made an especially deep impression on Naïma. The break was an especially sorrowful one when after twenty years of living in North Africa, the nun packed her bags to return to her native Alps. Determined, the young Tunisian promised to go visit her one day.

Naïma was to keep her word. Braving her father's outbursts, she arrived at Sion in 1979, by herself, to see her friend and at the same time to study the sanitational infrastructure of a Western country. It worked out well: the hospital of Sion had just opened its doors. Hired for a few weeks as an experiment, she stayed in Switzerland, where she still works as a nurse. Here she would marry Moshen, born in a village some ten kilometers from her own, formerly of the Tunisian Ecole Hôtelière and still active in the restaurant business today. Their Meyrinese children have lovely names: there is Hanane (which means affection), Wafa (fidelity), and Rafiq (companion).

Only Naïma's father's attitude has changed. Near-illiterate, but father of eight intellectuals trained abroad, he takes pride in his children's achievements. One of them, an aeronautical engineer, received a doctorate with highest honors from the Polytechnic of Lausanne. Tunisian television has even done a story on this humble farmer, father of doctors and scientists. Tunis has offered them brilliant posts which they, today scattered about the world, are reluctant to accept. For Naïma it's clear: her life is in Meyrin. Just in case she might one day have to help her husband, who would like to become an owner, she has taken courses in café and restaurant management and received a diploma that might well raise the curtain on a third act.

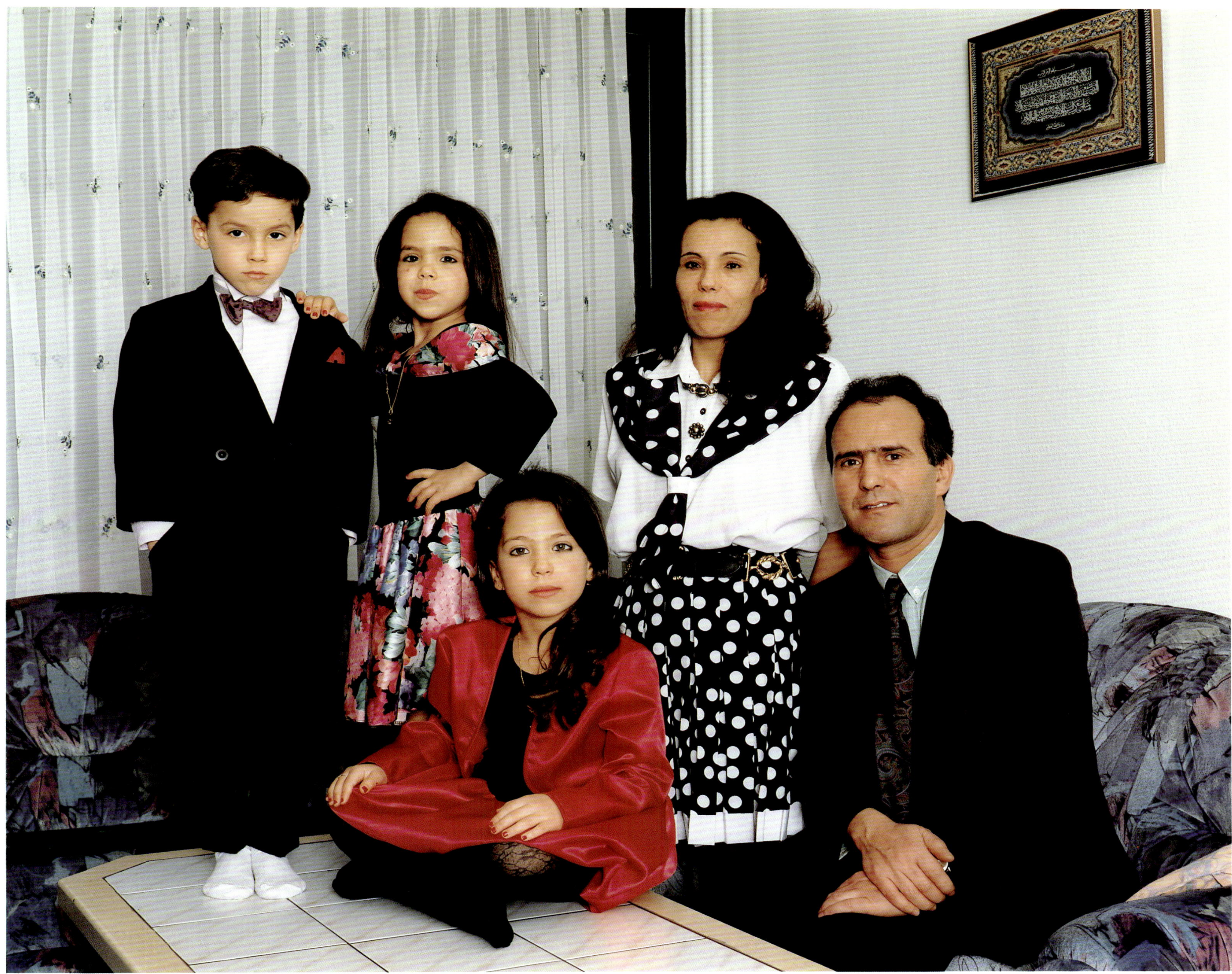

Iman and Wiesye Djuniardi, Indonesia

There are not a lot of Indonesians living in Geneva. Two hundred and fifty, three hundred perhaps. But they see one another often. Most of them are diplomats; those outside the international community are more rare. On Sundays they meet on the tennis courts or by the pool of a club they rent together. Twice a month the children can also take courses in history and national geography there.

Big Ben chimes the hour in the living room.

Iman Djuniardi wants to open a restaurant "of his native cuisine." This would neatly bring his story full circle: it was the restaurant business that brought him to Geneva in the first place. He wasn't yet twenty years old when he arrived in the distant, mythic country of the Alps. Since he had to wait five years before applying to the hotel management school of Lausanne, and since the one at Gilon is not within the reach of all scholarships, Iman Djuniardi chose the school at Geneva: thus began a long itinerary of study and patience, "Asian style," which would arm him with a double education. Each would complement the other in usefulness.

Big Ben chimes the hour again.

He is primarily a restaurateur. But he is also an economist. After two years spent learning French at a private school, he moved to Villars for a season.... He ended up staying three years, before going to a large hotel in Geneva. During this time Wiesye was studying in London. Her uncle worked in Geneva for an international organization. That's when Cupid intervened.

But how many times a day do they have to put up with Big Ben's chimes?

The problem, in the hospitality business, is that it demands a schedule that the nerves and sometimes the family cannot withstand. When Candy was born, Iman decided to leave the nest for a new tour of study—two years of business courses—and a re-orientation in banking. Thus he was in a financial institution when he celebrated the birth of his second daughter, Natasha (with an s to ensure the proper pronunciation of the name in Indonesian). His mother also works in the banking world.

It's really too bad that Swiss clocks are so loquacious.

Then nature took over again: with detailed resumé and financial plan in hand, the Djuniardis began making the rounds of the banks in hopes of finally opening their own restaurant. A stand at the Clés de St-Pierre and another at the Ponts de St-Gervais—at those memorable fairs organized for the restoration of the cathedral and the temple—had convinced them of the widespread interest in the cuisine of their native land.... With the blessing of their children, whom they had consulted, they thus cast the dice into a new career as restaurant owners.

Big Ben breaks the spell, roiling the flow of infinite sweetness emanating from Candy and Natasha.

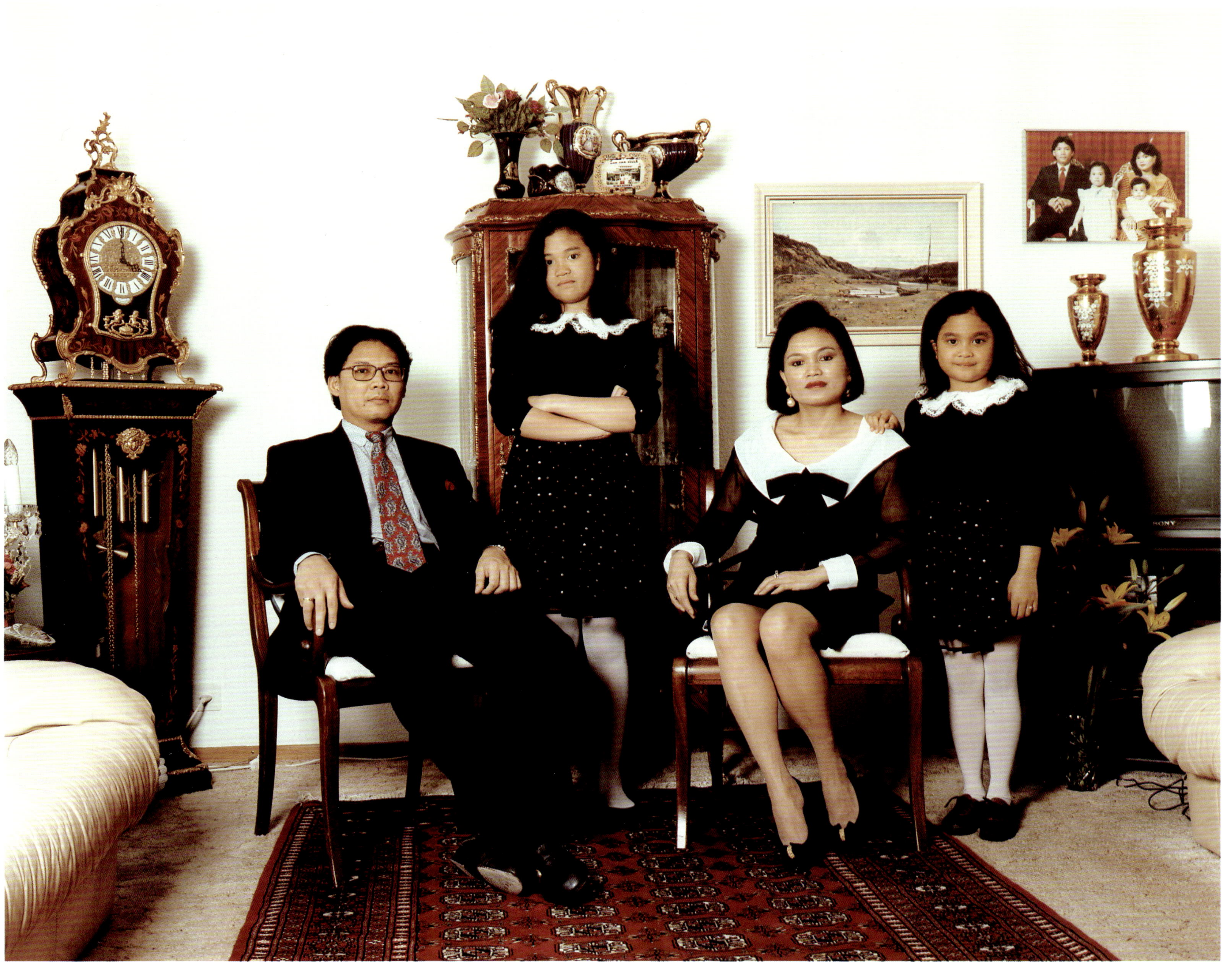
SONY

Inge and Eva Ekstrand, Sweden

Mention Sweden at an ordinary dinner-party. Words will stream out like symbols.

First they will say: Ikea, Volvo, Borg.

Others will say: Vikings, Olof Palme or Carl Gustav.

The best informed, or at least those in business, will add: Taxation.

Famous for their exceptionally high rates, Swedish taxes have driven enterprise into exile. Inge's employers in the oil business had thought of moving to London, then finally opted for Geneva. First Inge, then Eva and the children, made the journey the way one plunges into terra incognita.

A big jumble: he speaks English at work, she communicates in Swedish at home. But the children—Martin, Ingrid and Henrik—raised on Genevan soil, talk to each other in French. The eldest works in chemistry, hoping eventually to teach it, or, which remains to be seen, to work for environmental protection programs. His sister dreams of psychology. The announcement of her plan creates a stir in the living-room. As for the youngest, it's a bit early to decide.

They all like sports: Ingrid does aerobics and apparatus work, and also swims like a dolphin. The boys train around the ping-pong table. It is clearly in Switzerland that they will build their future, perhaps even with a passport bearing a white cross. For this to happen, Sweden will have to accept double citizenship, which its entry into the European Union should favor. And Switzerland, will it finally join Europe too? Martin is convinced it will.

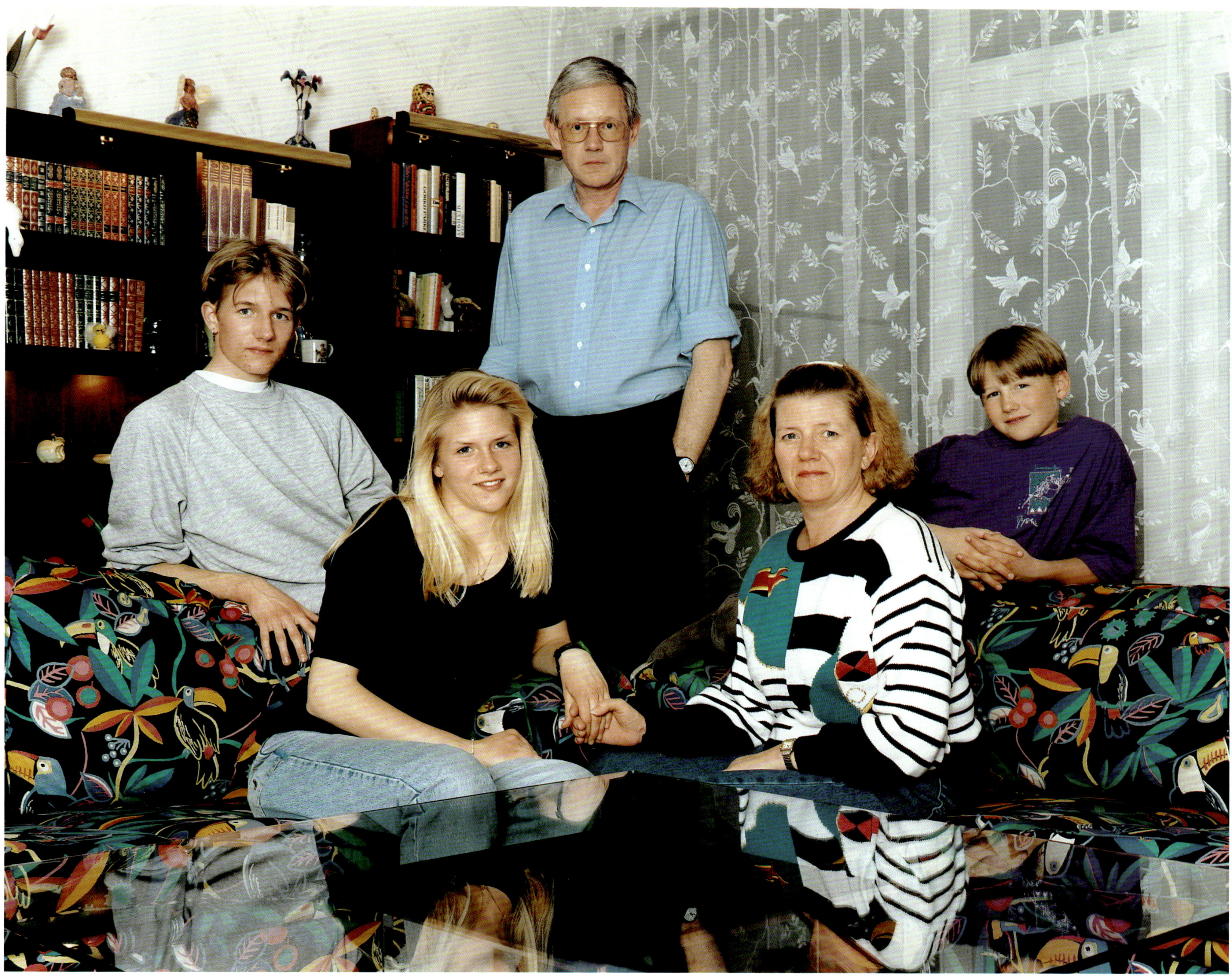

Cennet Evran and Mesut Güven, Turkey

There is a before and an after.

Before, the memories are sad. These two have suffered. In exile, separated.

After, they reunited in Switzerland. They almost got married, but the registry office required that they have papers issued by the Turkish consulate. Political refugees, of course, hardly ever frequent the consulates of the countries they have fled....

When homesickness really gets hold of her, Cennet walks along the Léman river. But she misses the waves of the sea. The water relaxes her.

Their son Onder wants to be a chemist or diplomat. Being a diplomat would be a bit of a paradox. But he's an optimist: this will all change, one day, he says. Or else, he will be the one to change. Like his mother who, as child, wanted to be ... a policewoman.

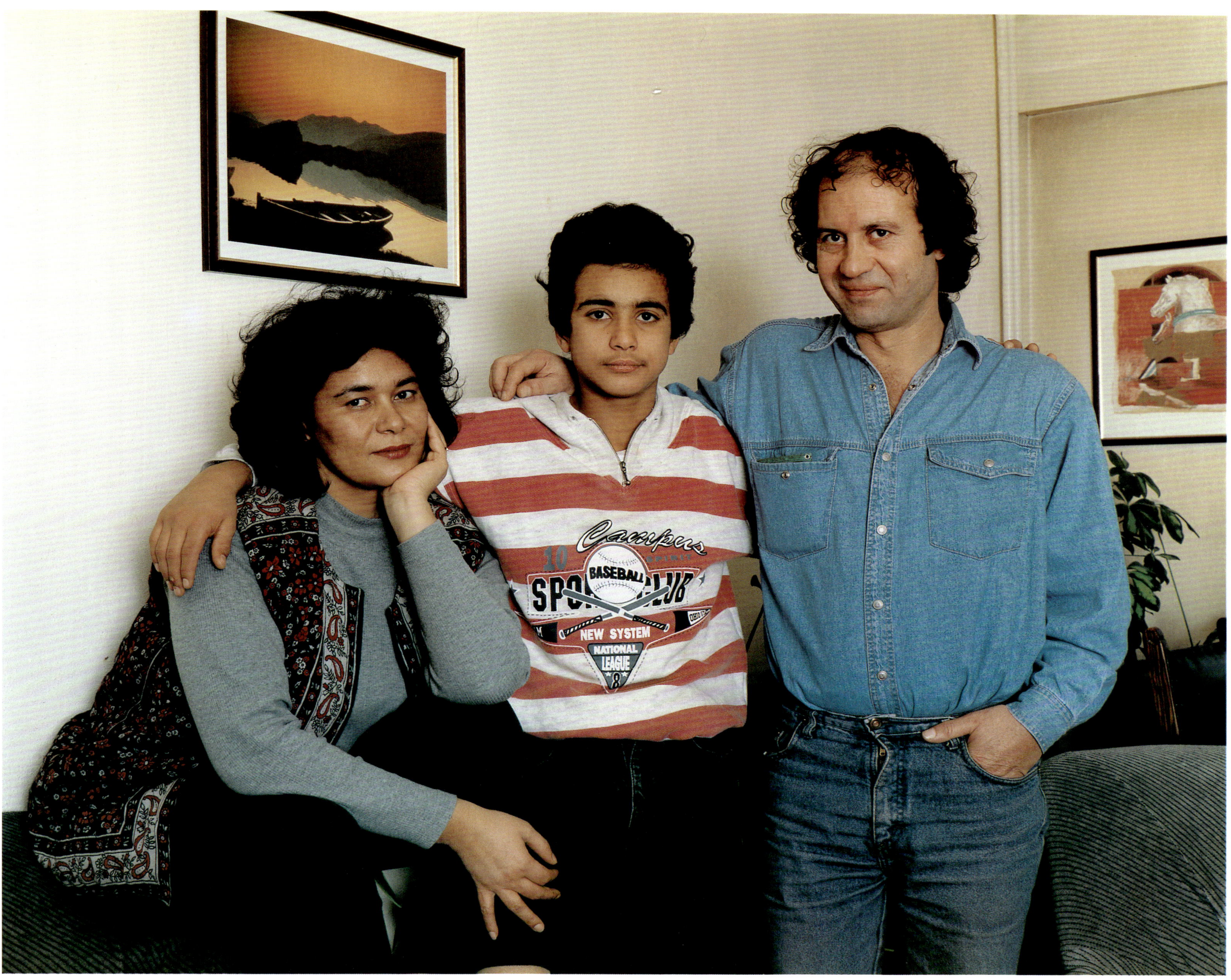
Campus
10
BASEBALL
NEW SYSTEM
NATIONAL
LEAGUE
8

Faez and Arfan Fahham, Syria

A kind of inborn wisdom drives the people of the East sometimes to express in few words the full depth of their gaze. That of Faez Fahham, for example, is precise as a laser and lucid as that of the cowherd who sees all but shows nothing. A placid man, he watches his children grow up, become adults—Swiss—and understands that it's not in Syria that they will raise their own families in turn. For this reason alone, which is as compelling as any other, Arfan and he do not plan to go back to Alep, their native city, the country's second largest and its economic center.

Roots must grow as people grow.

Syria, then, is the soil. But soil can be transported. The shoot has taken well to Meyrin, and it is here that the children's true roots will grow. Fouad and Chadi have only the vaguest memories of their earliest childhood; as for Hadi, she was born at La Tour. When it comes time to be grandparents, the Fahhams will have become Swiss themselves and will witness the growth of a new generation of pure-bred Genevans.

There are patterns that are not necessary to repeat.

The break, however, was desired by Faez. He fell suddenly in love with Switzerland, a country in which part of Arfan's family was already living, and then the representative of the Syrian industrial system also got it in his head to move there. Now all Faez had to do was find work. He found it first at the Syrian Mission, then at the ILO, where he works with documents written in Arabic. Arfan, meanwhile, works at the WMO.

An international small town: it's perfect.

He's been driving a long time, Faez has. This may seem a trifling detail, but for him, coming as he does from a large, teeming city, the calm of the traffic of Geneva borders on sheer happiness. Few accidents. Moves are well defined. And a very appreciable modesty with the horn. His children, who are more restless because it comes with the age, expend their energy in sports venues, practicing squash, basketball, martial arts....

That was how we overcame the generational problem. Sports protect children.

The concern for family unity. Let's take the TV: what about the programs in Arabic brought in by satellite? The Fahhams don't watch them any more than other programs. They go back and forth between the Television Suisse-Romande and the foreign channels and make their own synthesis of the news. Each channel in fact merely gives you the product of its own views. The children have been sensitized to this notion at school, and it is talked about at home among the family. It's a kind of apprenticeship. Conclusion:

Each bit of information has its own taste.

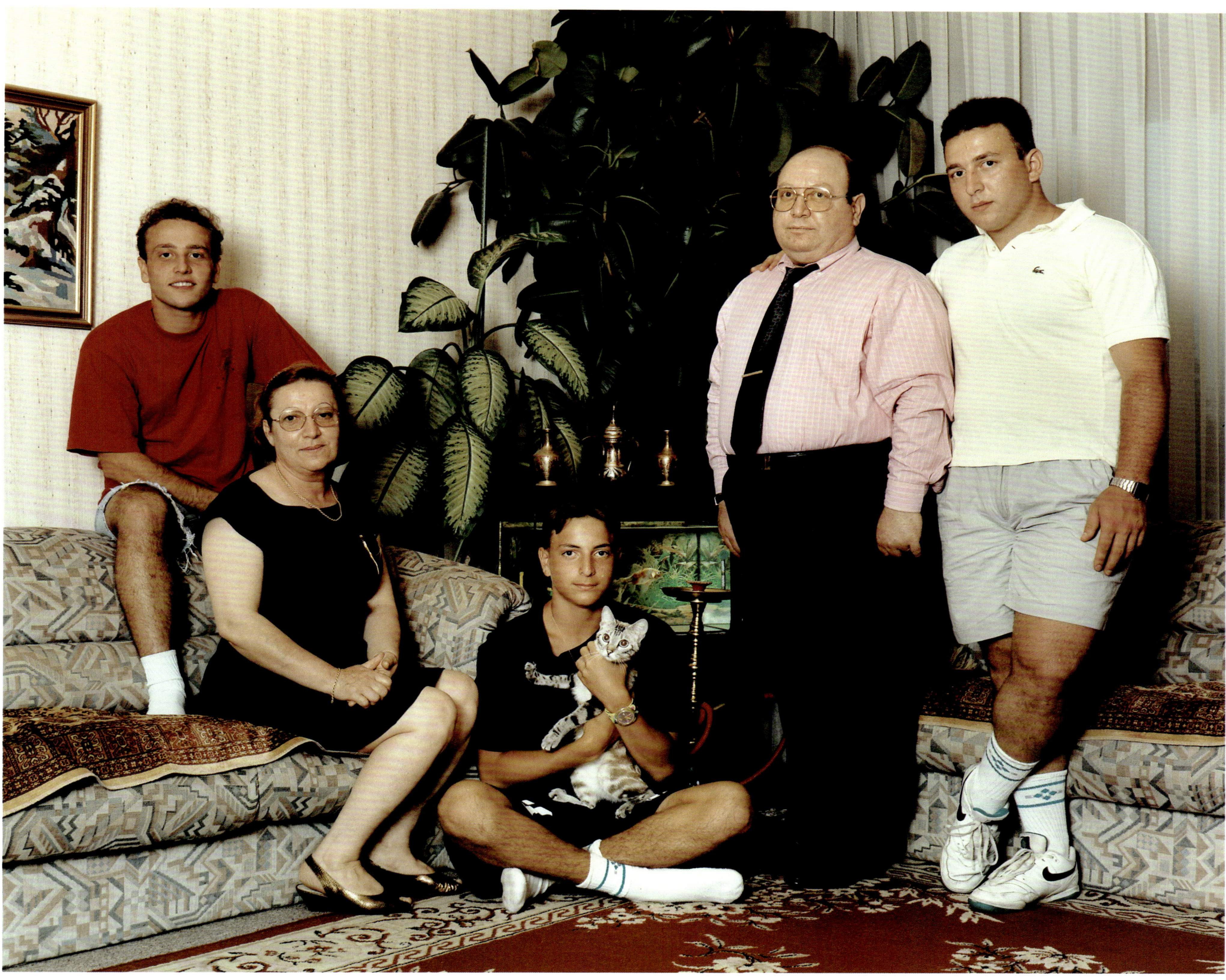

Franz and Brigitta Fässler, Switzerland

In their own fashion, they too had to be integrated. A Swiss passport means nothing when you come from Schwyz or Appenzell and you have to settle in Geneva, a distant city with a diabolical reputation. The Fässlers return each year to see their families, who have remained in the central region, but these reunions are a one-way street: the clan avoids this end of the country, which votes differently, sits on the French border and could easily not be Swiss and they wouldn't mind one bit.

In their inner, voluntary exile in Geneva, Franz and Brigitta chose Meyrin almost by accident. He was supposed to be sent by his company to England when a sudden death in the firm changed the course of his life. A change of direction, and the move to Meyrin was on. A studio had opened up. She, having come for her part to learn French, was to meet the man who would become her husband on the very day of her arrival....

The former member of the national discus-throwing team and the tennis-woman emerita did not leave town for very long, just long enough to move to Champel and come back. Since then their professional and social lives unfold entirely in the municipal area, since one finds everything there: business, recreation, services. Everything, for adults at least. Eric and Nadja, in fact, temper their parents' statements somewhat. Meyrin, in their opinion, is a daytime city. As a result, of tentimes the teenagers who go out in groups to discover the charms of the night prefer to "go into town" to party, and too bad for the *Graffiti* or the *Blue Note*, the local venues for youthful gatherings. All the same, while they may not know yet what to make of their future lives, they are no less certain of one thing: if they find housing there, they see no reason for leaving Meyrin. Typical adolescent paradox. When looking into the future, they downplay their present misgivings and reason like their parents: "Meyrin is peaceful, the countryside is a stone's throw away, and it wants for nothing."

On the attic terrace, Rita has three stories of planks all to herself. Rita is a rabbit named in homage of the Marley family—Bob and Rita Marley, reggae and ganja. In the living room, the walls are hung with Brigitta's paintings. A fine brushstroke. In one room, a bicycle. And trophies in the corridor. Sports run through this family's veins. Franz trains with dumbbells and is continuing his discus-throwing while adding the shot-put to his repertoire. Brigitta exercises in the gym and spins about on the courts. A retrospective comment: "When you leave your home region, sports can be a factor of integration. It makes barriers fall." Today, Nadja plays volleyball, Eric basketball, and the list of other sports they've dabbled in reads like the Olympic catalogue.

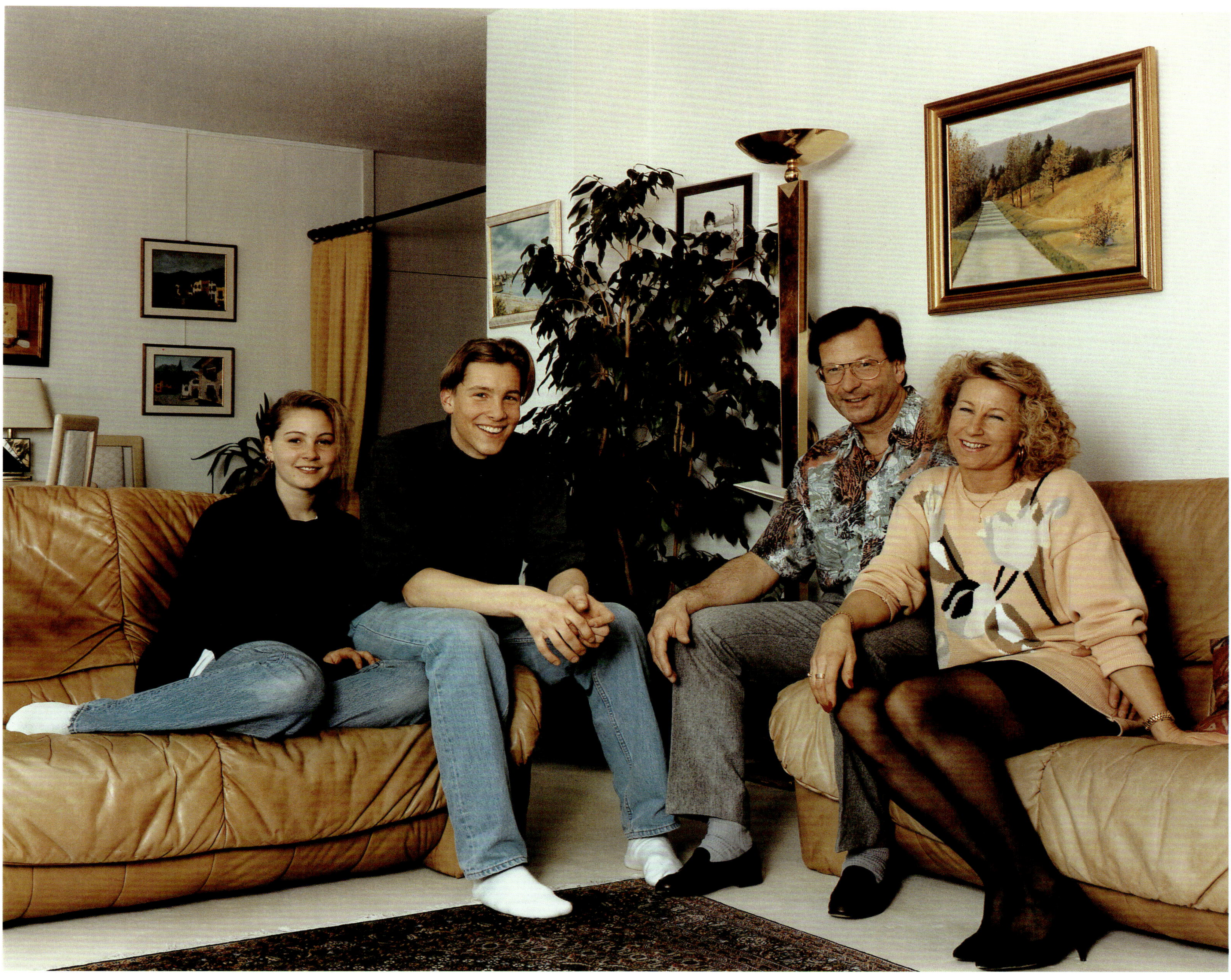

Etelvino and Maria-Luz Fernandez, Spain

Theirs is a story of brothers and the hospitality business. If Etelvino's elder brother had not left his native Galicia in search of work in Switzerland, the younger one would probably not have taken the same road. But it was tempting: in 1964, like a good number of Spaniards, he too left for the Swiss restaurant trade. While many of his compatriots were turned away, he slipped through the cracks and found his fortune at the Hôtel du Chandelier: a legitimate work contract for 350 francs monthly, room and board. As his boss's two brothers also ran restaurants, Etelvino, a good worker, soon made the rounds of the family holdings.

Maria-Luz Gomez, for her part, came to Geneva in 1967 with her widowed mother and like her, looked for a job. After various attempts, she landed a contract at the Beau-Rivage. A typical, ideal itinerary of '60s immigration: hard labor, then love and marriage with a fellow-countryman.

Today Etelvino works in the automotive sector. Maria-Luz takes care of them all, especially her mother, Manuela Gomez, who still lives under their roof. Monica and Philippe, the children, are wavering before two paths: will they live their lives in their country? And what is their country anyway, Spain or Switzerland? Grown up now, the children wonder and contemplate, bewildered, the unemployment figures so harshly affecting young people nearly everywhere in Europe.

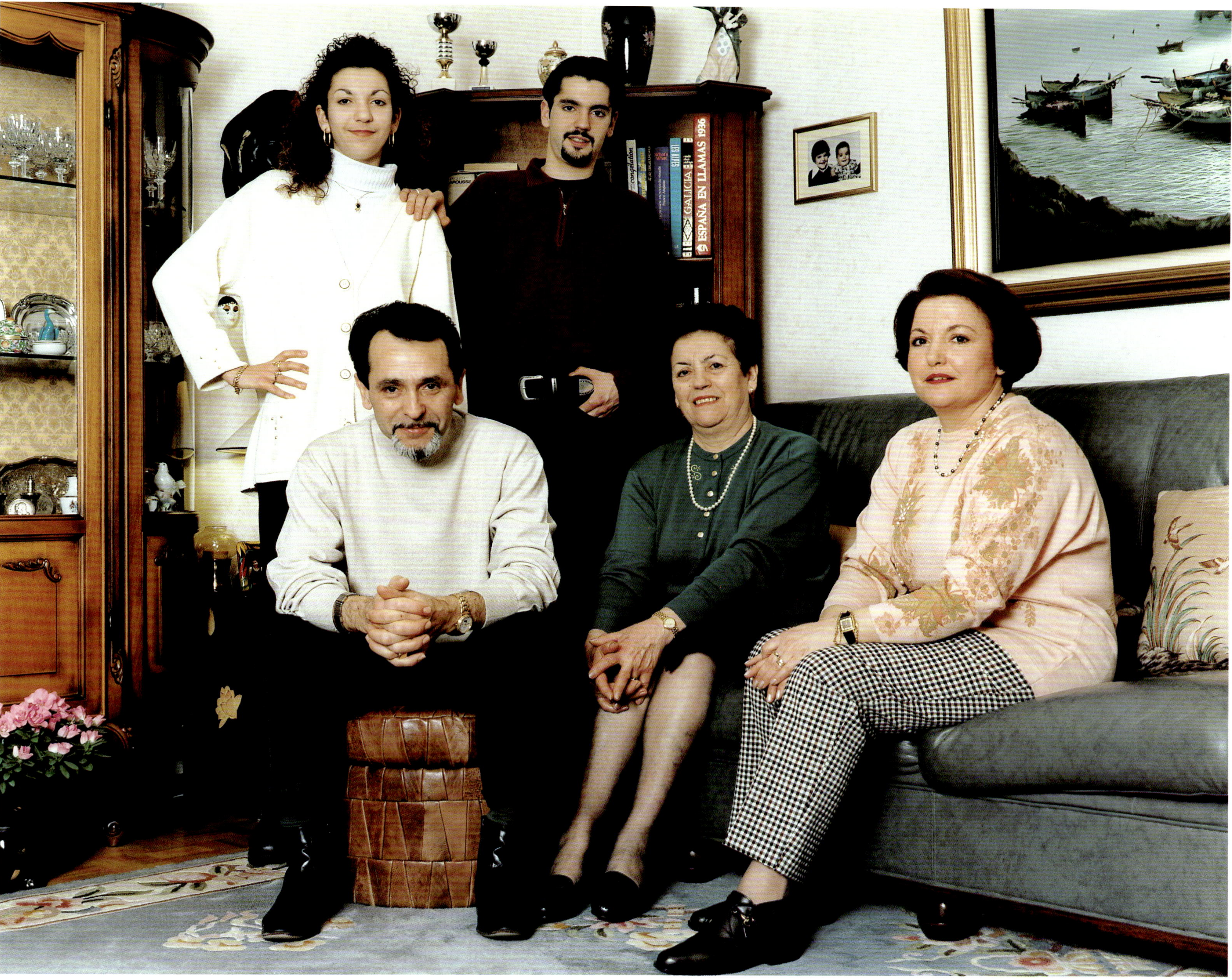
ESPAÑA EN LLAMAS 1936
GALICIA

Marek and Joanna Hagmajer, Poland

In Poland in the 1980s, one hardly ever came across colored people. At the most, a visiting politician would receive the brief homage or support of the reigning government; but as for the people, they were Slavs among Slavs. Similarly, except for Russian, one heard almost no foreign languages spoken in Warsaw. However, when Matylda, knee-high to a grasshopper, saw her first Africans or Asians here in Meyrin, it was the color of their clothes, not their skin, that she described to her parents.

This healthy reaction is most probably the result of her upbringing, which has taught her to respect others and affirmed the universality of the human race. Her parents used to say to her: In the end, it's only language that makes people different from one another. And so, when opening the door to their new Swiss home, Matylda would ask visitors: And what language do you speak?

While working at the Institute of International Affairs, a state organization charged with studying East-West relations, Marek was also working as a volunteer at the head of a non-government organization, the Polish Association for the United Nations. It is the national branch of a federation run from the United Nations building in Geneva, although it is in fact independent of it. Critical and supportive, it upholds and comments on U.N. activities while helping to convey that institution's message in each country. It was a holiday for the General Secretariat that prompted Marek to apply for the job among sixty other candidates—a simple political gesture, which amounted to showing that Poland knew what was what, despite there being no chance at the time that a Socialist-bloc country would be given this charge. At least that's what people said. To his great astonishment, Marek, on a lecture trip to Scandinavia, was welcomed there like the chosen one: he was, in fact, but he didn't know it yet. In Warsaw, Joanna, a high-level anesthetist, began, a bit shaken, to prepare for a temporary journey to Geneva.

Proust, a History of Geneva, the illustrated *Petit Perret*, and books of international politics adorn the white shelves of a white apartment. Beneath a Bosch triptych, a black cat with eyes so sparkling they compete with those of the mistress of the house—which are astonishing—is amusing itself retrieving the small objects tossed to him, not worrying too much about feline dignity. Cats are untouched by the servile sentiments dogs know so well. In this house, they have always been leery of prejudices and preconceived notions. An old souvenir of Warsaw.

Re-election after re-election, Marek Hagmajer has remained in place, in Geneva, where Krzyztof was born. In case they should one day have to leave, the children take weekly classes at the Polish school. The fact remains that such a departure would pose a problem.... Would it be a painful break, as Joanna believes, or simply an evolutionary stage that the children, with their formidable powers of adaptation, would easily get through, as Marek maintains?

In short, the parents are two of those international intellectuals who, having come to Meyrin "for a while," have put down roots here. And the children represent that second, bicultural generation waiting for a sign from destiny: they have no idea where they in turn will work and raise families of their own.

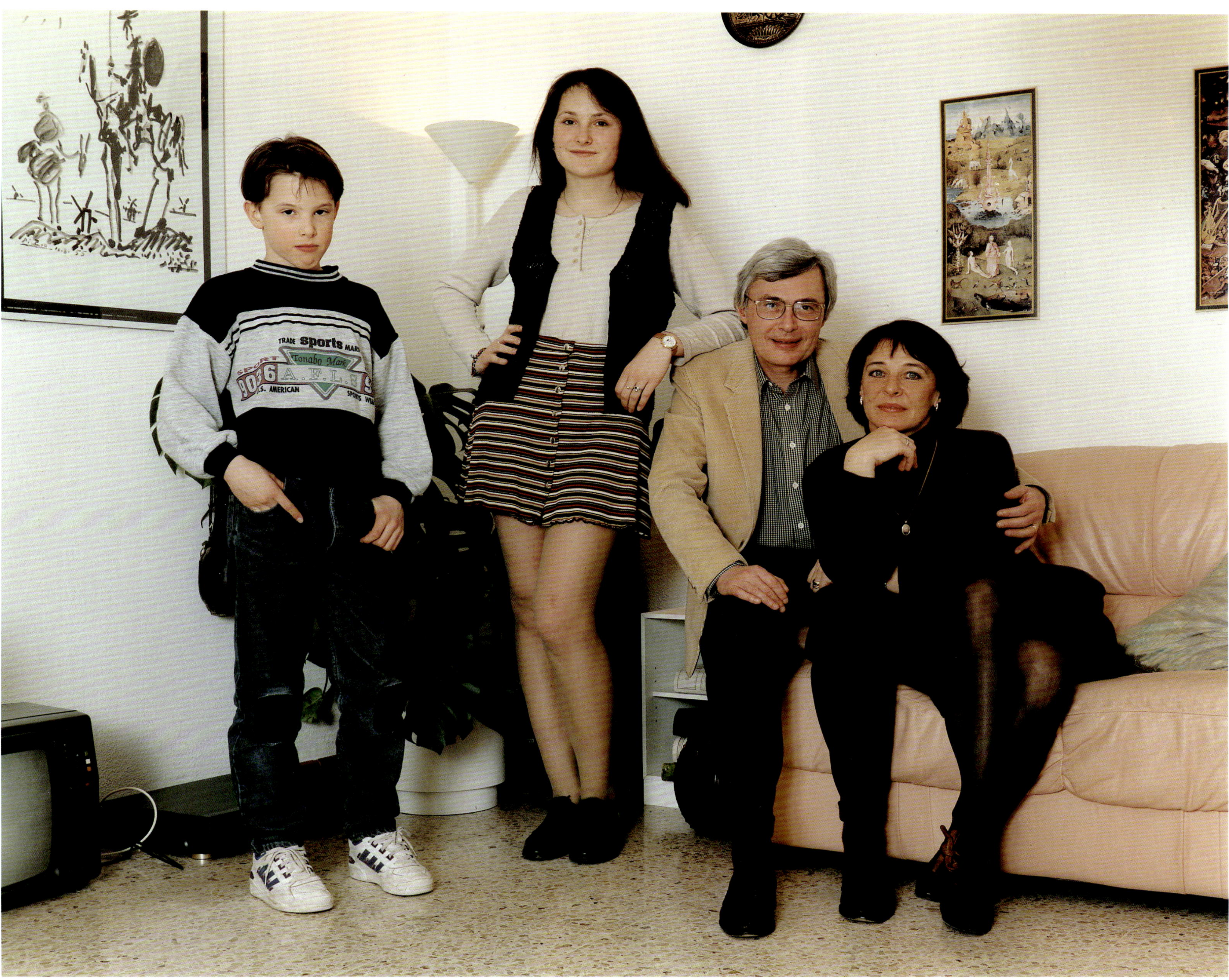

TRADE Sports
Tonabo Mark
A.F.L.
AMERICAN

Abdeslam and Hafida Halhoul, Morocco

Dear Mr Mayor:

Please allow me in my own way, which is certainly not Vian's, to write you a letter that you will perhaps read, if you have the time.

I have just come from the home of the Halhoul family. Charming people. A foreign family like so many others in Meyrin: modest, discreet, happy to number among your fellow-citizens. A family without history, whose third son, Karim, was born in Geneva. Abdeslam Halhoul is a chauffeur for the diplomatic mission of the Kingdom of Morocco, and his wife, Hafida, in the evenings, makes the empty offices sparkle. Probably their children will one day be Swiss; at least that is their fond desire.

You will tell me, Mr Mayor, that this does not fall within your power. You are right. But that is not why I am turning to you. Actually, I was struck to hear the eldest son, Mohammed, who is not in the photo, make an argument that I had already heard twice in my peregrinations through your town but until now had failed to pay any notice to.

Mohammed, like his group of adolescent friends, resent what they see as a lack of activities for young people their age. For my part, I am aware that Meyrin is actually one of the most dynamic communities in the canton in this regard. I am merely conveying to you the resentment of this age-group as I heard it: the *Graffiti*, an establishment targeted at this very group, apparently only opens its doors on weekends and the days before school holidays. As for the *Maison Vaudagne*, since it is institutional, it does not seem to fully meet the expectations of Mohammed's friends.

You see, Mr Mayor, Mohammed and his friends are some of the good kids of this community. They know that a bit of vandalism—not of their doing—recently cost the roads department a hundred thousand francs. They regret that such acts should have an effect on the way the authorities look at young people.

Is that why, they wonder, they are not accorded the right to organize a place that is their own and which they could easily manage themselves? Some old pavilions near the *CO collège de la Golette*, which they demand free use of, are scheduled to be demolished, they tell me. They regret this. They would have preferred to refurbish them, and probably would have put a great deal of healthy enthusiasm and energy into such a project. The youth of Meyrin are sometimes roaming the streets at night. But I have seen a few, in particular, who were positively consumed by a real hunger for building, in both a literal and figurative sense.

I know how difficult it is to administer an outlying city, and am aware of the efforts you have made toward the youth here, who indeed are well provided for. Still, I promised to communicate their demands to you, and that is why, with utmost respect, I am now addressing myself to you.

In the hope that you will show good will in hearing the voices of Mohammed and his friends, and thanking you in advance for your consideration, I ever remain

Yours sincerely,

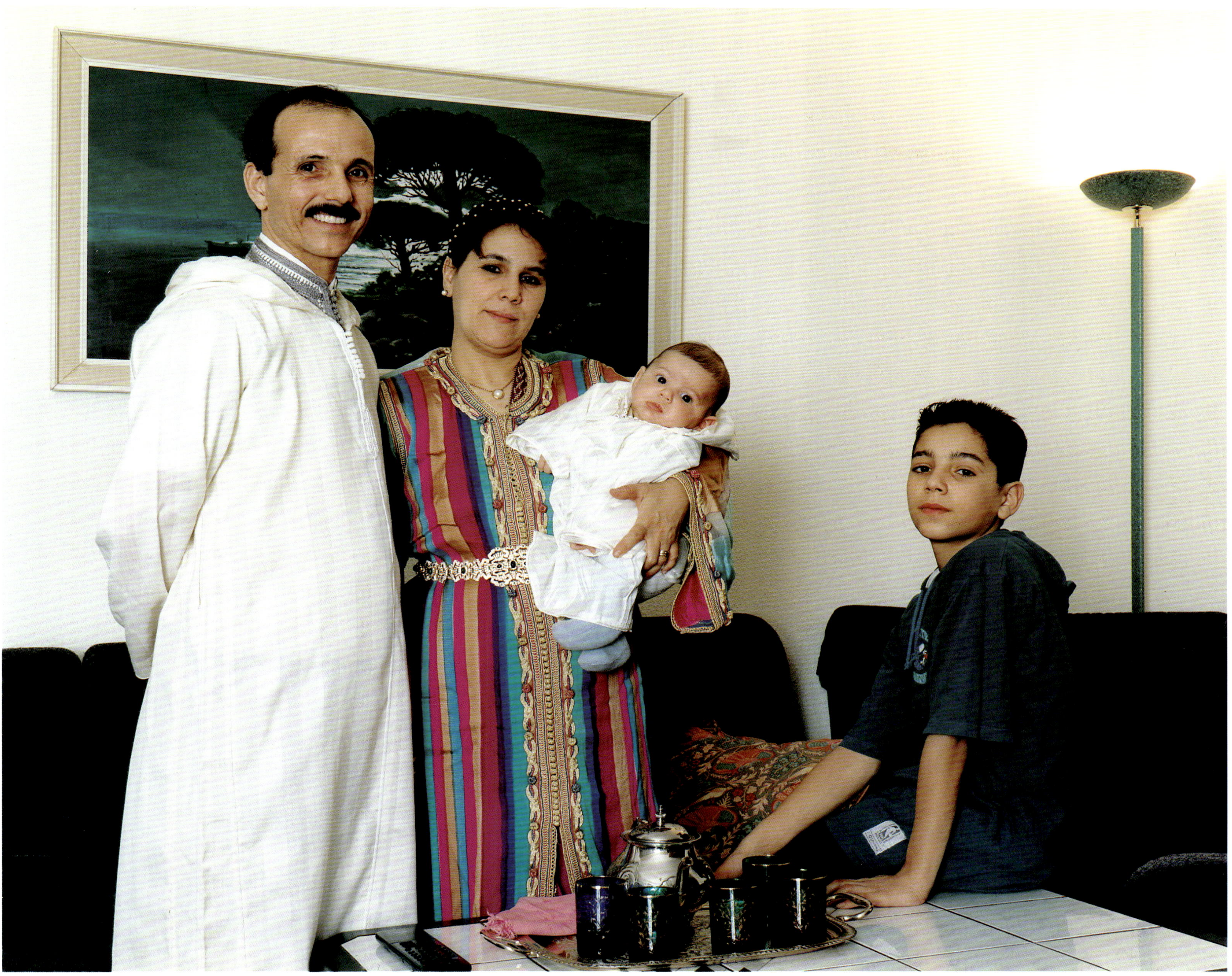

Barbara and Werner Hardt, Germany

Gigavolts. Electrons. Beams. Energy.
Process.
Weak forces. Center of mass.
Ring.
Particle, antiparticle. Proton,
antiproton.
Magnets. Reaction. Factors.
Refroidissement.
Percentages. Low energy. Storage.
Collisions...

In a soft, deep, slow voice, Werner Hardt explains his life's work to me, describing, growing impassioned, commenting.... But I don't understand a word of it.

So his wife comes up to me with her arms full of documents: "Look, it's all here," she says. "These are a few publications." In 1945, she left her native Silesia in painful circumstances. A nurse with a passion for the sciences, she met her future husband in 1952, in Bonn, at the physicist's ball. They moved to Hamburg and then, in 1964, left for Switzerland "for three years," to get in with the IAEA. Classic scenario.... The Hardts ended up raising their four children there, never leaving the country.

There is a specific science for the particle accelerator. By projecting protons the same way that one throws darts at a target in an English pub, one can obtain antiprotons. Not often, however. About once in every ten million tries. The main thing is to slow down their course in order to increase their conversion potential. To change it from a one-second passage to a four- or five-hour one. To do this, one creates complex rings in which the low-energy protons, lovingly nurtured by scientists, can change sex. The sex of angels. Afterward, the antiprotons must be stored and cooled down. The goal of the exercise is to increase the number of protons that will become antiprotons, then to keep them in proper form.

"What's the point of it?" I ask, to cut short this abstruse and fascinating stream.

"To keep scientists busy," smiles Barbara Hardt.

"Could I see your notebook?" Werner Hardt asks amicably, then covers it with formulas. Carrying on an intimate conversation with himself, he seems to have resumed his train of thought from zero. As if he had to verify one more time that it all worked, that there was no flaw in his reasoning.

Apparently, it works.... In 1984, Carlo Rubbia and Simon van der Meer were awarded the Nobel prize in physics for results obtained in the same area as that being explored by Werner Hardt. Why keep investigating?

Because that's the way of the researcher.

Barbara Hardt goes back to her puzzle boxes. Inside, well protected, are splendid religious images that she paints on old wood. On the wall, auras of icons, Orthodox Christian. In the library, a large biblical work. On the table near the entrance, the last issue of the *Revue Juive*.

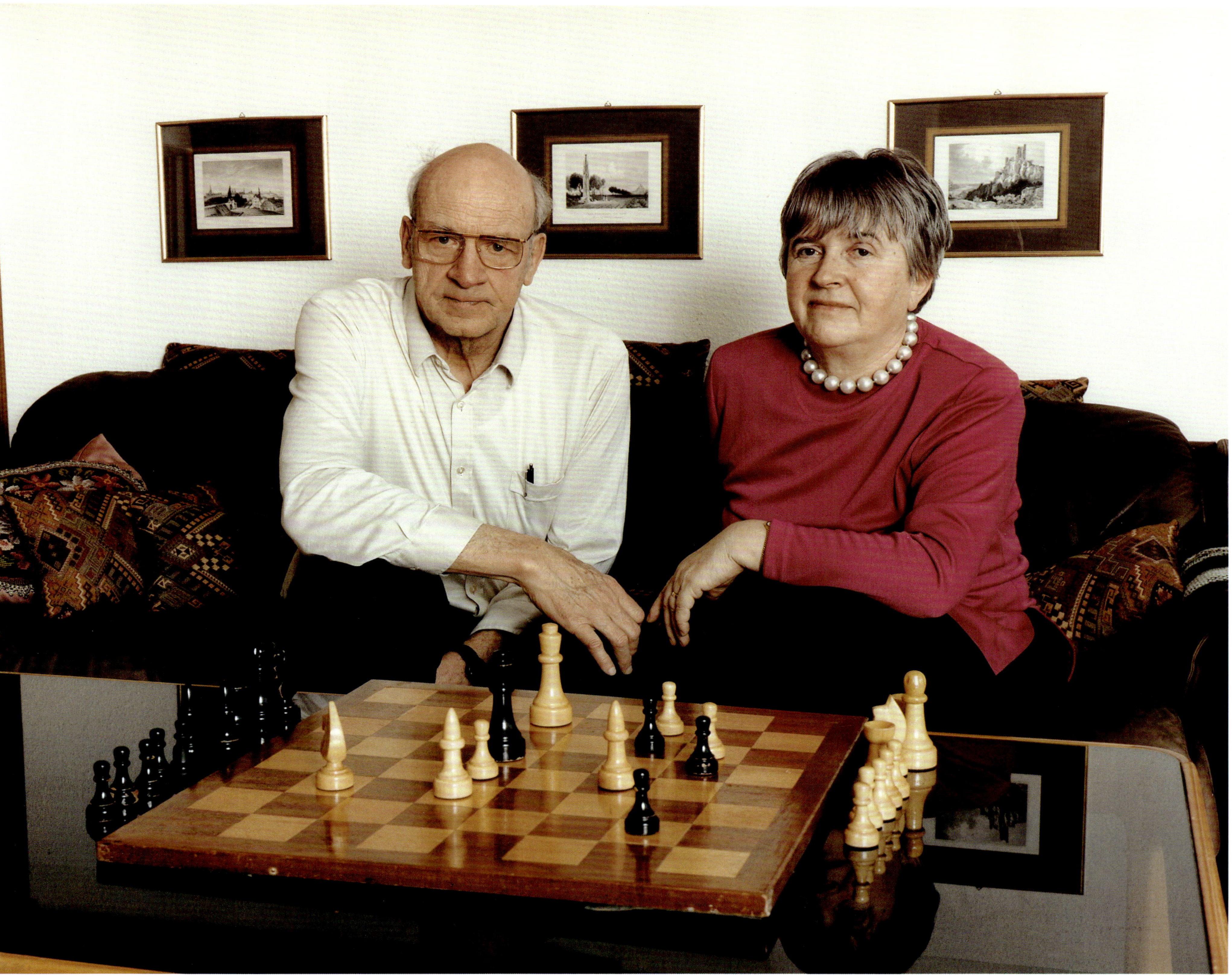

Donald and Maria de los Angeles Harlow-Powell, United States—Nicaragua

The game consists of putting the following elements back into a coherent order:
Frankfurt I David Niven I Rabbit Nostrils I Murders I *La Suisse*, a Newspaper I Lucerne Bridge I Tunis I Bike I *Queen of Coffee* I Mick Jagger I Somoza I Puzzle I Jazz Festival I Swissair I Girls' Boarding School I Magic Johnson I Baby-Sitting I Police Auxiliary I Connecticut I Mule-Safari I Benevolent Christ I Motorbike I Château de Chillon I Trilingual Children I Meyrin. The "beginners" version stops here.

Suggested response: Donald. The Sixties. Brought here on business, his father, an American of German-English origin, maintains close relations with Europe. All right, he thinks, why not live there? The stability of Switzerland and the charm of the Vaudois Riviera determined the choice of his landing-point. Donald was six when his parents moved to Montreux. A peaceful childhood. That old loner David Niven, a family friend, sometimes dropped in to see just what a typical family was like.

Maria de los Angeles was also in Montreux at that time, attending a fancy boarding school for girls. That's because in Nicaragua, under the Somoza dictatorship, things were not very pleasant. For her family, a renowned dynasty of coffee-growers, it would hardly be better during the Sandinista regime. In her town, Maria de los Angeles was one day elected *Queen of Coffee*, but in fact it was a life of oppression: eleven of her relatives are assassinated in a few years' time, including her brother.

At Montreux, the young Donald becomes a police auxiliary and parks cars on evenings when there are concerts at the *Maison des Congrès*. He meets Johnny Hallyday, Claude François and others. He finds show-business amusing. He works at the jazz festival as a baby-sitter, whispering to Joan Baez's and Melanie's kids and having drinks with Mick Jagger and Keith Richard. Then, as a tour guide, he conquers the Lucerne bridge and leads mule-safaris in the Valais. He even has a kitschy puzzle given him as a gift for his 500th organized visit to the Château de Chillon. In short, this American is more Swiss than the Swiss.

The couple leaves for Tunis, then Frankfurt. Donald works for Swissair. Ever ready to pack his bags. He loves travel. In Meyrin, in the beginning, he delivered *La Suisse* on his motorbike. Today he manages duty-free shops at the Cointrin airport. The children are trilingual. Ricky can even communicate with rabbits; all you have to do is move your nostrils exactly the way they do. In his room there is an autograph of Magic Johnson and over the main entrance, a benevolent Christ.

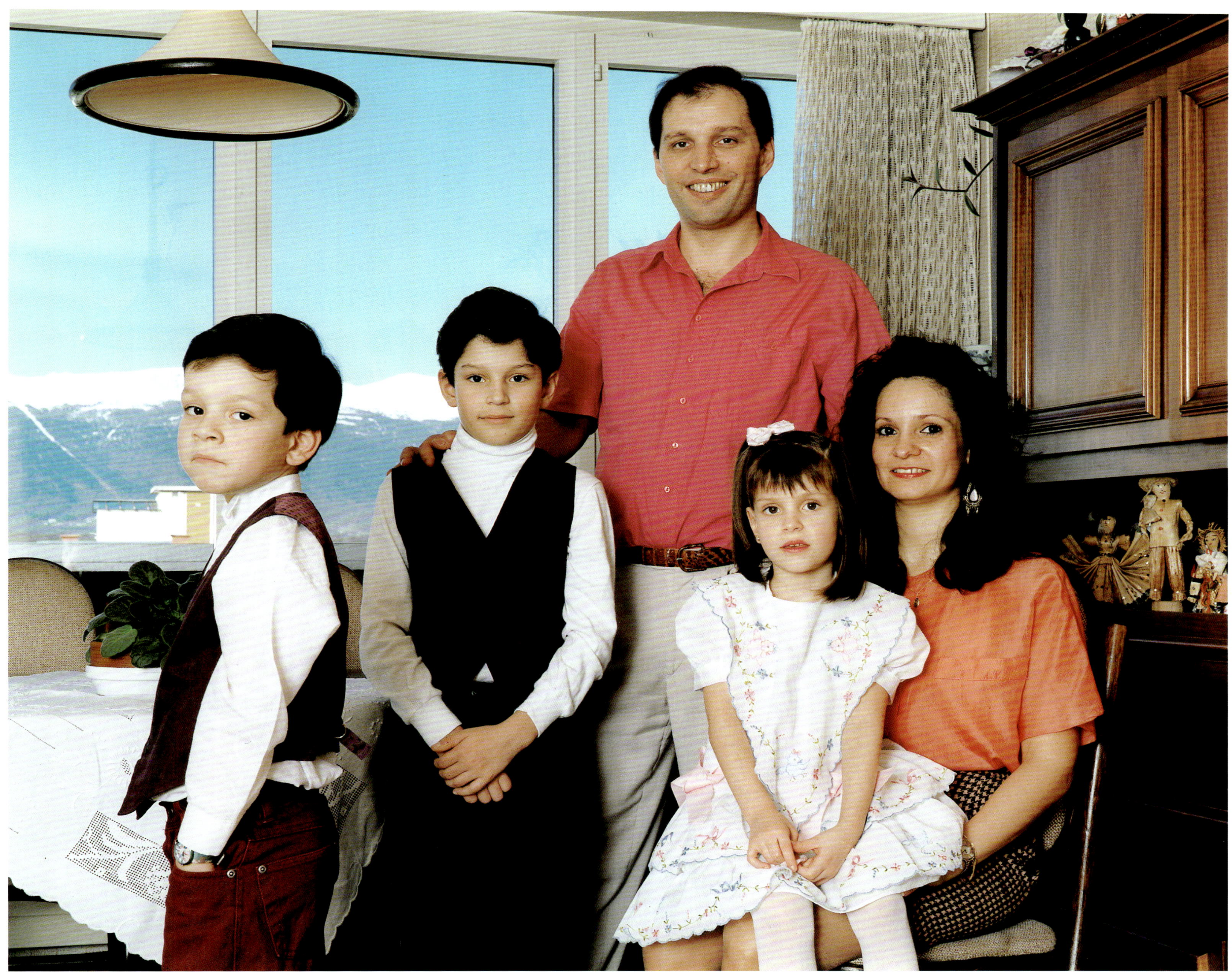

Harry and Sasà Hayes, United States—Italy

When he comes looking for his guest, lost in the city in a driving rain, Harry Hayes forewarns me, using Natel's formula, that he'll be "wearing a white coat." The statement already gives two clues. The first is his place of origin, betrayed by the accent. The second is that it seems perfectly natural to Harry Hayes that if he hadn't been forewarned, his interlocutor could only have difficulty guessing which person was he. And yet the crafts center is not exactly teeming with people in the evening. But the Hayes know that Meyrin is full of a thousand different noises, that passers-by are numerous, that those cats on air pillows are their neighbors, and that life pops up in the very places one least expects it. A motorbike buzzes past in the distance. A board on wheels is going "padam, padam, padam" over a surface that is obviously not smooth, and in one's head sings the voice of Piaf, who also knew how to play the crowd.

At the Hayes residence, all the paintings point to somewhere else. They were painted by Sasà. She comes from Turin, the headquarters of Fiat, for whom her father used to work. It was in fact Fiat that originally sent her to Geneva. Today she teaches drawing, one of the twenty-four skills for which apprenticeships are offered by the Association of Residents of the City of Meyrin, which she has headed for seven years. They have a thousand members.

"At first, when the association was born over thirty years ago, Meyrin didn't have anything. Just a few apartment buildings, a few others being built, no infrastructure. Of the first inhabitants, many worked for the IAEA. The city was being born."

The IAEA. He works there as an analyst. He is also a photographer and publishes a magazine, *International Review*, which gives him a forum in which to express his pacifist sentiments. He knows Cambodia and Vietnam. He conducted humanitarian missions there, frequented Edmond Kaiser, founder of Terre des Hommes, and Bernard Kouchner, the "French doctor" become minister. But he knows Vietnam best of all. Like all Americans of the Kennedy years, he speaks very little about it: "The war is over." He spent two years there. After that, he was named head of security for the American Mission in Geneva. Then came the second half of the story. At an American picnic in Geneva, he met her.

Since the time of the "boat people," they have worked with relief networks. When the war was raging in Afghanistan, they took in a wounded man for ten months. The Hayes get involved everywhere: with the inhabitants of Meyrin; with the American community (in preparing the national holiday); with organizing a comic-book festival, and country music concerts.... Their son, trilingual and trinational, recruited into the Swiss army, is a chip off the old block. At the moment, he is waking up. He had fallen asleep over his biology book. Exam-time is near.

And what do you want to do in life?

I don't know. Something useful.

Useful? What does that mean?

The environment.

All the while one can hear Mama growling in the kitchen. She will not come out. America has not really got the upper hand.

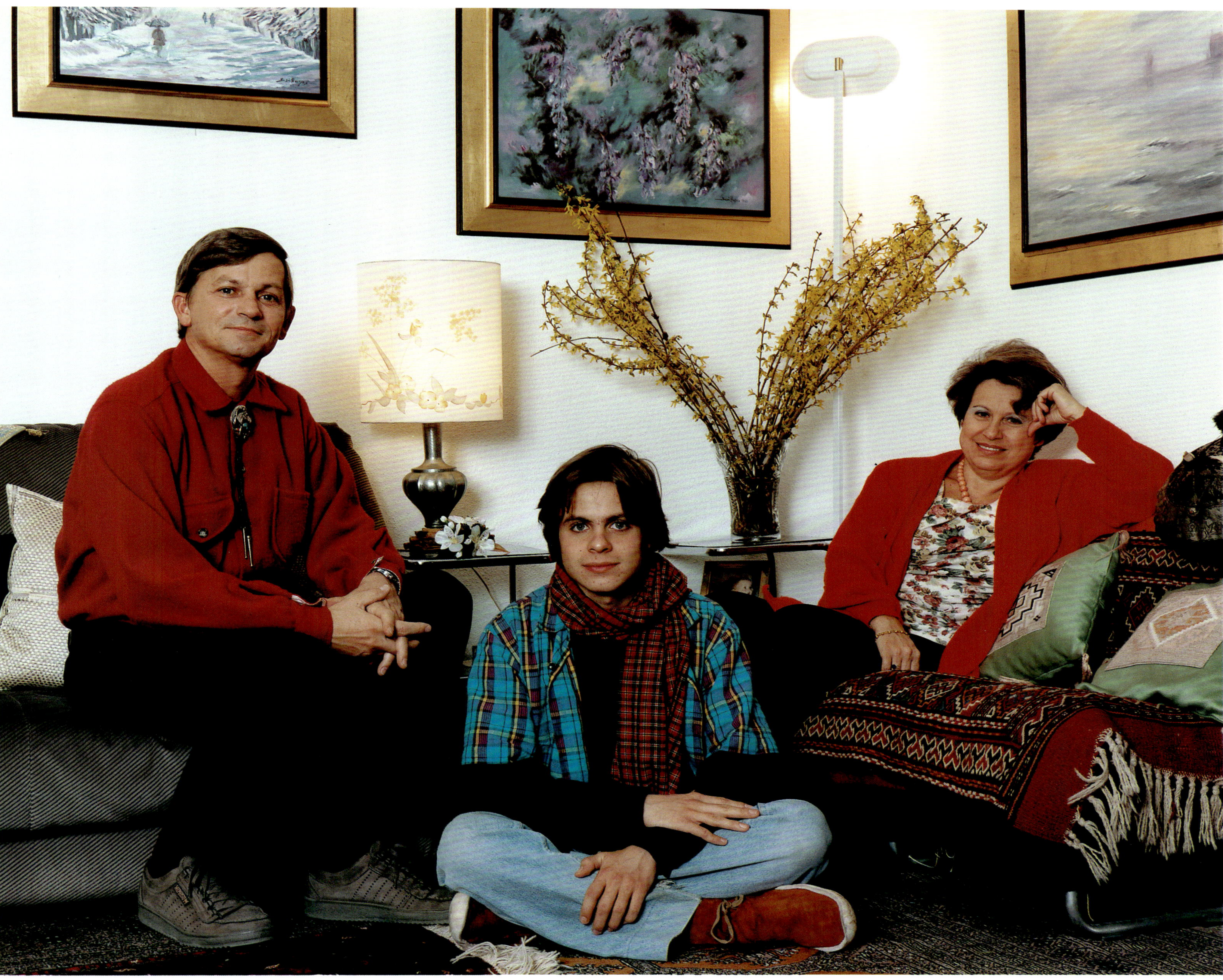

David and Jaqueline Hillman, England

On a stretch of inhospitable land near a prison, is a barren hill crowned by an old church. Nothing else around. Not even a road leading up to it. Legend has it that the church was originally built at the foot of the hill but a malevolent spirit, just out of spite, decided to shunt it to the summit, among the brambles. It was there that David Hillman was baptized. According to the local people, only the children of robust families are baptized in this church, for only the strongest mothers manage to climb up there with their babies in all weather. A photo guished in the hall conveys all the anguish appeal this house of God might have for the lost traveller.

A man in another picture is playing the bagpipes in black and white. A former military man. He too is a force of nature. Fighting on the European front during the War, he escaped from Nazi stalags no less than seventeen times. Between escapes, he was building stills to make whisky on the sly in the workshops where the Germans enslaved their prisoners of war. By the end of the war, he was hiding in a lost corner of Poland, not even noticing that the cannons had fallen silent. A helper in the Resistance who would go on to become a star bagpipes player, summoned to perform for high dignitaries and recommended to the film industry as a specialist extra, Jacqueline's father was a phenomenon.

Things smell new in the neighborhood around this house, which David, a former copy editor, was able finally to buy after working his way up to being publications director of the UN. A swimming pool laps lazily in the small garden. In London, in the old days, David and Jacqueline's house was rather more modest. At Meyrin, the Hillmans have since founded a large family: after Neil, who studies Fine Arts in England, there is Asha, who comes from India. The Hillmans wanted "to give a home to somebody who didn't have one." This was not without its complications, "but," the bearded giant smiles, "that was in 1979: the international Year of the Child!" Then came Martin, who welcomed me into a home where the child is truly king, and Robert, a sweet English-speaking boy who wishes he could participate more in the conversation. The chatter of adults is a hard thing to bear when you're a child.

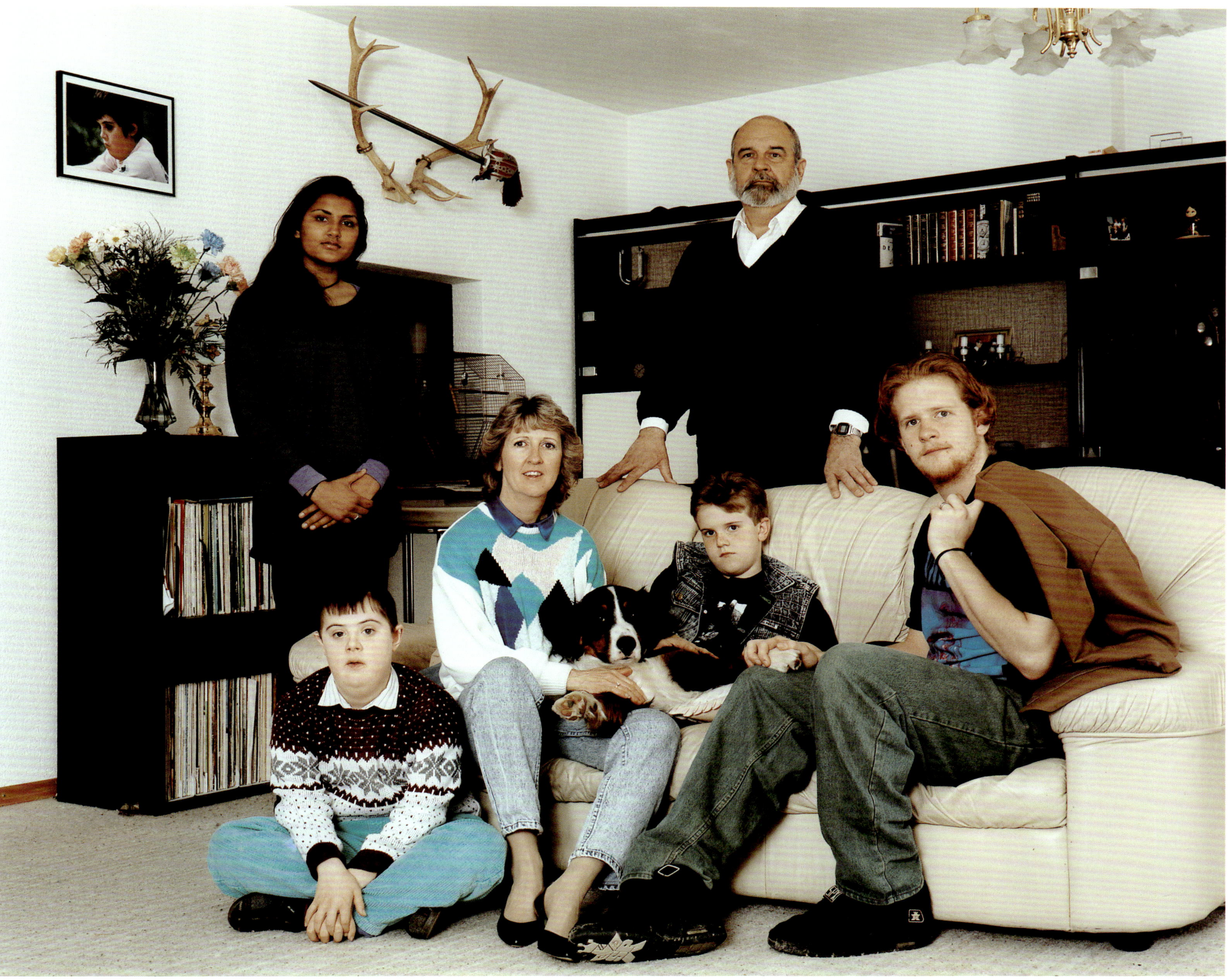

Soe and Daw Hlaing, Burma

Burma, a west Indochinese country, is a federal republic that includes the former English colony of Burma, various states (the Chans, Kachins, Karens, and Kayahs) and autonomous territory of the Chins. 670,000 sq km, 35 million inhabitants.
Capital: Rangoon. Language: Burmese.
[...] December 1973: new Constitution instituting a single-party regime.
Petit Larousse

Though he agreed to be photographed with his family, Mr Hlaing, foreign representative of the Burmese Government, asked not to be interviewed by a journalist.

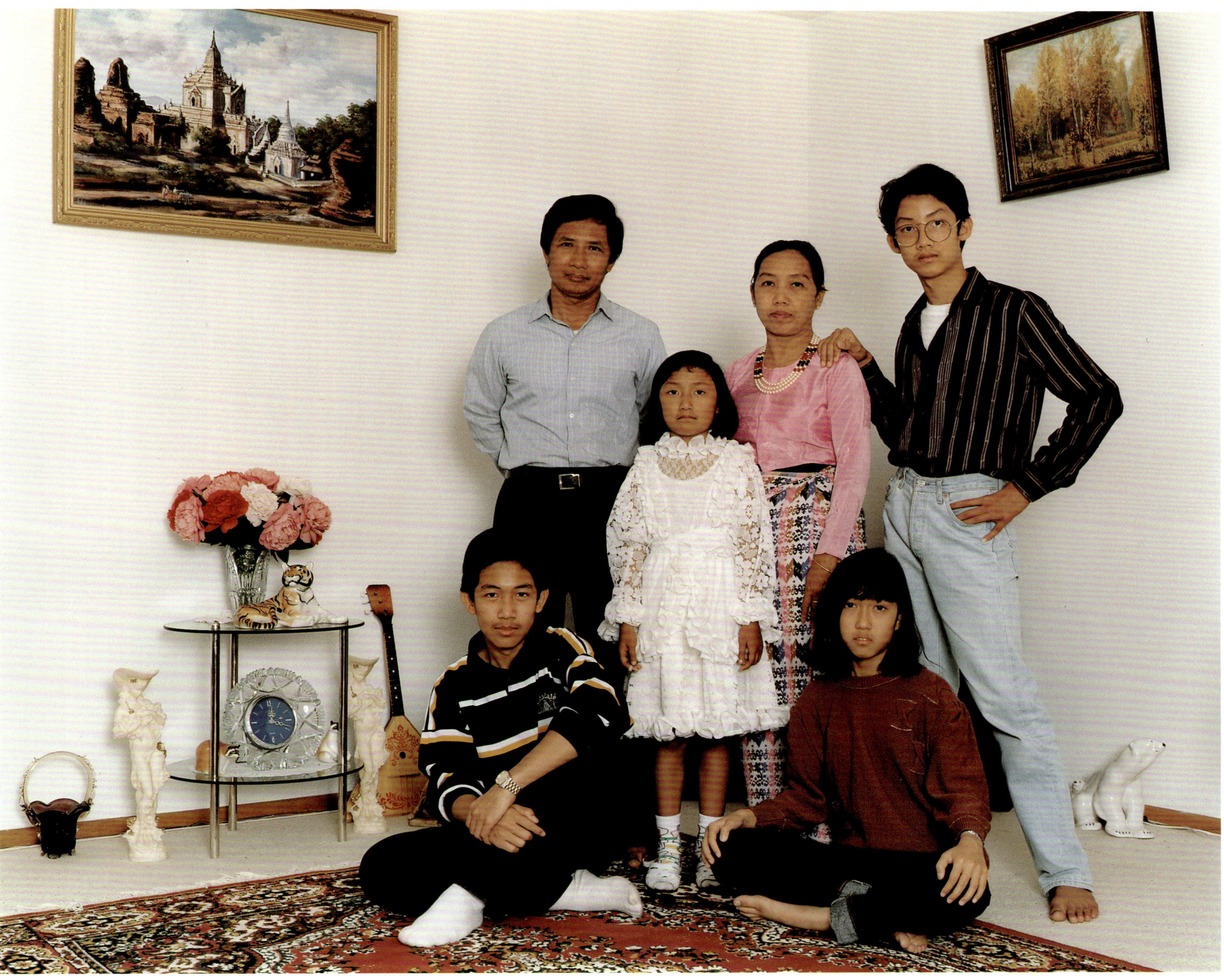

Vilay and Sengsomchit Inthavong Phrakonkham, Laos

I feel like talking, he says.

And he tells of his fear of politics and soldiers, who used to fire into the air to frighten him when he went fishing; of his brother, who suddenly left with only one bag and some communist friends; of the offers he was made to run a football club if he would also agree to become politically active; of his departure, in 1968, to an early refugee camp; and finally of his return to Laos in 1975. That year, Vilay marched in the streets in his first demonstration. Sengsomchit was also there, but the two did not know each other at the time. Then, as the army was becoming more threatening, another departure: in 1979, Vilay reached a camp in Thailand, carrying nothing but his three tattoos.

When Vilay arrived in France as a political refugee, Sengsomchit was already living in Meyrin. She was even supposed to get married there, but as soon as the banns were published, her fiancé skipped town without warning. Finally, at a New Year's party in February near Annecy, she met the man who would become her real husband.... "But not for five years!" he stipulated. Time enough to learn a trade.

She works for Rolex. He also used to work for a watch-factory, but lost his job and has now been unemployed for a long time. The day the letter of dismissal arrived, his life suddenly changed direction: his only hope now is his son Marc, who at age five speaks Laotian, French, and Thai—and he still has a dream, still vague and much cherished, of some impossible return to his native land.

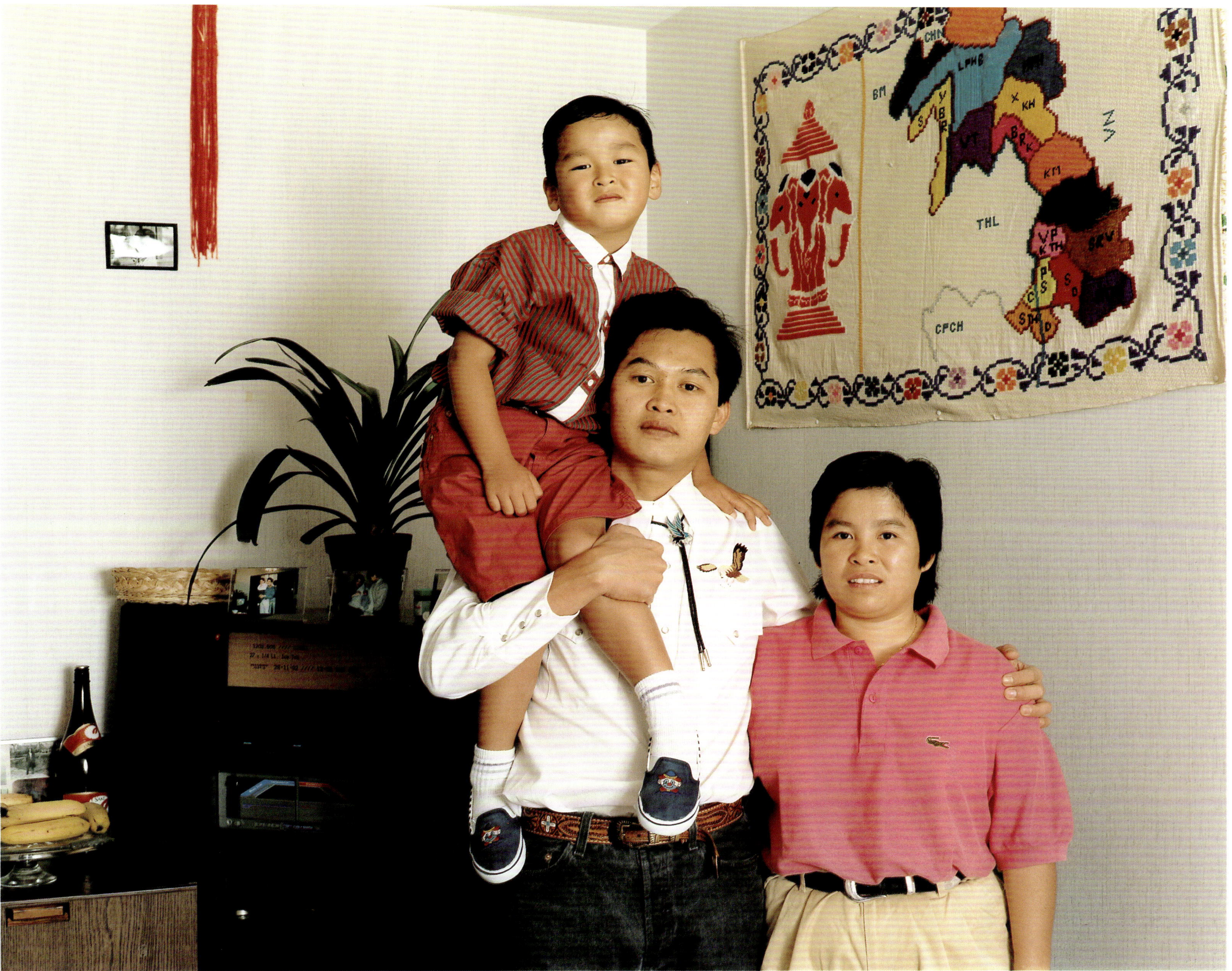
CHN
LPHB
BM
KH
KM
THL
CPCH

Ohran Islamovic, Bosnia

The Look
With his cowboy boots, double-breasted suit and sumptuous handkerchief, Ohran Islamovic strides about Meyrin, mobile phone in hand. He eyes his fellow townsmen, watching over them like senator. A popular character. Yellow Ray-Bans, aviator style. A cross between a fashion-plate and a Christmas tree, he's a close cousin of the peacock.

The Chalet
His three-room dwelling is entirely wainscotted inside, transformed into an Alpine refuge. Very Swiss, with flags, cuckoos, and panoramic views. "Your country is the one you feel good in!" There's a smell of pine in his chalet. On the wall, a placard warning the visitor: "Here, one must speak the truth!" His office-living room has something of the feel of a drinks cabinet.

The Office
"I spend 90 percent of my time working." On the landing-door, near some other placards banning smokers and solicitors, a sign informs the visitor point-blank: "Bureau Islamovic." Everything here is conceived "for business." Calculator, dictaphone for an absent secretary, banking advertisements hung like diplomas of excellence.

The Bank
A certified middleman. Soul-soother. Lends on the basis of one's word. "I like to serve my fellow man." As he crosses his fingers, his rings gleam like a thousand fires: "I'm a prudent man. I lend only to the rich. The poor are a source of trouble, since they don't always pay you back!" To them, on the other hand, he lends his "risk-free" advice free of charge.

The Women
A notorious lady-killer. He cultivates this reputation studiously and directs his oglings at the cuties "as an homage to their beauty," but claims to have stopped chasing them. Cold turkey? "Well, I've stopped… taking an interest in other people's women!" He'll never admit that he's actually looking for the great love of his life. The beautiful bird is loath to turn around in its solitude.

The Car
He likes power and the unusual. His car is the hi-tech counterpart to his rustic chalet. "I get a new one every year!" Sporty, racy, a Corvette ZR-1. White. A leather-upholstered rocket. Priceless. In the front seat, American and Swiss flags. In a nearby garage, a Fiat 500. "Me, I'd rather walk than drive a mosquito like that!"

The Past
He had wanted to be a priest. Having become a state functionary under Tito, he fled his country a few years after it broke apart. "I've always had a good nose. Professional idiosyncrasy." Later, his son would fight in the suburbs of Sarajevo. Not he. "War is useless. In business, they know that race and color are of no importance."

The Future
Sometimes, Orhan Islamovic grants himself pause, to read a book of psychology. "It's very important for business!" He lives on dreams. "Building the future is the only valid motivation in the fulfilment of the present." What about private life and recreation? "There'll be no retirement. I'll work until my last breath."

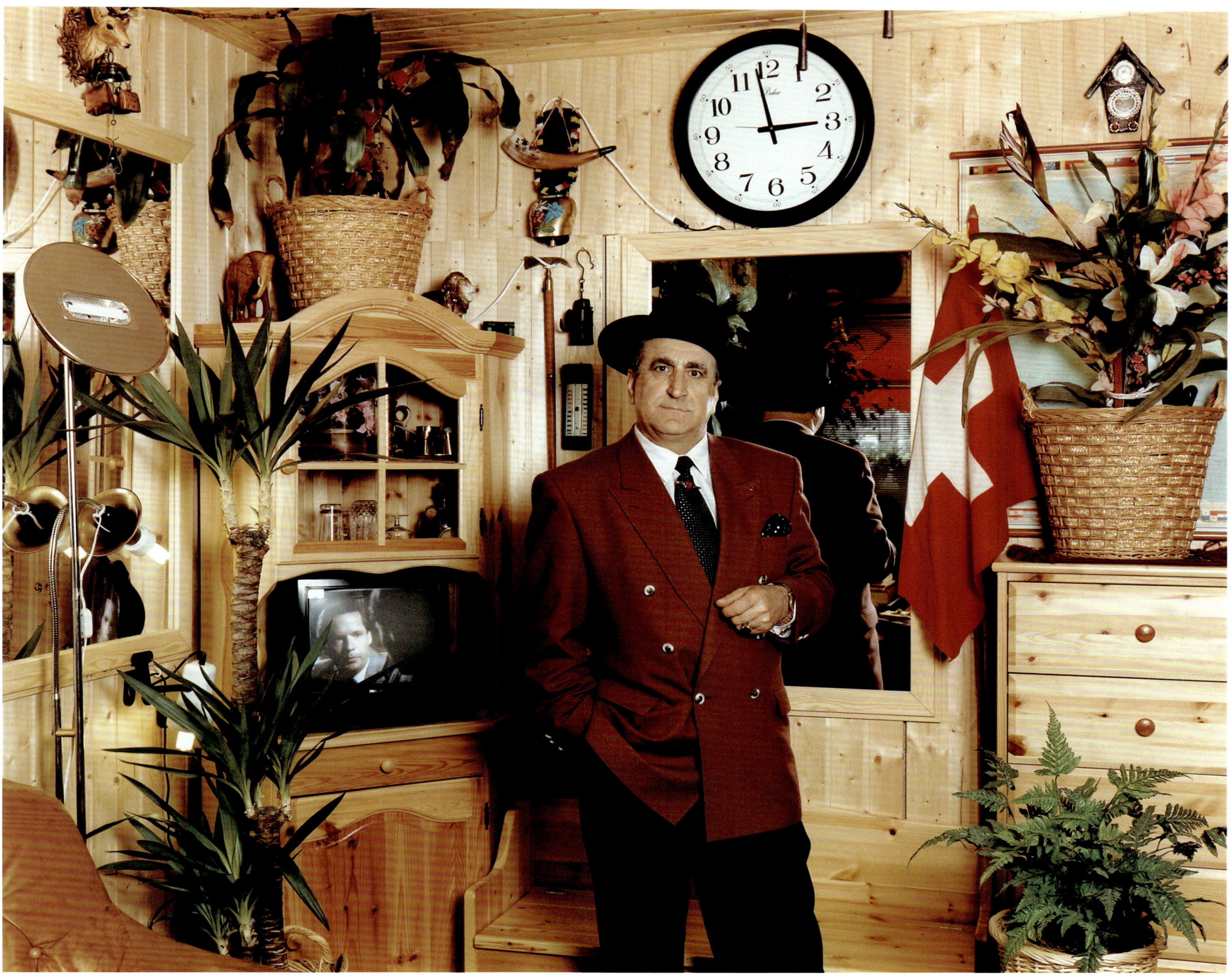

Denise and Jaime-Haïm Israël, Israel

"And you shall hang them over your doors."

Two oblique nails indicate that a mezuzah, a small oblong box containing a sacred text, had once been hung near that door.

A few days after moving in, the Israëls noticed it had disappeared, but didn't rush to any conclusions.

"Sometimes people think it's an alarm...."

The Egyptians downstairs, like the Syrians upstairs, are friends. The neighbors have picnics together regularly. There's no problem.

In Morocco, in 1956, it was different. The riots and the exile of the king, protector of Jews in Arab lands, triggered an emigration in all directions.

"Everyone feared serious problems."

The Israëls too packed their bags. In 1961, six-months pregnant and with another child under her arm, Denise and Haïm left for the country bearing their name with no precise plans.

They headed for Rosh Pina. No one had ever seen an immigrant from Morocco there before. They learned the language, worked in the fields, then in the factory, then took intensive courses.

"I had the family to provide for. I had to buckle down."

An insurance broker who became a peasant, then a laborer, then a foreman three months later, then a chauffeur, a volleyball instructor and accountant, he also ran two companies.

They lived everywhere. Bath Yam, Akko, Nataniah, Tel-Aviv.... But as the economic pressure was mounting, they took to the road again in 1980.

"My brother-in-law was living in Switzerland. A peaceful country."

Supported by his friends and steered by a former Chancellor of the Republic, who sent him to Meyrin, Haïm Israël looked for work with insurance companies.

At first, polite refusals, and they didn't try to hide the reason: that name! Then, a job. There was a problem, however: foreigners are not allowed to sell door-to-door.

"So I'd had enough. We looked elsewhere."

She went back to Israel, he prospected in Caracas and New York. Passing back through Switzerland, he was taken on as accounting analyst at a firm where he still works today.

Their four children are grown up. A fourth grandchild is on the way. The Israëls are going to become Swiss. They are gentle and strong of character. Haïm: that means "life" in Hebrew.

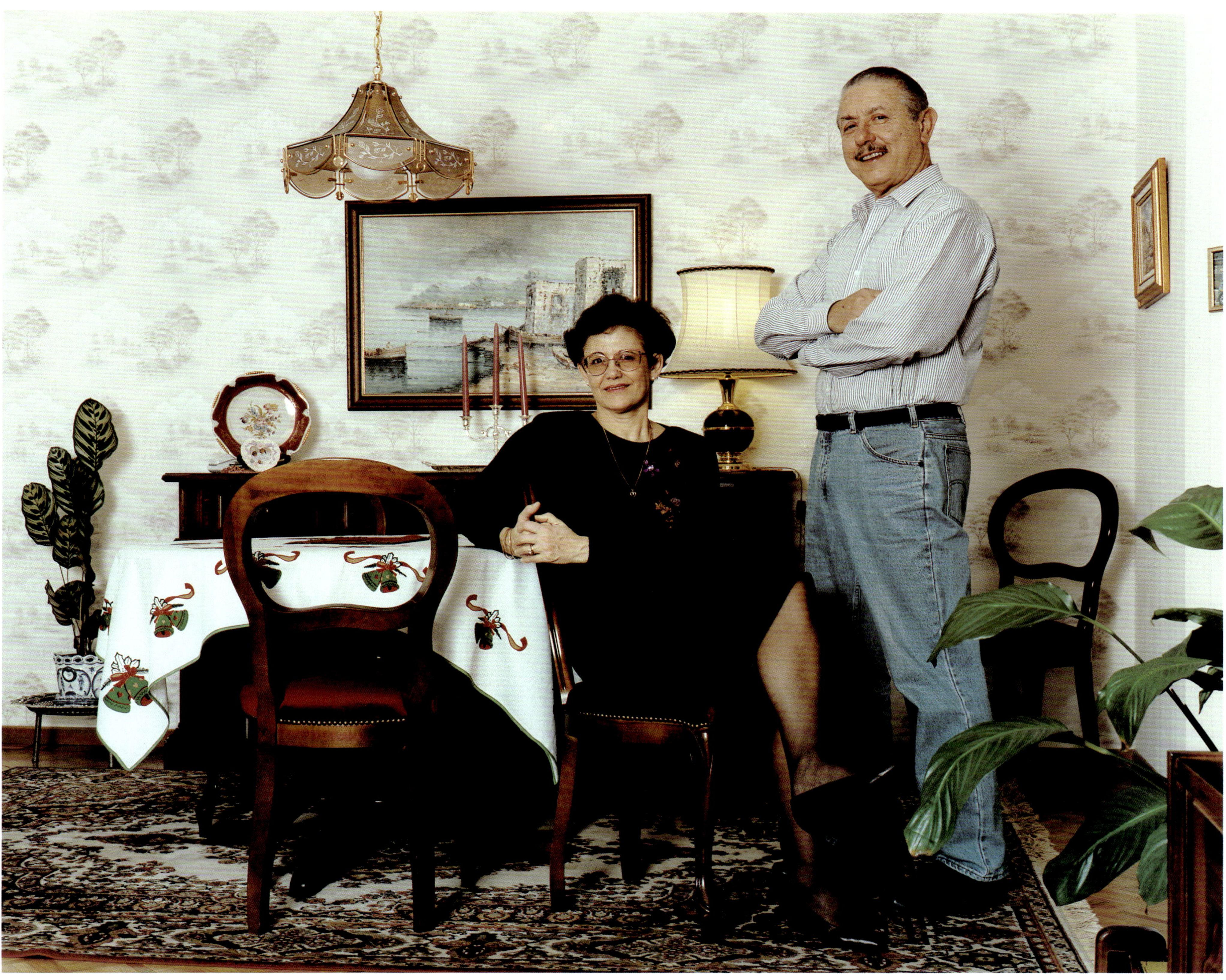

Jacqueline and Charles Karekezi, Rwanda

Kigali, capital of Rwanda. The classic scene unfolds at the airport: great crowds of people, families coming back together for the duration of the holiday, eyes seeking other eyes, hands reaching out to other hands. A little girl breaks down in tears. She is Angélique Karekezi, unexpectedly struck by the fact that all these people are ... black. All of them. Not like where she comes from. On this day, as she is setting foot on Rwandan soil, her sense of proportion is suddenly teetering, and she feels disoriented.

The memory of this scene is one of those that have led the Karekezi to meet regularly with other Rwandans of French Switzerland to teach their children the rudiments of the national language and culture. Sometimes, the group dances at a guest-house. It has also come together on the occasion of the 700th anniversary of the Confederation, and has even been seen on television. These Rwandan children of Swiss culture have learned to appreciate their roots and round out their experience; in a word, they are able now to situate themselves.

Like so many other people in this book, Céleste, Angélique and Grâce are fully children of cultural crossbreeding. What twist of fate determined that they should be born in Meyrin? Since one is readily fatalistic in Africa, it doesn't matter. It's an act, a matter of destiny.

Destiny, for these people, has shown its face three times. First, when Charles and Jacqueline crossed paths. Charles had obtained a bachelor's degree in literature in Zaïre before going to teach in Burundi; he was then awarded a scholarship enabling him to study in Paris toward a degree in educational science. Jacqueline was also a teacher in Burundi. Likewise the beneficiary of a scholarship, she went to Rome. Then came the second stroke of destiny: while passing through, a professor of the CHUV invited her to come to Lausanne where he was teaching a course in family planning, the path she had chosen for herself. She became a midwife, and then—the third stroke of destiny—the hospital of la Tour offered her work in Meyrin. Charles followed her and worked for eight years for official institutions for the protection of youth, then for the UNHCR.

Six months before the outbreak of the Rwandan civil war in 1994, which would take a million lives, she had said to me: "There are massacres on the horizon."

Six months after the horror, Charles, now a consultant for Rwanda at UNICEF, counts the relatives he has left. His mother is dead, his brothers too. And everyone else. There were sixty-six of them; now only three survive. Back home, they have counted 100,000 utterly traumatized orphans. Many have seen their parents raped and killed. Others are still wandering in the hills. They must be found and re-integrated into life. That is what Charles is involved in. In Geneva, the girls have cried a lot. They don't understand the wickedness of men. Even lions only kill when they are hungry.

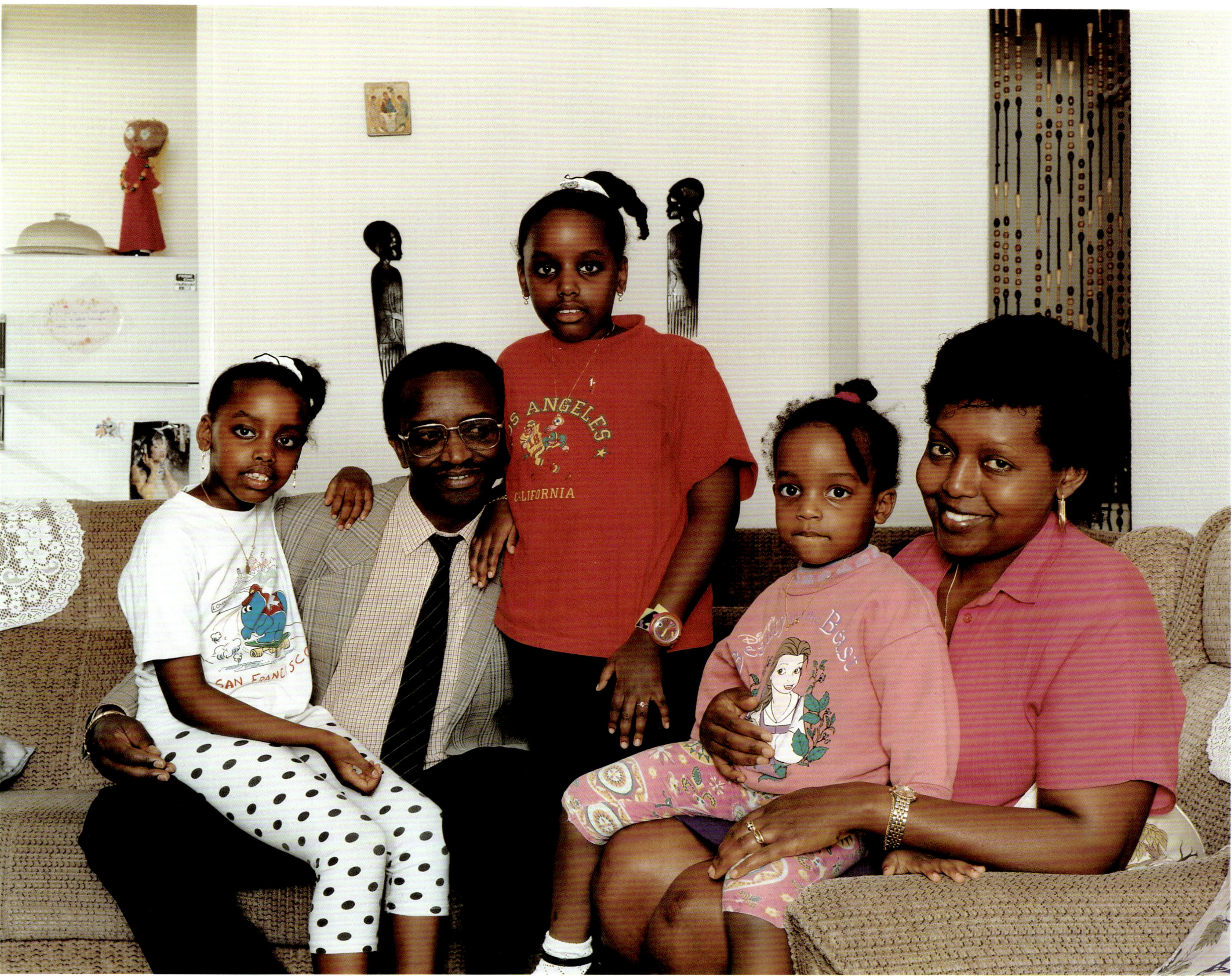
ANGELES
CALIFORNIA

Ernst and Theresia Kaufmann, Austria

When the mayor of Meyrin, Joseph-Hyacinthe-Victor Perraut, went to Ferney on an evening in March 1813 to sit at the table of an Austrian colonel serving in Napoleon's armies, it was in the hope that the 12,000 men of the Count of Bubna would turn away from his town. "I am hopeful... God willing," he wrote to his adjutant. But God was busy that evening and didn't hear him. As Meyrin at the time was under French administration, the Austrians were going to pitch camp there. It was, as Eugène-Louis Dumont writes in his monumental *Histoire de Meyrin*, a terrible time, made particularly difficult by the burden of taxes imposed. By inviting themselves into the natives' home, the Austrians, who were getting ready to enter Geneva in December through the Cornavin Gate, left behind a very bad memory of themselves. And a bill of 24,551 francs.

In his August 1, 1990 speech, another mayor, Pierre Paschoud, recounted this anecdote. Ernst Kaufmann was concerned. A Meyrinese through and through, co-founder of the residents' association, active samaritan and president of the Society of Austrians in Geneva, this electrotechnologist of the IAEA could not stand the idea of a debt—perhaps more a moral than a financial debt, but a debt all the same. On the occasion of a colloquium on Austro-Swiss neighborliness, he approached two ministers from Vienna at a bar in a hotel in Zurich: "We must pay them back," he said. "Not as a war debt, of course. But what would you say to creating a cultural fund in Meyrin?"

The miraculous occurred: Austria accepted. And Ernst Kaufmann obtained from the Meyrin mayor's office the promise to match the amount. And in addition, to round out the figure to 50,000 francs, the IAEA personnel association would contribute another 3000.

The book you are now browsing through has come into being at the same time as the *Meyrin Forum*. This cultural center has a library, and on one of its shelves sit sixty-six finely bound books all signed by Austrian authors. It was a gift from the city of Vienna to the city of Meyrin. As for the 50,000 francs, they will be used to finance student exchanges, which will follow those that Kaufmann has already organized between Swiss and Austrian Samaritans.

It is a wonderful story, one perfectly in keeping with this generous, attentive family, old-fashioned but also contemporary. Theresia has always cultivated the ancient truth that holds that when the mother of the family is in good spirits, the entire home should feel it too. Their daughter is today a medical assistant. Their son sells his country's attractions. Which country? As proof of his totally assimilated Swissness, he has become director of the tourist office of St-Luc, in Valais, a canton where, they say, it is not easy to fit in with the locals when you're not from that neck of the woods.

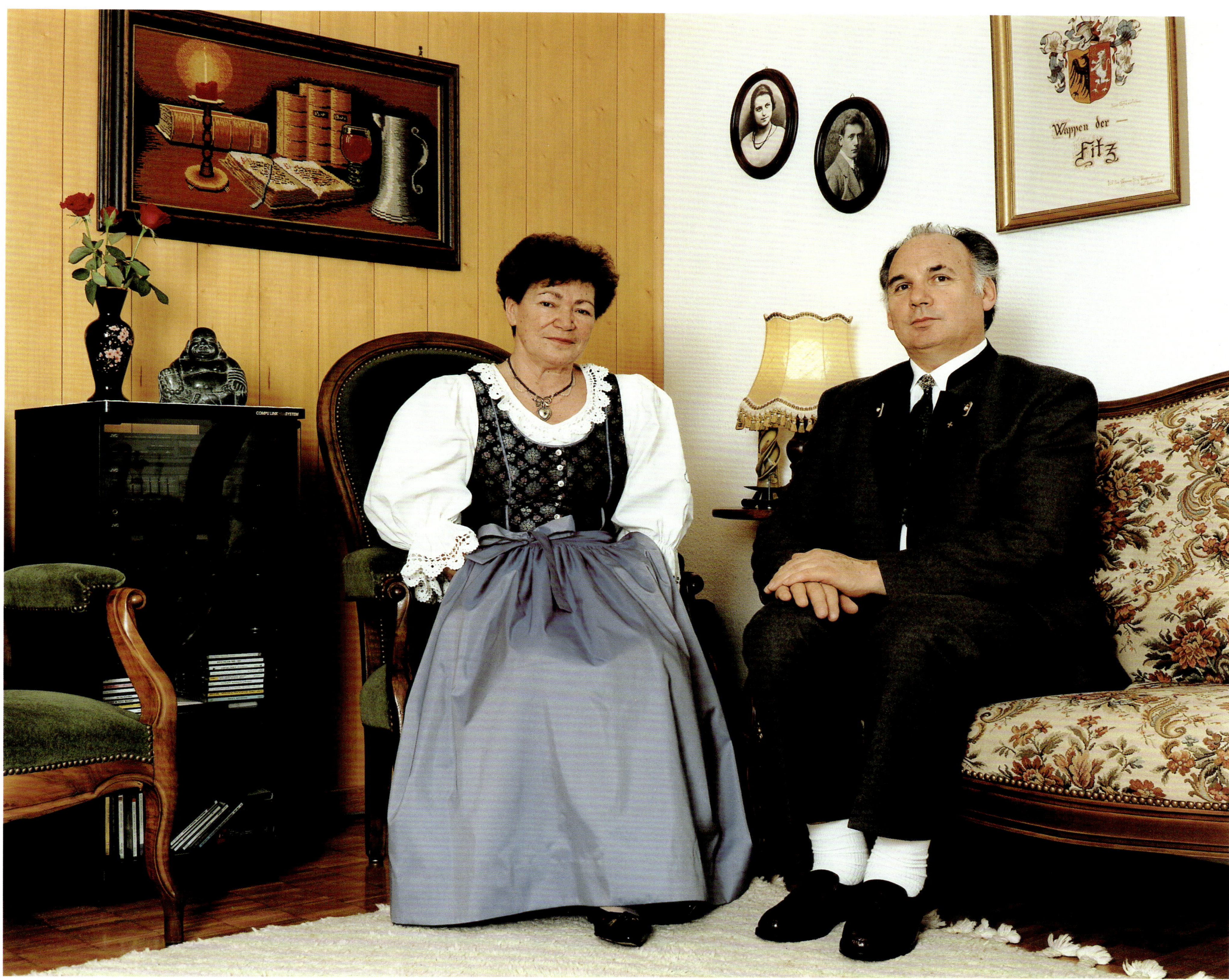
Wappen der —
Fitz

Alexander and Nathalia Leukhin, Russia

When a Westerner talks about the "changes" that have come about in Russia, he means: the fall of the Wall, which is certainly no small thing, but rather reductive all the same. The reality is more subtle than that. My question was therefore rather idiotic:

"Did you leave after the changes?"

"Which changes? You see, there were changes every other day for weeks on end...."

In fact, Alexander left the USSR at the very beginning of the great upheavals that were to astonish the world with their swiftness and symbolic power. Mikhail Gorbachev was still Secretary of the Central Committee of the Communist party of the Union of Soviet Socialist Republics, thus "Master of the Kremlin," in Western dramatic terms. He wanted to institute "openness" within the Soviet apparatus.... It was the age of Perestroika, that new wind which, signalling the end of the Cold War years, would scatter the USSR into a hail of smaller states.

Alexander was a functionary in an organized Soviet cooperative system, "much like a Swiss Coop," he says, which bought and distributed goods. Sent by Gorbachev to represent his country at the Secretariat of the World Union of Cooperatives, he stayed on, at Geneva, that is, and launched into business, like his son Nikolai. Comfort, luxury, and outward signs of wealth emit a subtle perfume around this Russian who, as a middle man between capital cities (ex-Soviet) and capitalists, earns commissions from the fruitful deals he promotes.

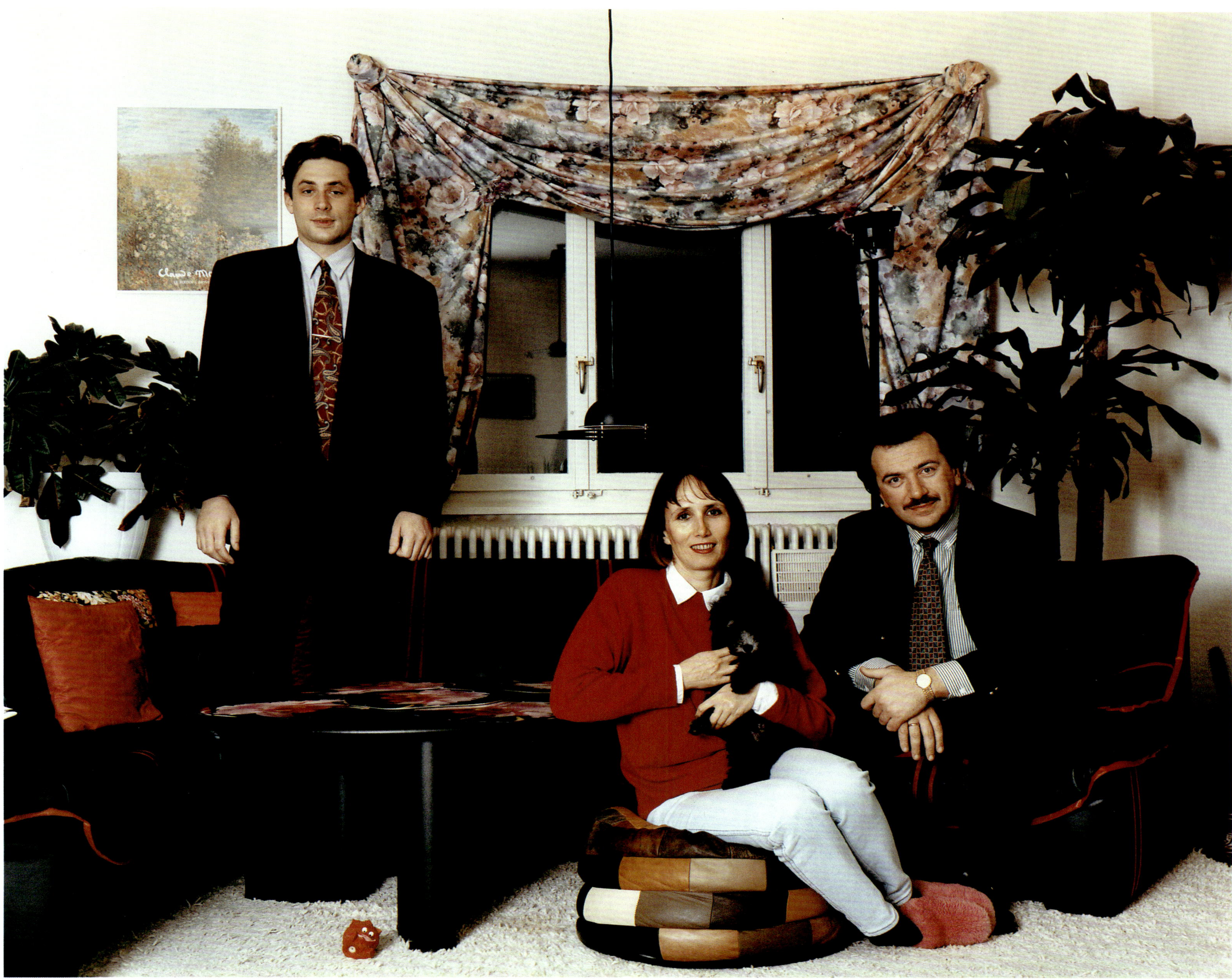

Jiahao and Maolan Li, People's Republic of China

Jiahao Li
Principal adviser
Bureau of cooperation
for development
and external relations
with Asia and the Pacific
World Organization
of Intellectual Property

His calling card displays three languages: recto, French and English; verso, Chinese.

For learning French, his wife Maolan found the best possible approach. She had, of course, taken courses at the parents' school at the Cycle d'orientation de l'enseignement secondaire upon her arrival in Switzerland in 1985, and still others at the Women's Club of the IAEA.... In 1990, however, she decided to offer an exchange of services:

Teach me French and I shall show you how they cook in my country, the vast province of Szechuan.

An interpreter helped her out during the first lesson in Chinese cooking, which she gave to a group of Meyrinese women gathered round her in the school kitchens. Afterwards, she went at it alone. And it continues to this day: Maolan Li now has one hundred and fifty students, most of them loyally attached to her, to the point where they hope to visit China under her guidance and to feast at the finest tables. Which are every bit as fine as Maolan Li's.

The Chinese cooking she prepares at her home is intended for her foreign guests; to her compatriots, she offers raclette instead.

Exchange means learning and teaching.

This is indeed one of Jiahao Li's professional goals. A lawyer formerly in the service of the Chinese patent office, today he works for the WIPO on relief missions and programs of aid and exchanges of ideas. For six years he was the only Chinese functionary employed by that organization. Today China, among other countries, is part of his sphere of activity. Whenever he goes back, people ask to see photos of this "garden of the world," where watches grow in all seasons.

Their two sons, Hui and Tao, both study at the engineering school of Geneva; the older one makes pocket money on weekends working at McDonald's. They will probably go back to China to live later on, hoping to take advantage of their know-how. Their decision will also determine whether or not the Li parents are to go back home when it comes time to retire. By then China will have further opened up to the world, a goal which Jiahao will have spent his life trying to attain.

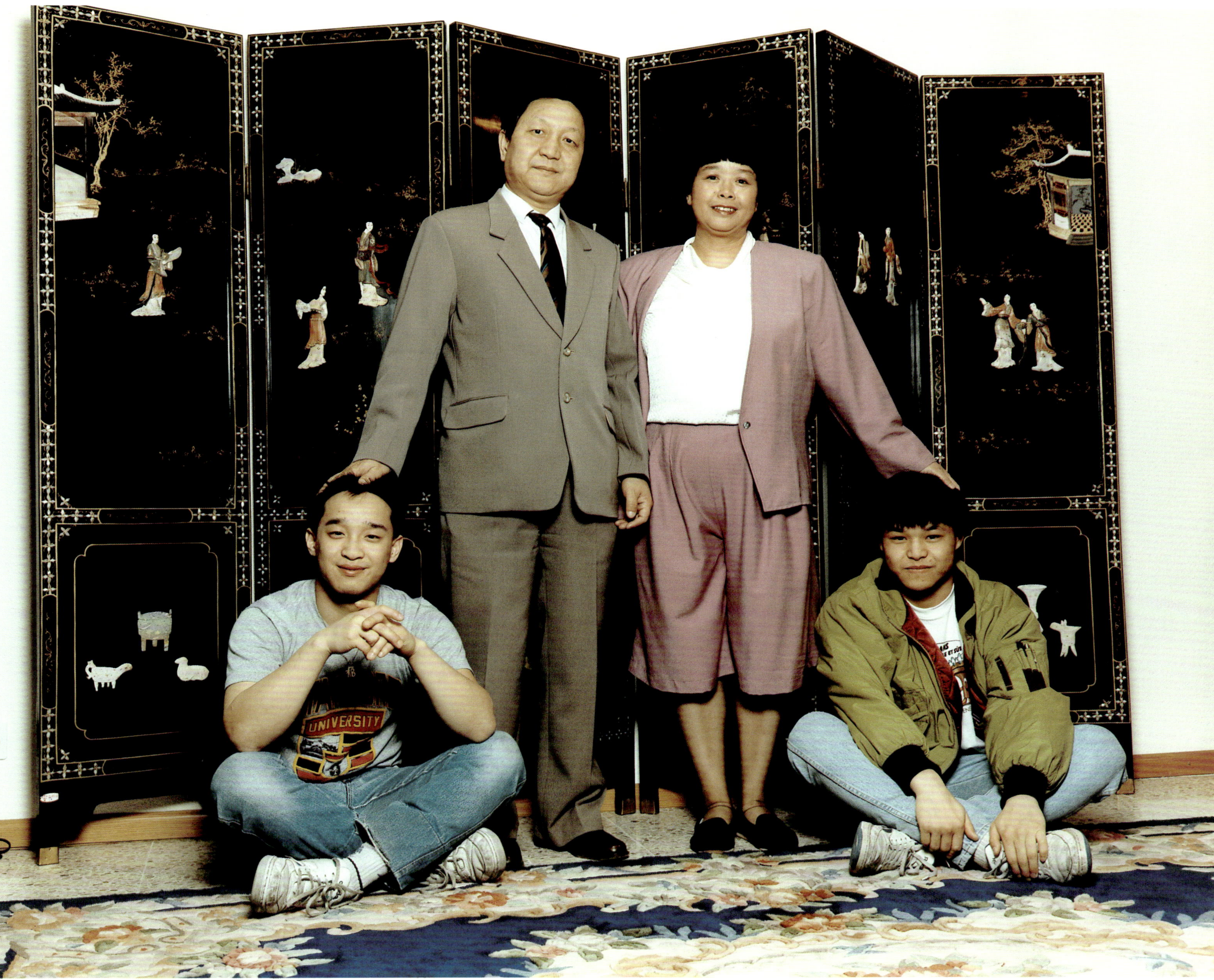
UNIVERSITY

Eugène-Dominique and Zeineb Louemba, Martinique — Eritrea

Eugène-Dominique came
to Switzerland during
the Eighties
from France,
married.

Zeineb came
to Switzerland during
the Eighties
from Italy,
a homemaker.

He from Martinique,
she from Eritrea,
their paths followed
those of their colonizers
in reverse.

Their households
broke up,
they found one another,
got married,
moved in.

Alain Emmanuel
and Nadia
frolic
in a whirlwind
round the flat.

The parents work hard
He
a chauffeur
she
a packer.

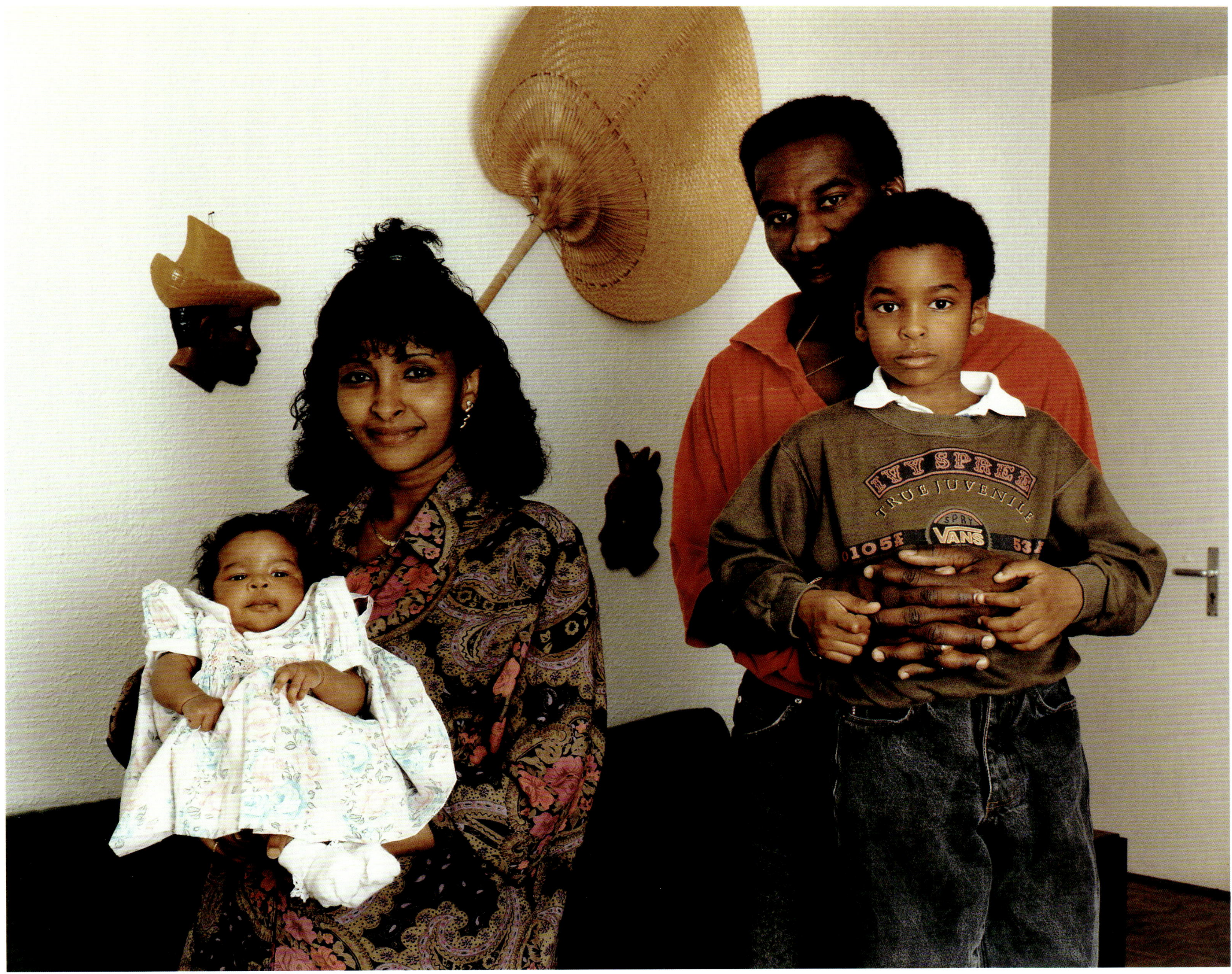
IVY SPREE
TRUE JUVENILE
SPRY
VANS

Mohammed and Nasira Majeed, Bangladesh

Showing me an article from the French daily *Le Monde*, which serves as an exception, Mohammed Majeed, international representative of Bangladesh, expresses a regret: "They only talk about my country when it is ravaged by floods or the typhoon," and not when indicators point to a growing economy. It's true that many Europeans and Americans have a confused notion of the country called Bangladesh. Worse still, for those of my generation, now pushing forty, the name evokes a vague memory of electric guitars and terrible images of a devastating famine: George Harrison, Ravi Shankar, Mick Jagger, Bob Dylan and a few others giving what was to be the first multi-media concert of a genre that has since become "the charity business." This was 1971. The adolescents of the time carried gunny sacks as an act of solidarity with the culture of a country that to them seemed emblematic. By now the moments of that event have irreversibly become part of the history of rock'n'roll. The discs were even re-issued in 1991.

Today what Bangladesh fears most are floods. When they overflow their banks, the Ganges and Brahmaputra wreak havoc. Near Khulna, the native city of Mohammed and Nasira, large forests protect the land more or less from such scourges. The people have mastered irrigation and are able to obtain an optimum yield from the protected rice-fields. The textile industry is also growing, but not as fast as the population which by 1993 had reached 116 million. One need only look at Mohammed's household: he has seven brothers and sisters. Nasira has six. In Meyrin, however, after the Swiss fashion, they are modestly raising two children: Tanjema, who wants to become a doctor, and Tanvir, who is still a bit young to know what he wants to be.

Mohammed left his country in 1973 to study in London, where life is not always easy for those of Asian origin. Having later gone to Geneva to work for the Bangladesh mission, he turned to the United Nations, where he works today. Nasira, a historian by training, has chosen to devote herself primarily to her family.

On a table, in the middle of which sits a trophy won by the Meyrin soccer team, for which Tanvir plays, the egg-coated aubergines, the fried ground beef and onions, the coconut cakes and noodles with sweet milk and cardamom welcome the visitor in accordance with the immaculate rules of traditional hospitality. Another image illuminating the living-room: the Majeeds have hung their children's smiles on the walls.

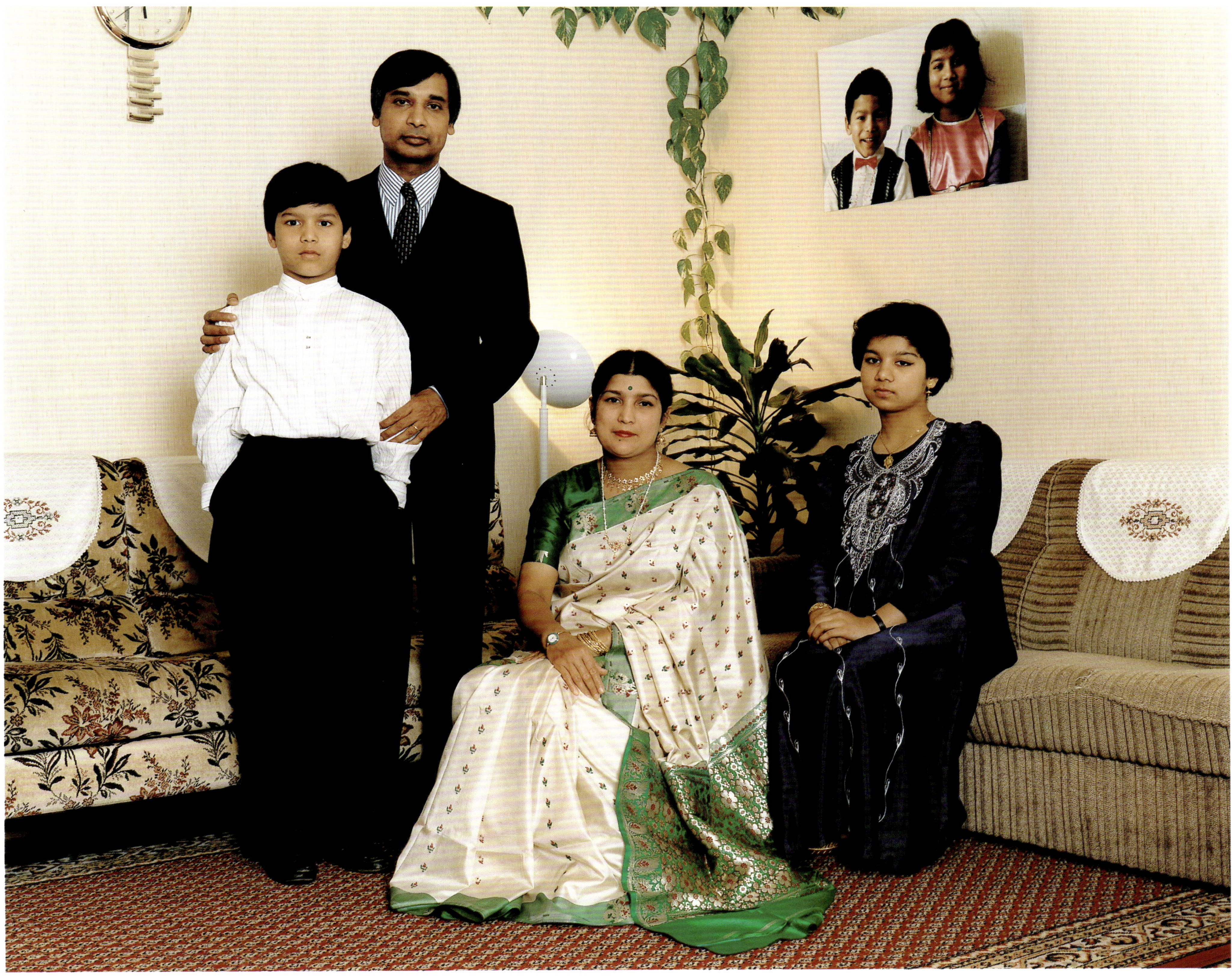

Kimvuka Henry and Kafuti Malembe, Zaïre

Nicolas had told me:
And I was left alone
for about an hour.
Everyone had vanished
to dress up like princes.

The nobility of poverty.

When I arrived
(on another day),
there were friends there,
but not the father.
No longer so ready to talk.

The humility of poverty.

And so I drank some juice,
admired a baby.
A rather modest dwelling.
Told nothing,
understood everything.

The elegance of the excluded.

Disarray and dignity
command respect.
The role of father,
the sense of family—
and no jobs.

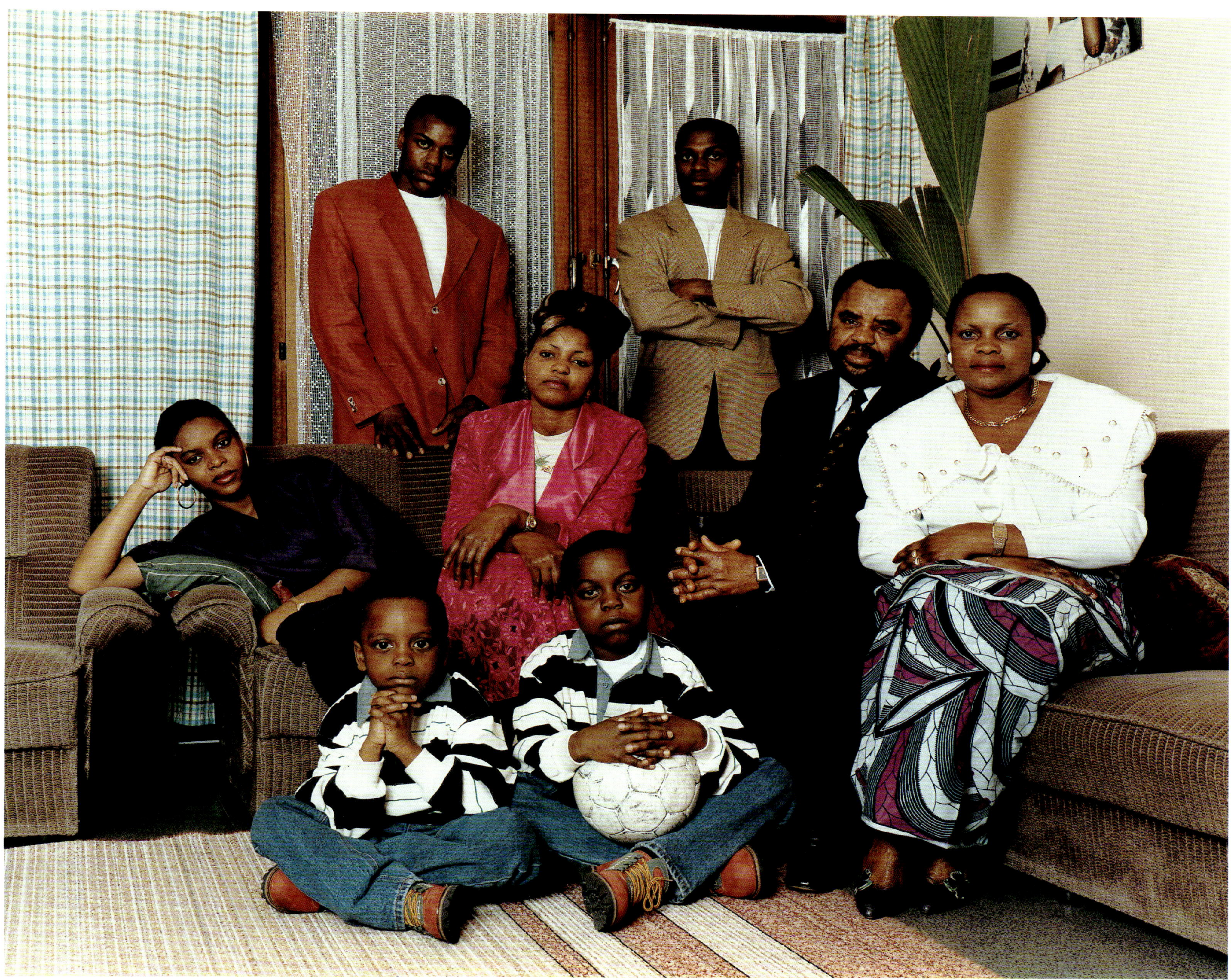

Najah Maroki, Iraq

The Gulf War brought the West together against Saddam Hussein. A modern conflict, a battle of images: the stripes of SCUD missiles tracing their deadly rays in the black sky, the oil refineries on fire, the televised speeches of American officers, their chests puffed out, describing their "surgical strikes." These powerful images form part of the collective memory of the late 20th century. But that memory is a bit short. It forgets that beyond the ambitions of states and their leaders, there are people, and that among them the Iraqi people also suffered deeply. Might this ordeal have been the cause of the extreme reticence of the Maroki family? All we know is that, having been called to Baghdad during the war, then moved to Basra, the family lived some terrible hours there. They shared them with a people that loved their leader, this Saladdin of the modern age, with such a love that, when the fire began to rain down on him from heaven, it was as though the earth suddenly began to turn upside down. Battered by the bombs, starved by the embargoes, the Iraqi people suffered more than was necessary—and they weren't alone—for all human vanity is embodied in a small handful of leaders.

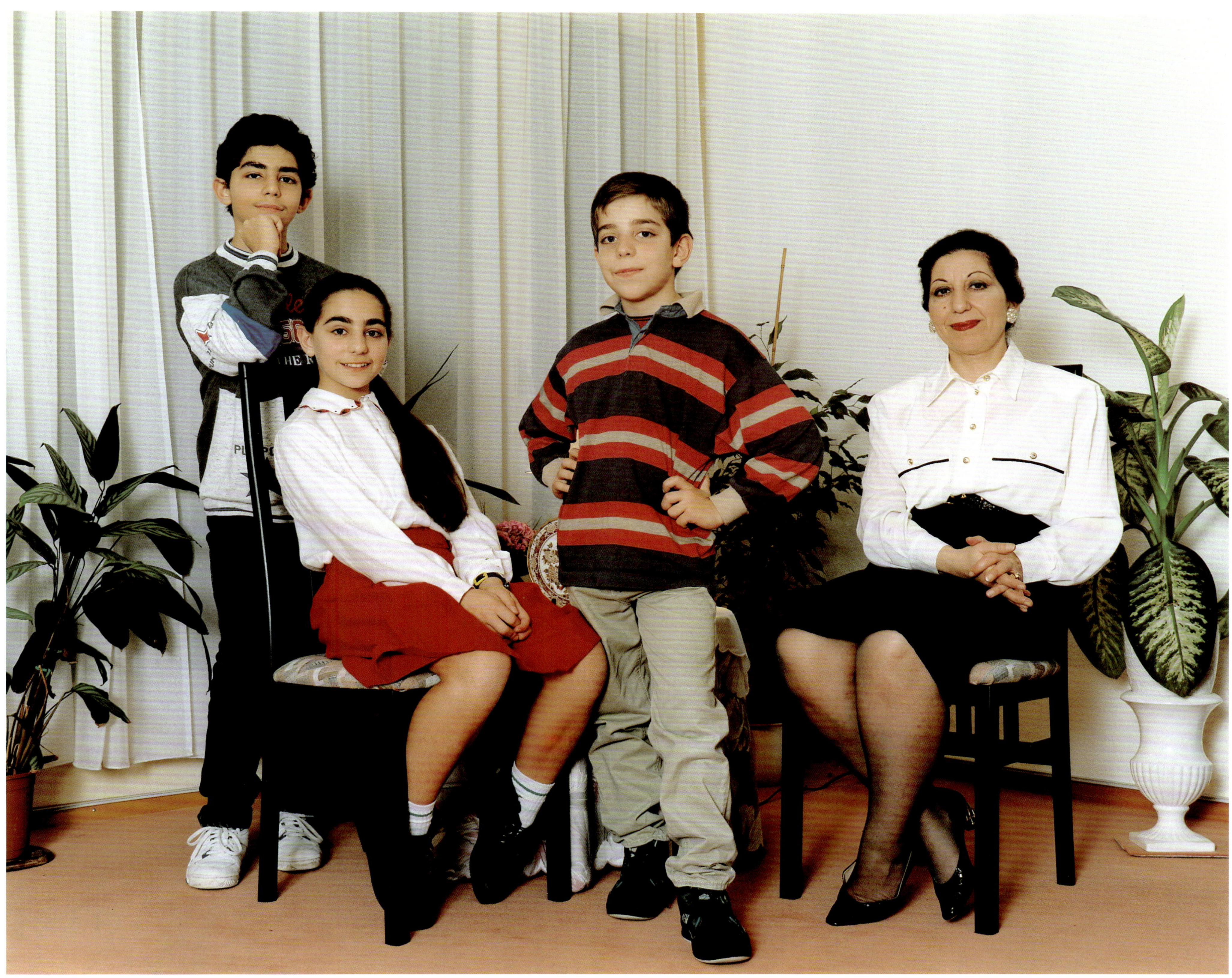

Thelmo Martinez and Lulieth Gonzalez-Martinez, Colombia

When one becomes a doctor, one promises to uphold an oath. In defining the terms of this moral pact, Hippocrates put the mechanics of the body and soul under the obligation always to seek the good of their patients, the betterment of their state, the prolonging of their life, if possible, and in the best conditions.

Doctors practicing in troubled parts of the world can become inconvenient to some people. When clans clash, when bullets bring their destructive power to the human machine, the physician's activity can get in a way. If the doctor is caring for someone whom Mr So-and-so wants eliminated, then he too becomes an enemy. If he cares for people regardless of their camp, their clan, their personal ideas, he becomes quickly catalogued as a traitor to the cause, which he has chosen neither to defend nor to combat since his only real concern is to safeguard human life. In such conditions, the situation of an independent spirit can quickly become untenable.

The Martinez-Gonzalez family chose Switzerland somewhat at random. No doubt that country's ambassador to Bogotà appeared more receptive than the others. And when the couple landed in 1990 at Kloten with Andres—a year and a half old at the time—*Amnesty International* was waiting for them at the foot of the ramp. As the family spoke neither German nor French, they chose to learn French, since with its common Latin foundations it better suited their convenience. Having first moved in to a halfway house at Verrières (Neuchâtel), it wasn't long before they tasted the benefits of the Genevan administration, the canton that finally accepted them.

In Columbia, this medical couple enjoyed a comfortable social and economic situation. In Switzerland, they have moved into one of the most modest apartment buildings of Meyrin. It's a paradoxical situation: at night, to earn his living, Dr Martinez worked as doctor-on-call; during the day, he returned to the university as Thelmo the student. He was required to obtain a Swiss equivalency certificate and federal diploma. Today he has new responsibilities at the cantonal hospital. Lulieth is a dentist. They must certainly be excellent doctors: "When you have suffered yourself, you better understand the suffering of others. Our past enables us to see life differently...."

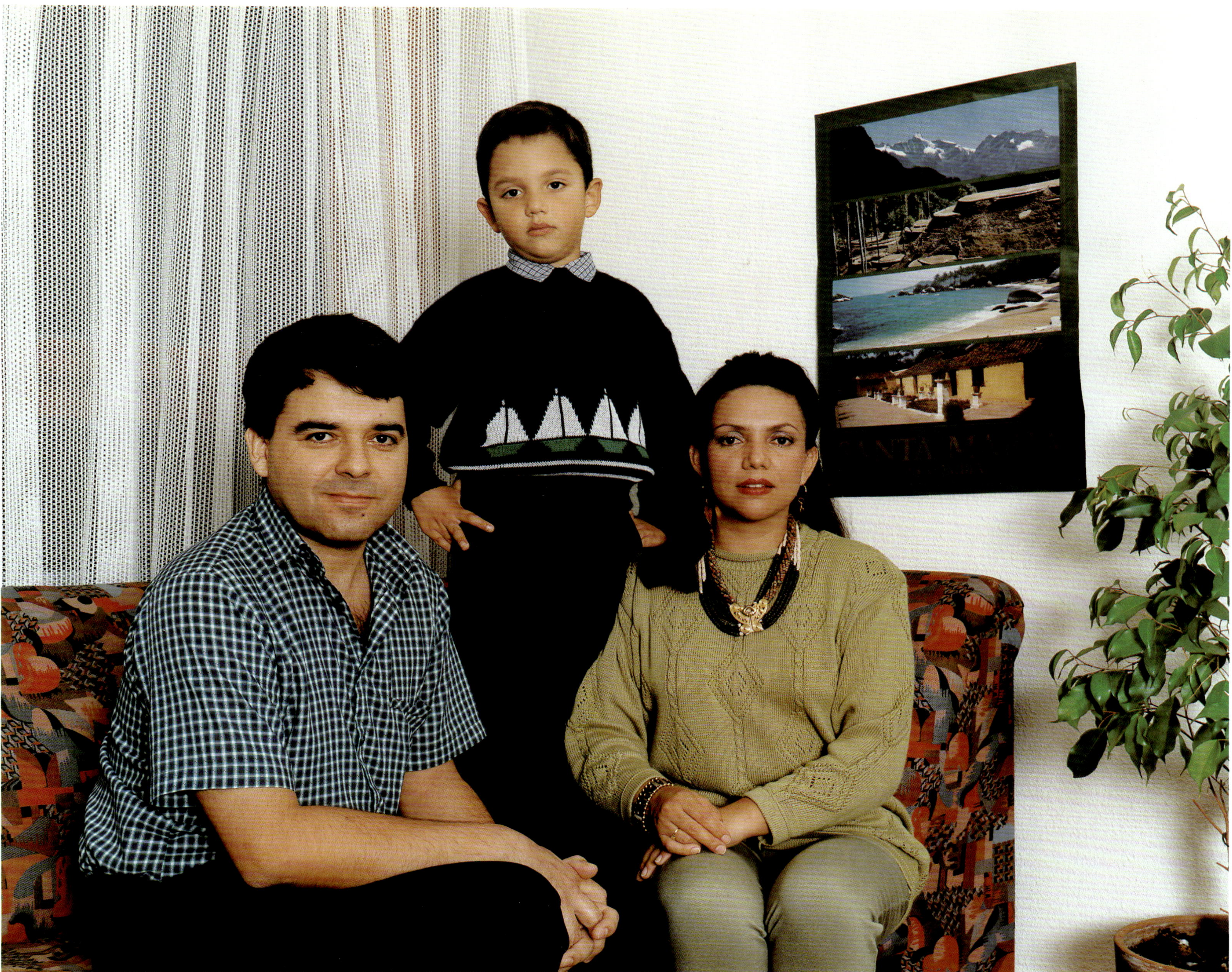

Mojtaba and Mina Mashayekh, Iran

A captain in the Shah's air force, Mojtaba lived through six years of war against Iraq—a war he secretly opposed—fighting for a regime that was not the one to which he had originally pledged his service. Thus, two serious conflicts of conscience lead to a plan to escape to the United States, a country he knew from having done part of his aeronautical studies there, and where he still had some friends. Of course the United States had no diplomatic representation in Iran.... At the time, it was Switzerland that was representing the interests of the despised Uncle Sam in Iran. Thus it was that the Mashayekh arrived in Geneva, on a temporary basis—or so they thought. Without refugee status—Switzerland concurred with the Iranian view of the pilot as a deserter—and in the face of the Americans's refusal to grant them a visa, which was almost as much of a shock to them as their decision to go into exile, they were left with little choice but to make their nest right where they were, with their children Shirin and Shahrzad. Mojtaba hooked up with *Intercontinental*—he has just obtained his civilian pilot's license—and Mina works for *La Placette* as a saleswoman, a far cry from her former employment in the secretarial offices of an American company in Tehran before the revolution.

Even as I am writing these lines, Switzerland has asked the Mashayekh to try to re-obtain their Iranian citizenship, since the Islamic republic has recently granted this right to exiles, even political ones. It's quite incongruous. A former officer turned political exile cannot frequent without risk the consulate of the country he has fled. They still cry, sometimes, in this close family perfectly integrated into their new city, within whose walls a harsh wind one day deposited them.

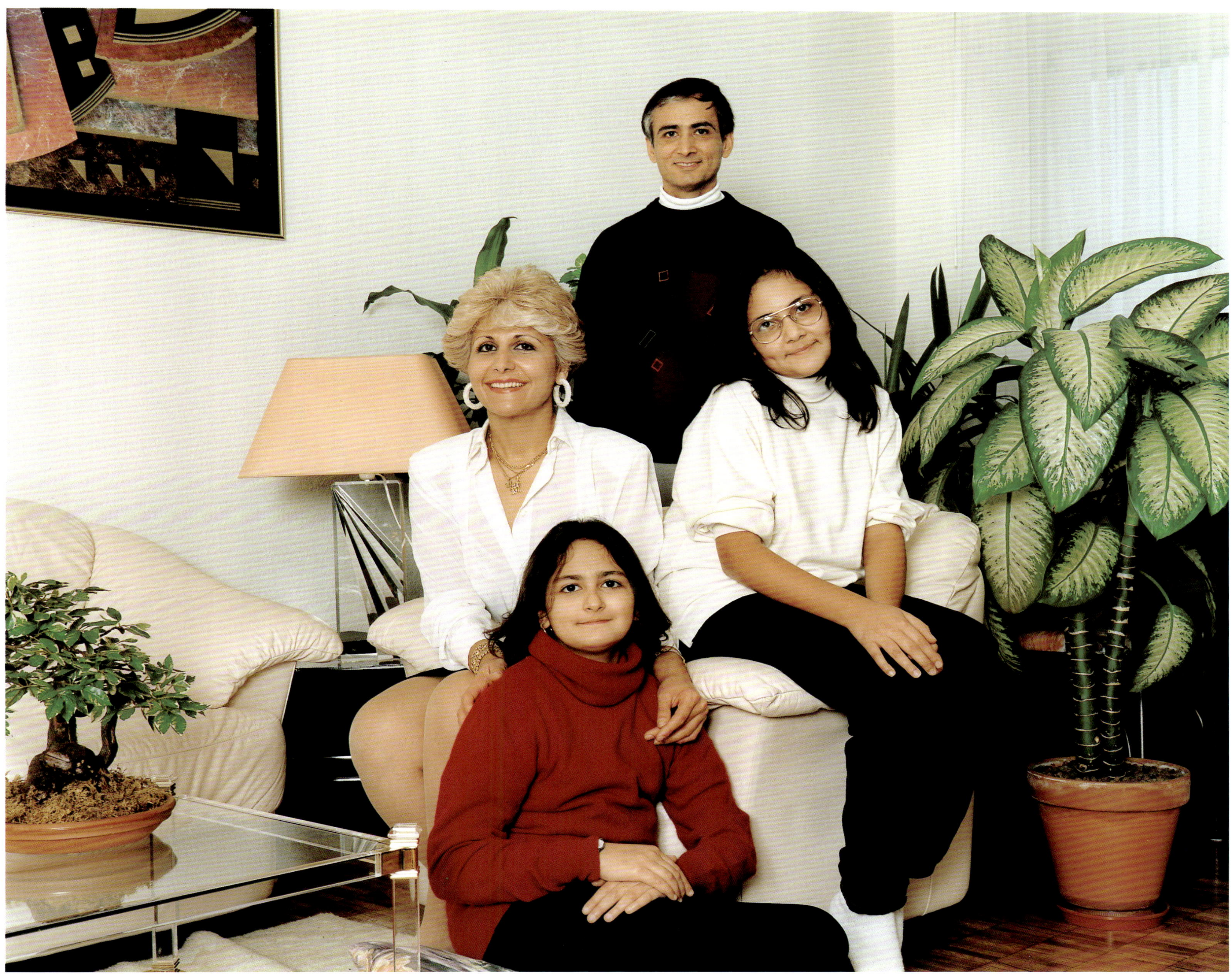

Carlos and Josephina Matute Irias, Honduras

In this country where the exportation of coffee, bananas and textiles represents the bulk of the economic resources, and where the average income is 500 dollars a year, multinational business have long called the shots. Today a subtle balance exists in Honduras.

The country owes a good portion of this stability to a man who, in 1974, when 70,000 workers in the banana business revolted (at that time no labor laws existed), was able to find a point of agreement between the all-powerful foreign banana companies and the workers. In gratitude, the government sent this providential advocate post-haste to Harvard. He was to study economics there, in the service of his country.

In fact, his personal itinerary overlaps with the construction of modern Honduras. He was in fact a minister for five years; his socio-economic development plan has become a model for Latin America. He has also taught at the university and was involved in farm loans. But it is outside the country that he has been most active. At first this was not a choice but a necessity: Carlos Matute did not agree with the military government. A typical diplomat's understatement.

Two small suitcases asleep on the rug.
A large Honduran flag.
On the walls hang nothing
but a standard art reproduction and
a portrait of the President of the Republic,
an old travelling companion.

After arriving in Geneva in 1973 and moving into a furnished apartment, he became adviser to international organizations responsible for business with developing countries, then director of a program on multinational corporations with the UNCTAD. The typical story: his first contract in Switzerland provided for a six-month engagement that would be systematically renewed until 1985. When democracy returned to his country, the government would ask him to enter GATT as an assistant to the ambassador.

Today, he's the ambassador. GATT has given way to the World Commerce Organization. He is in fact the de facto dean of the diplomatic corps. Rather than go back to being a minister, Carlos Matute preferred to remain in Geneva; his children are Swiss. One of his sons is chief of gynecology at the cantonal hospital, another works for a large bank, a third has created an international company oriented toward homeopathic and biogenetic specialties. Only his daughter has returned to Central America, to Costa Rica. He knows he owes a lot to his wife, "doña Josephina, without whom nothing could have been built."

A specialist in international commerce, financial affairs and development, Carlos Matute knows the path he will take when the time comes to quit his post. He could preside over a foundation, and he is already cultivating ideas on the subject. On one condition, however: that he have the time to read and write, to meditate and share his experiences.

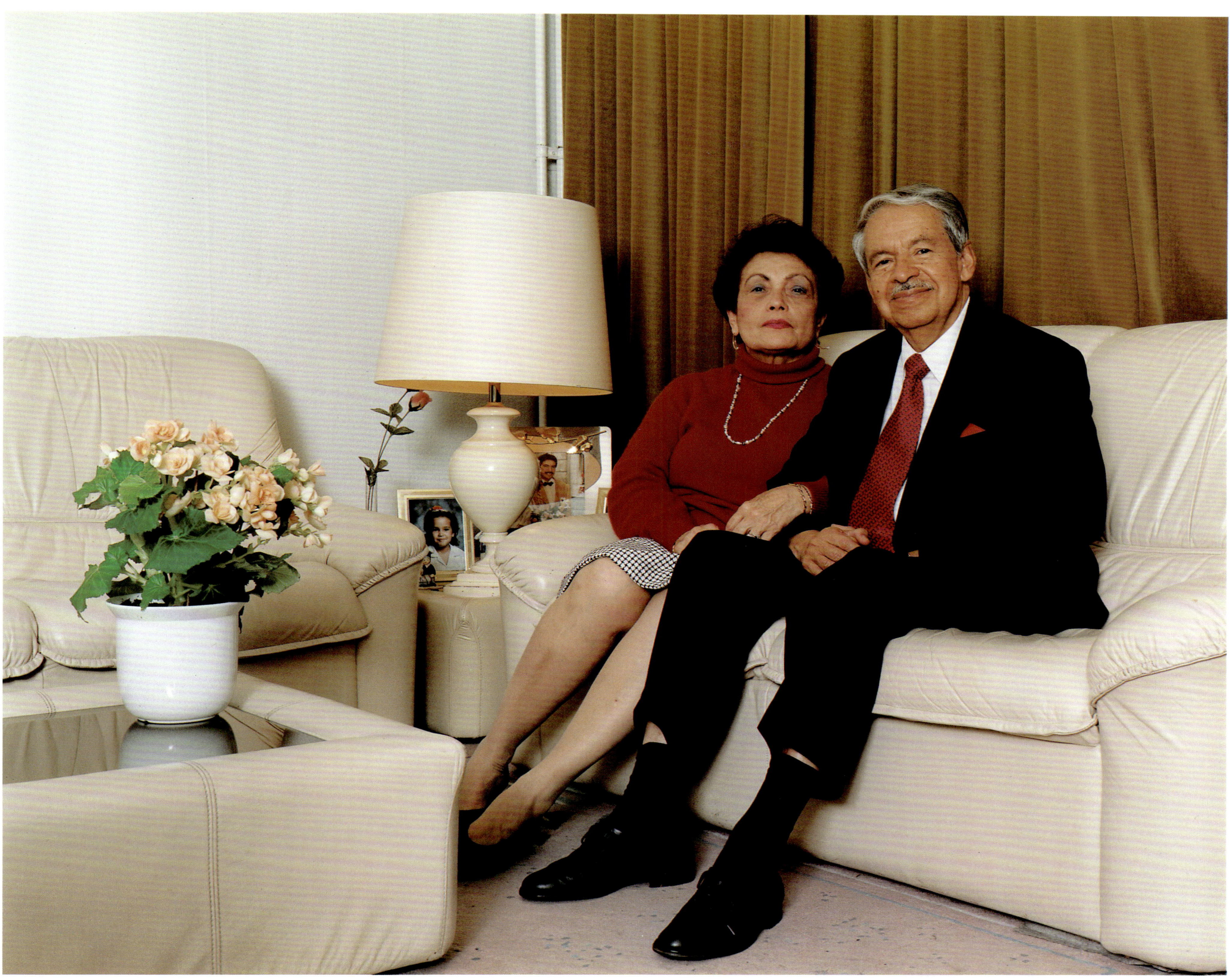

Eric and Patricia McIntosh, Scotland

The damp, misty Scottish air has left its mark on this familiy that loves to swim, dive, surf and fly—to say nothing of the mournful sounds sometimes heard emerging from a strange-looking pouch-flute. Yet it wasn't in Glasgow that Eric began playing the bagpipes, but in Geneva. Maybe it was out of a need to reconnect with his native land, its culture, its customs, from which his move to Geneva—to work for the IAEA—had seperated him? Today pipe-major, Eric McIntosh is overwhelmed with requests for performance, from which he picks and chooses, favoring social institutions and events. The *Pipes and Drums* ensemble for which he is a driving force has had a good bit of success over the years. And when he sheds his kilt in favor of trousers, this mathematician works on creating information networks, the same path his daughter Fiona has set out on.

Alan, for his part, is quite a case. His first interest in aviation dates from childhood. A builder of scale-models and pilot of remote-control airplanes, he distinguished himself at a very young age with a very interesting experiment in free glide: he jumped off the fourth floor of their apartment building with a homemade parachute whose cables, for lack of rope, consisted of bands of computer paper, of dubious solidity. It was his first crash. With only a broken wrist to show for it, he was exceptionally lucky. The intrepid imp had leapt forth with such vigour that instead of landing on the concrete, where he probably would have been smashed to pieces, he reached the grass, which was sodden with water from the morning's rain and just sufficiently muddy enough to give this Sunday Icarus the lesson he deserved, without seriously hurting him. Later, a scholarship with the RAF and an education in Britain would better teach him how to stay airborne, notably at the commands of a Boeing 737 and an Airbus A 320.

Meyrin is, in part, the airport of Cointrin. It is also, of course, the site of the IAEA. Two good reasons not to budge from there. It's also a border community. This has its practical advantages: when teaching English, Patricia often crosses the border, because in France she encounters fewer administrative impediments than on Swiss soil. Geopolitics can be sometimes rather tortuous indeed. No matter. Borders cease to represent much when one looks at things from above. Around her neck, an airplane; on the tea tray, an airplane motif; on the living-room table, yet another airplane.

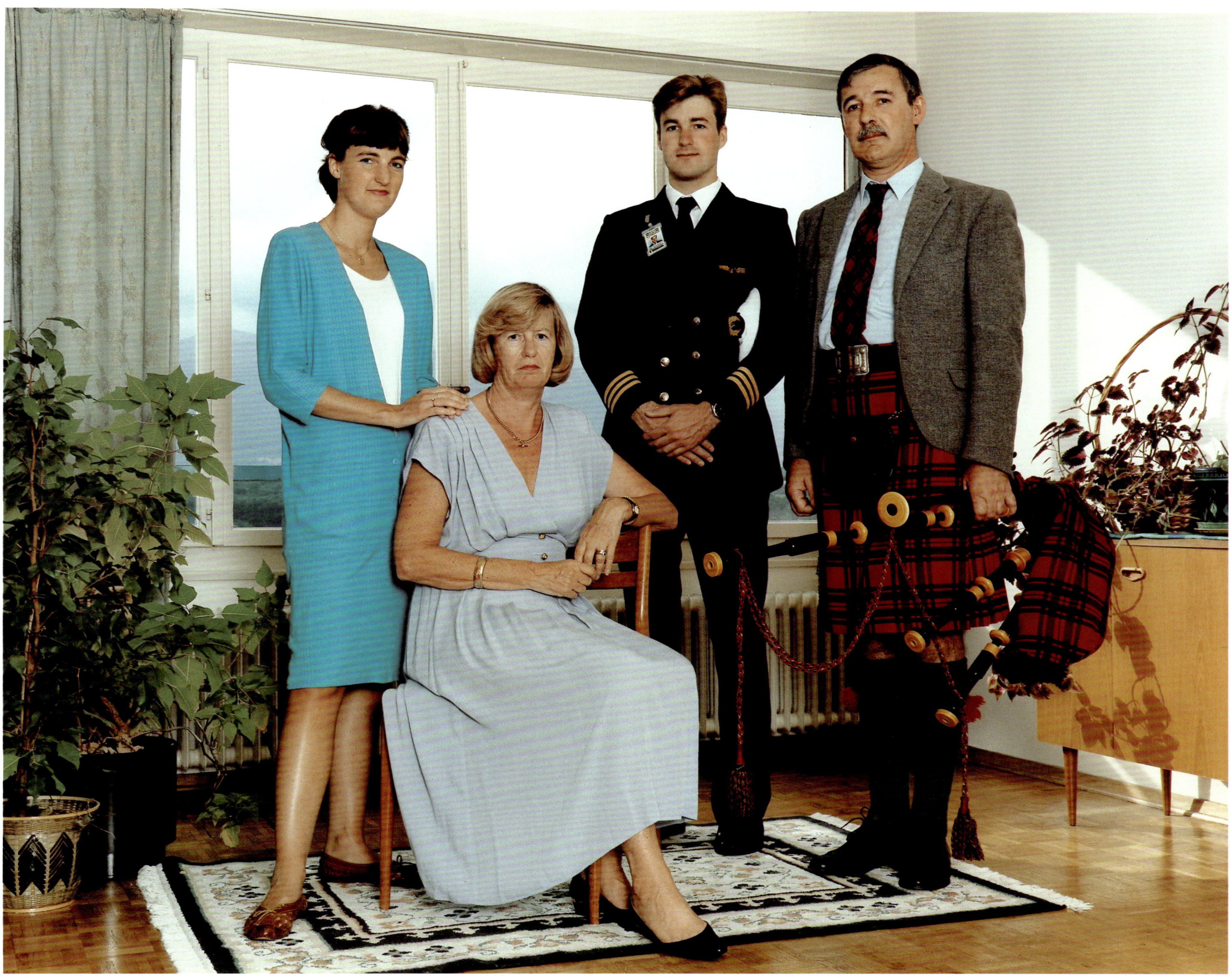

Carlos and Sonia Mendoza, Salvador

The life Carlos Mendoza came apart on a day in April 1989 with the explosion of a bomb that had been planted at his home and programmed to go off at midday, the hour of the family meal. As a high-profile intellectual and professor of philosophy, student and disciple of Francisco Peccorini, who himself was shot to death, the very Catholic Carlos Mendoza says it is a miracle that he survived. It was nevertheless as a disfigured, partially paralyzed man that he arrived in Switzerland a few months later. When his life took a turn for the better in April 1990 with the birth of his fourth daughter in Meyrin, Sonia and Carlos named the new gift Abril.

The destiny of men is often strange. At present Carlos, hardly predestined for such a career, is Salvadoran ambassador to the European Office of the United Nations, in Geneva. And Sonia, a journalist, no longer works outside of her home, which in its modesty is a far cry from the pomp one imagines as the lot of the diplomatic high life. Philosopher and diplomat: the two callings must be compatible after all. With an unshakeable faith in the redemption of his fellows, Carlos continues to encourage dialogue, reflexion, and the peaceful confrontation of ideas. His home is full of symbols paying homage to the Virgin and Child. The walls are covered with photos and a few diplomas—all that remains of a once peaceful life in a hot, volcanic land.

The green of Meyrin has helped him recover his strength. Of his numerous bus trips—so precise and exact in Switzerland—he retains the memory of a land ideal for reflecting on human nature. And his daughters, avid for literature like their parents, and likewise haunted by memories of friends who were assassinated, bask in the hope of a country finally rebuilt, grown up.

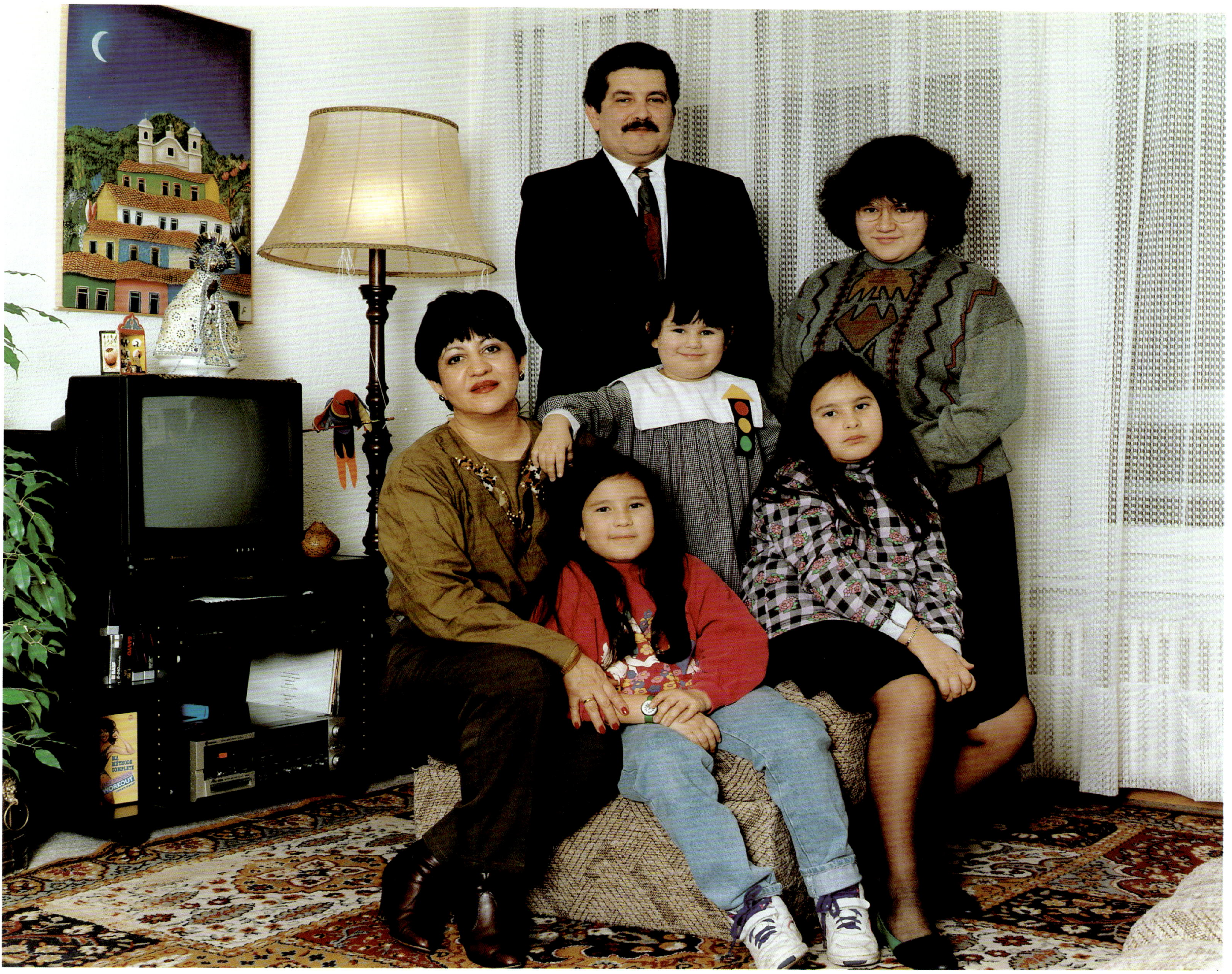
MA
METHODE
COMPLETE
WORKOUT
BASF

Ibrahim and Agnès Moussa, Egypt—Switzerland

God gave to each his own
He a Muslim, she a heathen
He's religious, she's an atheist
All is necessary, says the surah.

When Ibrahim came to Switzerland to open a branch for a Cairo company, he knew neither the language nor the customs of the land of cows. His only baggage, the residue of sojourns in the United States and in Canada, was a certain sense of displacement. Pharaohs are not timid. They learn fast and know how to listen.

When Agnès informed her loved ones of her intention to marry this philosophical Egyptian, whom she had met at a party, the Cassandras and old wives had a field day. Marrying an Arab, they said, you don't know what you're getting into. You'll be less than nothing. A bedmate, a baby-maker, veiled, hounded, totally ruined.

Nonsense. When you're in love, you give in, she says. Love has no boundaries, he adds. Thumbing his nose at his uncle, minister of foreign affairs? He's not interested in politics. It's all prejudices, lies.... He's not cut out for it. Business, that's his line. Stones and a variety of goods; not a trade for angels, in any case.

Then there is Rozanne, Jehane, and Shady, the boy. Around her neck, Jehane wears a medallion given her by her grandmother, like the blessing of the Nile. During Ramadan, when Agnès is cooking, Ibrahim lets his family do as they please, but he abstains from eating before nightfall, as the law requires. They love and respect one another. Mektoub?

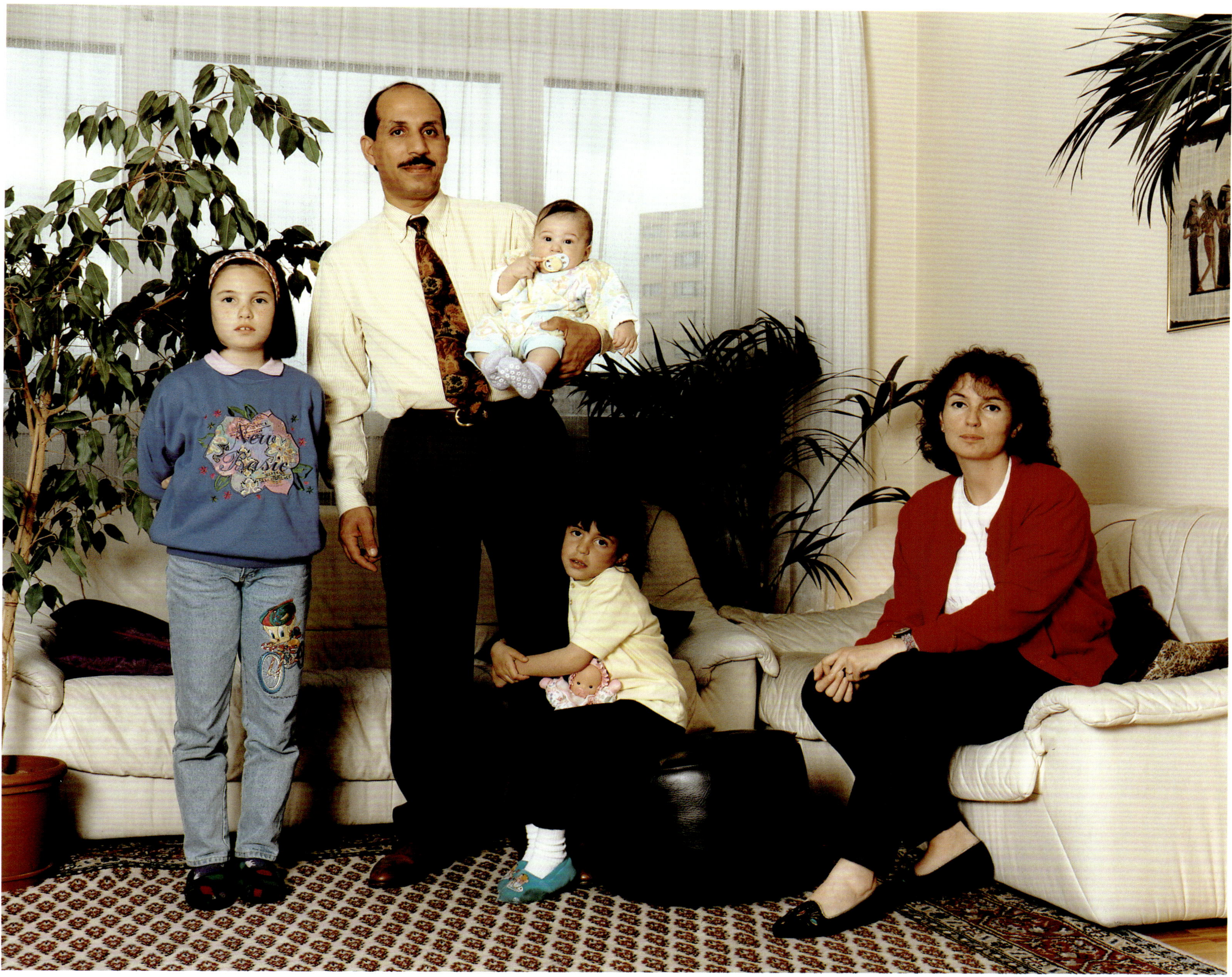
New Basic

Beryl and Janet Mutambirwa, Jamaica—Zimbabwe

The supercharger here is Nehanda. Her energy is flabbergasting.

My mother loves to eat. I love to eat too.

Janet grew up in Jamaica before going to the United States, where she met Beryl, a Rhodesian refugee and history professor at the university.

My two grandmothers are dead, but my grandfathers are still alive and living in Jamaica and Zimbabwe.

In 1980, after Zimbabwe gained independence, the Mutambirwas spent six months in the country before going to Switzerland, to work for the Ecumenical Council of Churches in Geneva. In their home, the COE initials adorn a corridor crammed with books in English.

My aunt has four dogs: Putsch, Daisy, Dapsy and Hitler, the killer.

They've had some nasty confrontations with racism. In the United States, jobs with unequal pay, marked ostracism in the formation of work teams, employers practicing discrimination. In Geneva, a restaurant refused to serve Beryl because he is black: the story made all the papers. This gentle, peaceful man has fought too hard for civil rights to believe everything he is told.

Ob-la-di, ob-la-da... Tral-la-la-li! Ta-ti-dada-ti-tsuin-tsuin.

Nehanda belting out Ringo Starr. A photo of Bob Marley calls to mind Jamaica and the singer's message: "change your mind." Free yourself of imposed fetters. The king of Kingston, prince of rastas, remains a common value among upstanding people in Jamaica as well as Zimbabwe.

Hey! Want some chewing gum? My daddy buys me chewing gum and I don't have any cavities.

Her mother has taught her to brush her teeth, a utensil she herself did not have during childhood.

Beryl now works at the ILO, Janet is active with the World Association of Young Christian Women, and their home—fifth-floor, standard flat—breathes with intelligence, curiosity, openness.

I would like to have a dog that would never bite anyone.

Beryl offers to take me to hear Meyrin at night.

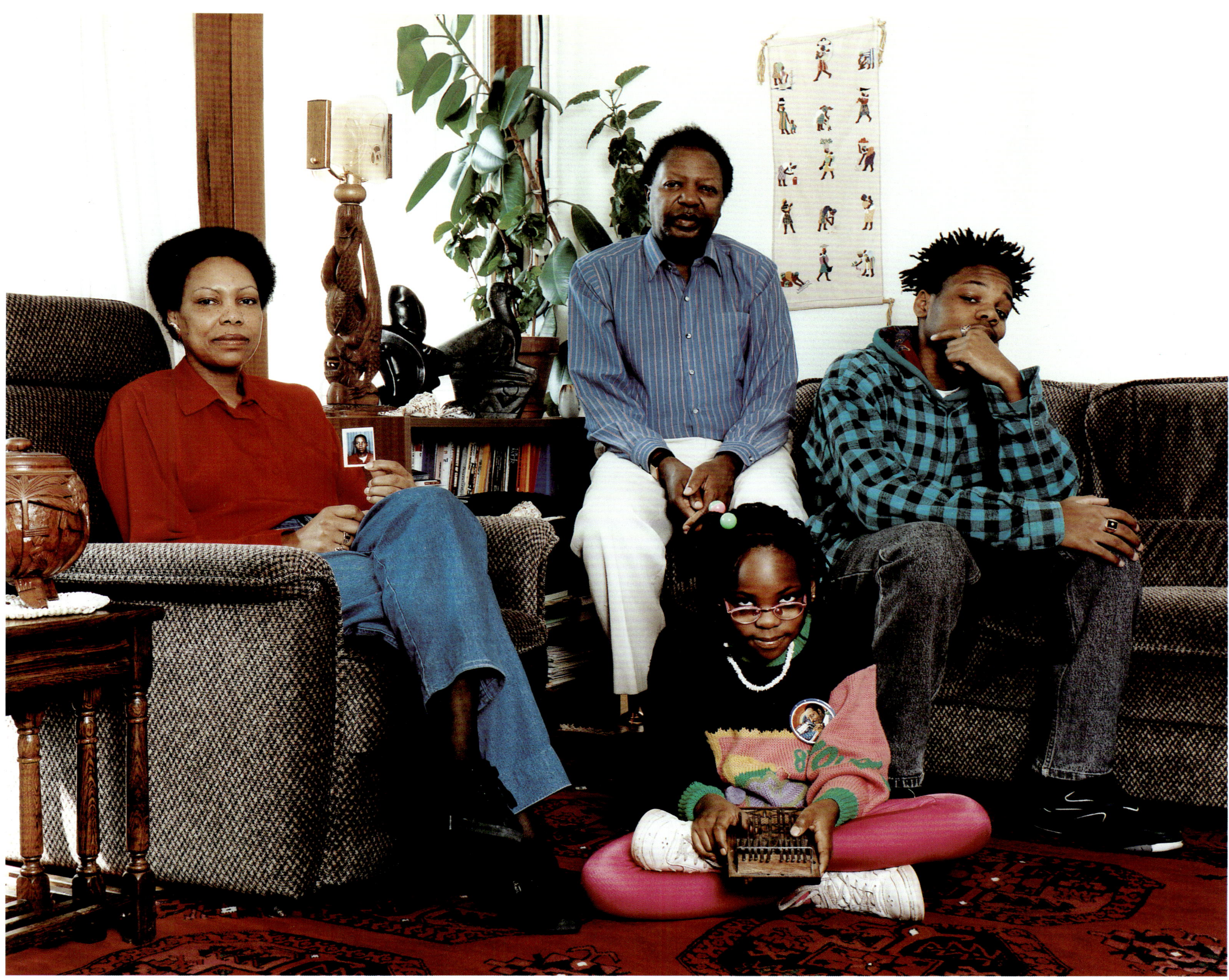

Colette and Stephen Myers, Ireland

To my son, who has come along for the visit, Stephen Myers explains his work in simple terms:

You see, beneath Geneva and in nearby France as well, there is a twenty-seven kilometer ring, buried under the ground and full of magnets. But it's not a toy: it cost 1.3 billion francs. Almost 900 people work down there. They take protons and positrons, which are tiny, basic little particles of life and then make them circulate at very high speeds, to see what will happen when they collide. And in so doing, they try to understand the origins of the world.

This reminds me of a remark Dimitri made one day in a café: Papa, the toilets haven't been cleaned since the beginning of Mankind! Perhaps, but there were already protons and positrons invisibly leading a joyful dance.

I've never understood the first thing about physics. I could never pay close enough attention. And yet, listening to Stephen Myers, one of the chiefs of the Ecole Polytéchnique, it really seems all very simple. Except that we still haven't quite figured out from what the world was born.

The Myers left Belfast in 1972. It was the peak of social and political unrest. The bombs would echo one another with their blasts. But that wasn't why they left: turning down an offer to teach at the university, Stephen opted instead to orient himself toward research and take on a post with the IAEA. Since the organization owns furnished apartments in Meyrin, that's where they ended up. Later, they would make their nest on a plot of land they bought, on which a fine house has since sprouted up. Curiously, they have a swimming pool in their yard, but the boys prefer the municipal pool. No doubt you can swim greater distances there.

Colette is a secretary with the World Health Organization. Catherine is going to be a doctor. Her younger brothers haven't decided anything yet. Perfectly bilingual and partial to reading the classics of each language in the original, two of them already have Swiss passports.

The house is a veritable airport, and the family is endlessly passing through in search of some exotic relaxation. You see, it's rather vast, this family: Colette and Stephen together have thirteen brothers and sisters.

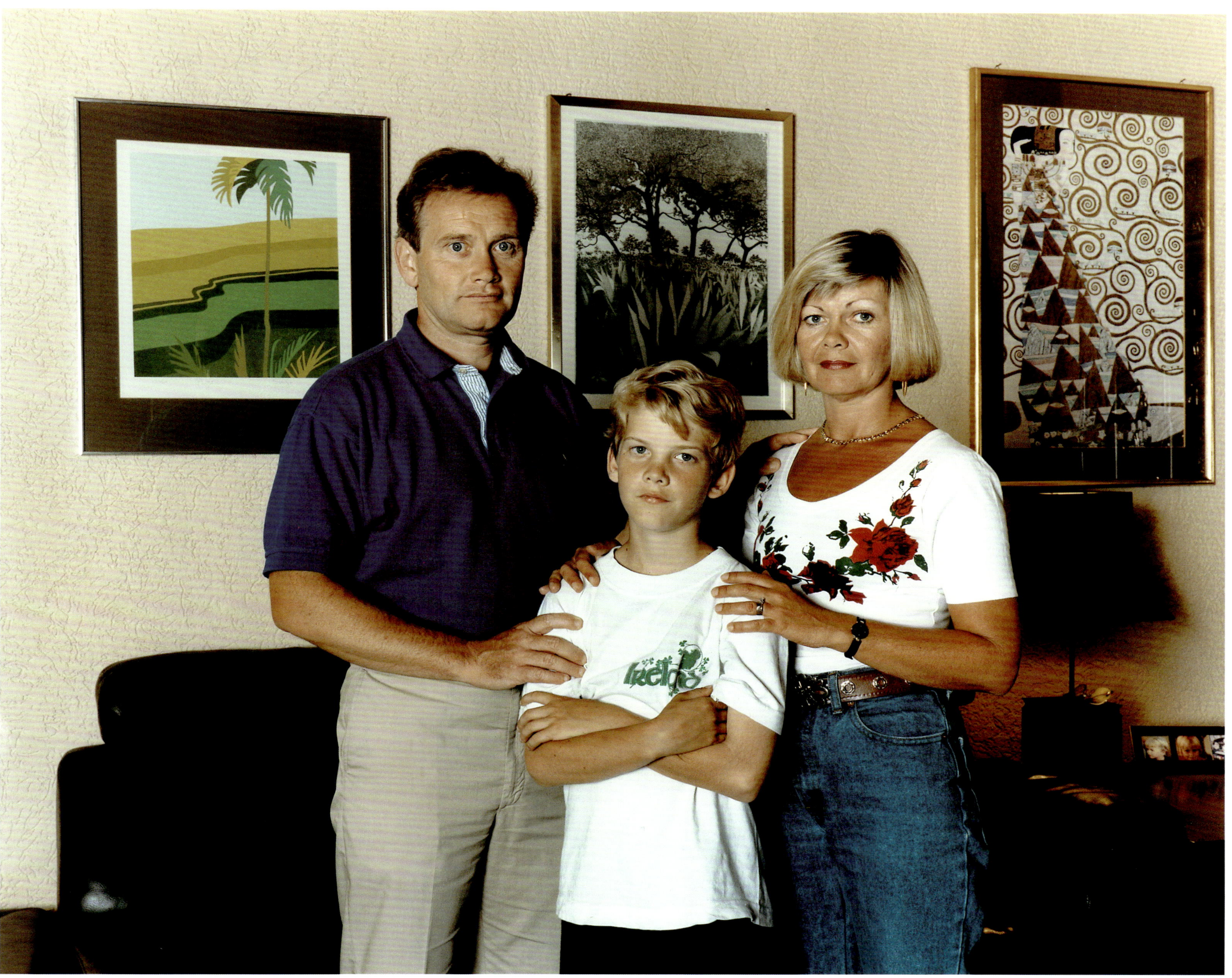

Patrick and Lucretia Myers, United States

Bio I
Patrick Robert Myers was born in Bern because his father, a diplomat, was stationed there. He has studied in Washington, Paris, Neuchâtel and Geneva. He has a doctorate in international law and works in Meyrin at the European office of Hewlett Packard.

Bio II
Lucretia is an English teacher. She has taught at the Meyrin Residents' Association, at the Hospital of la Tour, at the ILO, and also teaches future teachers.

Anecdote I
It happened one Halloween during Lucretia's childhood. She went and rang the doorbell of a certain person—Richard Nixon—to get the customary sweets. It was a meagre harvest. For revenge, she papered the Republican's yard with stickers glorifying his rival in the presidential election, John F. Kennedy.

Anecdote II
One day when the Myers were looking for names on the Vietnam War Memorial, they crossed paths with another well-known individual, a contemporary of Patrick's who also became President of the United States, William Clinton, out for his morning jog.

Black Hole I
In his youth Patrick R. Myers was opposed to the war in Vietnam. It was while he was studying in Paris that he received his draft notice. It was a difficult blow, but he did not refuse to serve. Happy ending: he was not sent to the front.

Black Hole II
In childhood, Patrick O. Myers was stricken with a brain tumor. Junior struggled for three years before recovering his health as well as his size, which had been compromised by a slowdown in his growth. Happy ending: now recovered, he hopes one day to become a doctor, like his sister.

Housing I
Without a penny in their pockets, the Myers started out living in tiny little low-income apartments. That's what brought them to Meyrin, a community of low rents: "the worst of America, but in Geneva," they said.

Housing II
The Myers have changed their minds about Meyrin. There's no longer any question of leaving. They have created a rich social life for themselves here (one can't even accompany Lucretia shopping without greeting thirty different people on the way) and have even bought a house.

Fact I
They ate hamburgers today for lunch.

Fact II
They offered me some Coca-Cola.

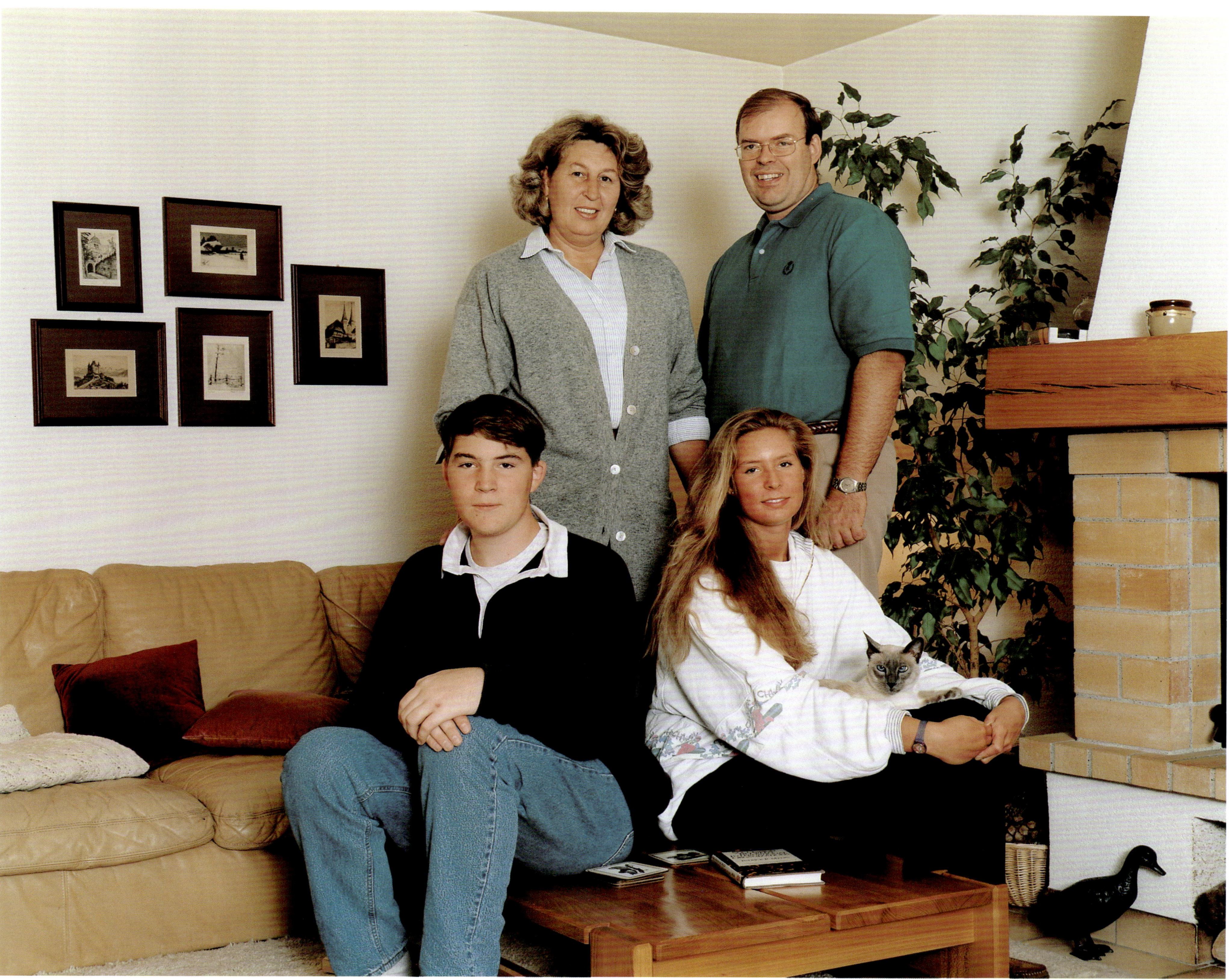

Sassy and Awa N'diaye, Senegal

When one finally manages to get a hold of Sassy N'diaye between two flights to invite him to talk about himself, and one listens to his memories unfold as he sits regally in a shady garden where one of his children is playing diabolo, only one word comes to mind to define the string of events that make up his life: destiny. The question is to find out how this man born in the heart of Africa in a village of seven hundred inhabitants, who was supposed to tend cows like his father, ended up in Geneva as head of the Africa and Indian Ocean department of the IATA. Nothing predestined him for such a life.

School? In Sagata, "the whites' school," also called the French school, did not have a good reputation. Respectable families were loath to send their offspring there, to the point where they sometimes sent the children of families in their service to be educated in the place of their own children. A situation where the whites got the best of it without upsetting the established order. The son of a stock breeder, Sassy, according to the rules, should thus have never attended the school. But his friends went there! To meet up with them there, Sassy, having no one to play with in the clearing, defied his father's prohibition without a second thought, just to be with them.

What about his promotion to the higher grades? An accident. Sassy was not enrolled and the inspector didn't want him to be. The teacher, however, promoted him, to the great dismay of his mother this time: "No way I'm going to send my son sixty kilometers away from the village" to the local chief-town. "I'll give you the land and you can build the school here if you like!" Sassy went anyway.

The airplanes? Another "chance occurrence." After completing his studies, which had taken him to Dakar, one of his friends who had a passion for aviation but was drawn to Saint-Cyr suggested he show up at a competition for which he had registered. Goal: Paris, a school of aviation administration. Sassy was accepted, and that was when he left his country. Each stage of his life has involved a geographical and cultural expansion of his field. Upon returning to Senegal with his diploma, he took part in the development of Air Afrique, while his friend completed his military studies at Saint-Cyr in full regimentals....

Geneva? From one international conference to another, the respected Sassy N'diaye managed to get Senegal into the council of the International Organization of Civil Aviation. This honor for his country, which would win him personal congratulations from president Leopold Senghor, should have propelled him to Montreal, but it was actually in Rio that he ended up, and then in Geneva, at the whim of the winds.

That's the story. The village couldn't get over it when he went back for the first time to look up his old childhood friends. The conversations went something like this:

So, are you an important person?

If you like.

Do you make a lot of money?

I can't complain.

So why aren't you married?

The reply is beyond the pale in Africa. The truth would be incomprehensible in Sagata, but could be summed up as follows:

I haven't had the time.

He did know Awa, however, a distant relative who had also left the country to study French literature at Aix-en-Provence. They crossed paths a few times in Africa and finally got married. She then joined him in Geneva.

Since then, the prodigal son returns often to his village. Sagata is indebted to him for its well, a project for which he pleaded in every ministry imaginable, and a pharmacy. He will also find the money needed to repair the small mosque, which is greatly in need of it—so say the old people, under the conversation-tree, when the earth is cold, they who have never boarded an airplane.

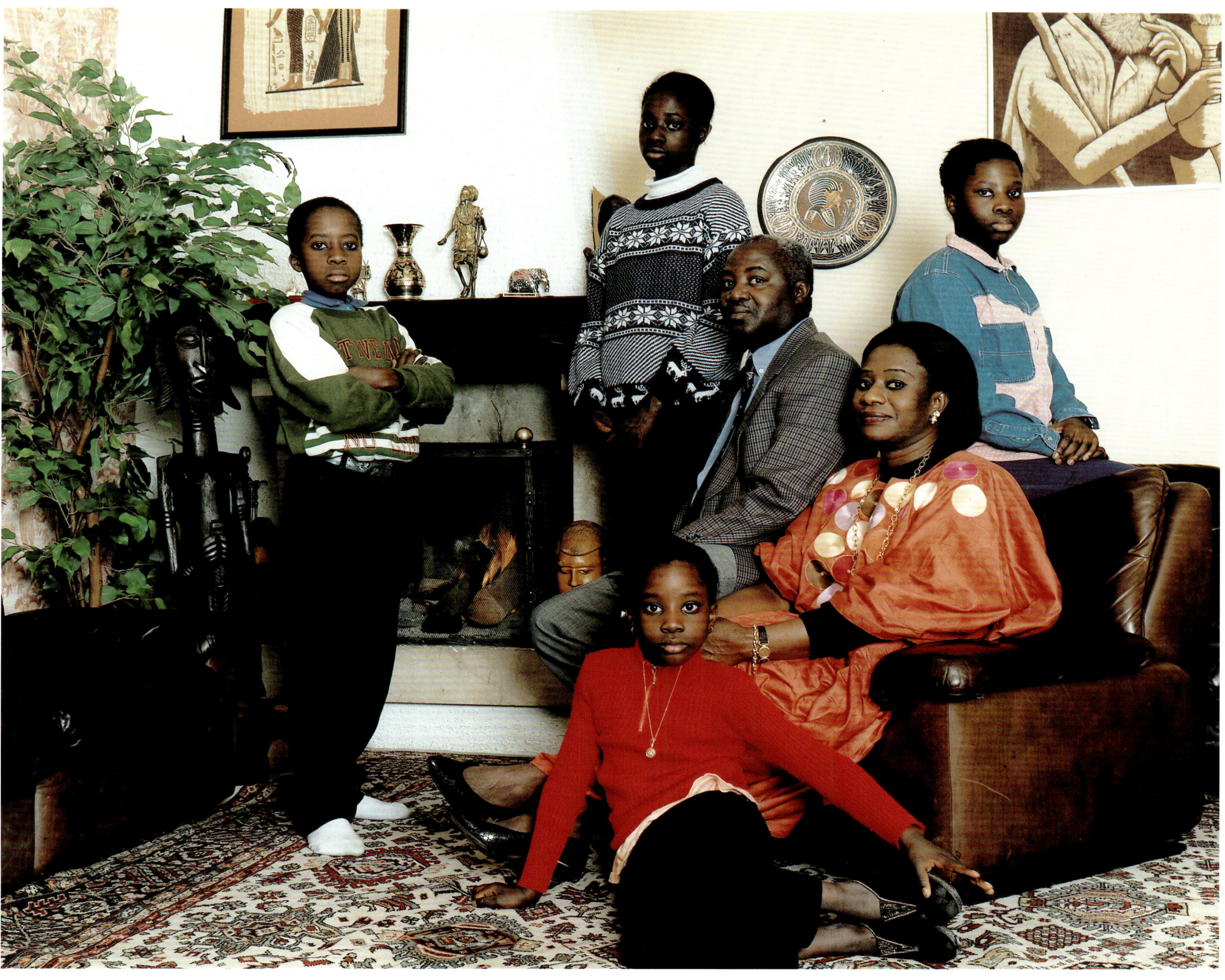

Hiroshi and Mishiko Nakajima, Japan

Sent to Michigan by the Japanese Karate Federation, Hiroshi Nakajima there developed the art of the Chidokan school, the Shotokan style, before coming to Switzerland in 1974 for the same reasons. A world-class referee, 7th dan athlete, trainer and coursemaster—for the Swiss national team, among others—this karate professional spends his evenings, weekends and holidays on the tatami. The rest of the time, he works full-time at the Japanese Mission.

The two met in Geneva. She had come there to learn French, and set up a software business in passing. Neither of them imagined they would settle (perhaps definitively) in Meyrin, where they have now bought a house. Today a journalist for Fuji TV, stationed at the Palais des Nations, Mishiko Nakajima works the international beat during the week; on Saturdays, she gives lessons in Japanese history.

He
"When I'm at the Mission, it's my preference. When I practice karate, it's my preference."

She
"The cultural difference? In Japan, he who speaks little has that much more value."

The Student
(attempt at Haiku)
A couple.
Two beings.
Four lives.

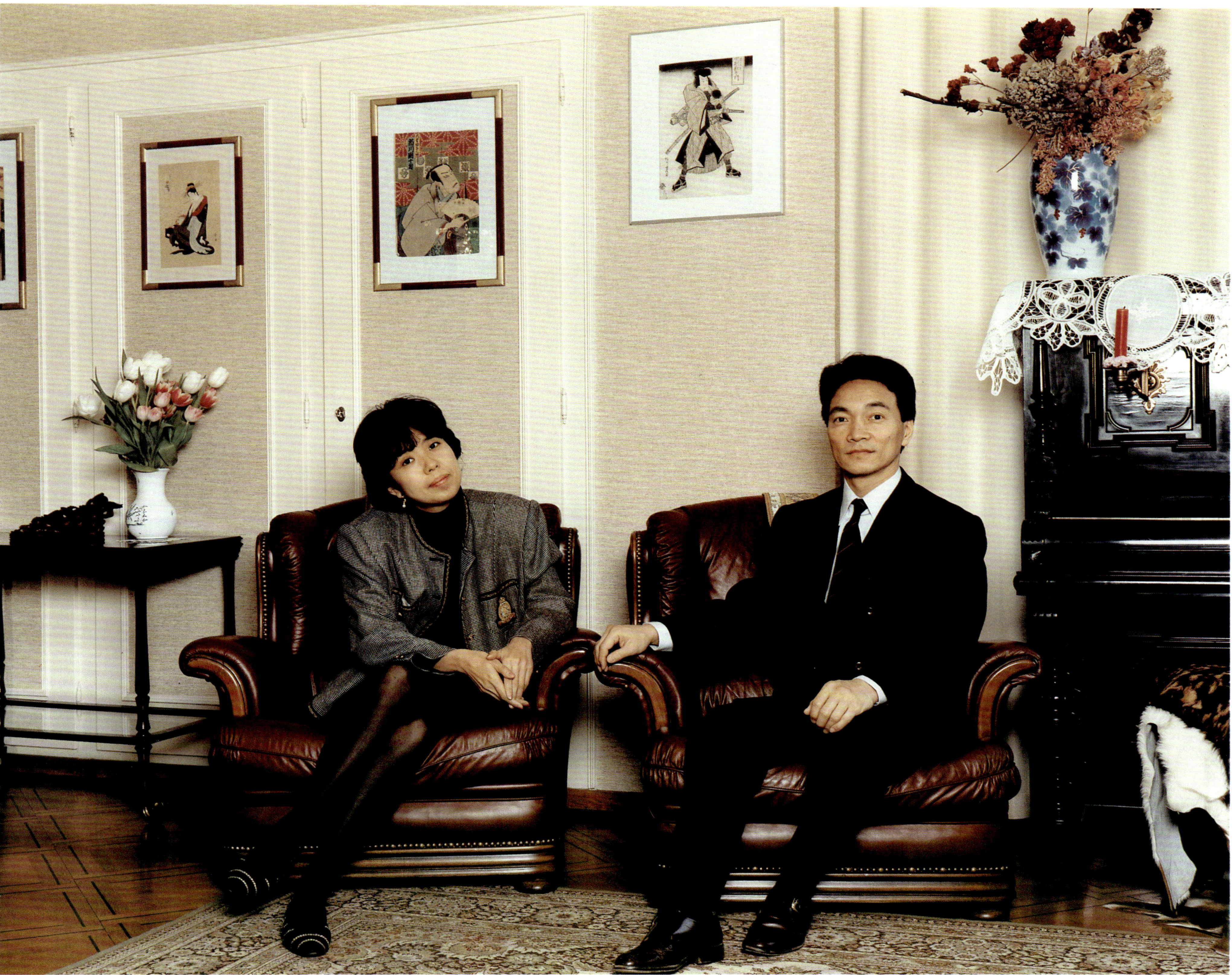

Shekhar and Sharadha Narasimhan, India

Sharadha will never wear a diamond. Too many crimes and injustices have been committed in traditional India for her to possess one of these carbon remnants that shine like a mirror. At bottom, it's a dowry matter. One doesn't marry a woman without dowry. When families arrange a marriage, it's actually one of the first questions put on the table: how much and what sort of goods and jewels will accompany the chosen girl into her new home? Even today, in certain regions, it happens that, by some "stupid accident," a woman guilty of poverty will be burnt to death, doused with kerosene. The diamond, which is fire-resistent, symbolizes this deadly form of dowry.... Sharadha herself had made it clear: My family's circumstances have nothing to do with the fact that I myself refuse to be associated with any possessions whatsoever! Today she may well be the only Indian woman in Geneva never to wear a diamond, but to her it's a matter of principle. An accepted gift will come out of the chest in due time, when her daughters Shubra and Shreya come of age, so she can pass them on—but not before telling the girls of the evil spells the stones too often cast.

Sharadha and her husband Shekhar were educated Brahmins. They know the literature, the religions and a few of the fifteen official languages of their country, to which are added the dialects as well. Their families were in immediate agreement on the principle of not giving or receiving dowries. The promise was even made rather directly: her first words were to inform Shekhar, the Chosen one, that on this matter she would not budge. But she was also able to articulate her reasons well, and he, being rather progressive, understood them perfectly.

Until that moment, neither knew the other except by a frozen portrait on paper. As the horoscope, in the end, proved favorable, and the man was likeable and, most importantly, a Brahmin, she said yes. Yes to the ends of the earth, even as far as Geneva. Why Geneva? It was there Shekhar's father, a high Indian functionary, spent the last years of his life. Shekhar came to Switzerland, where his brother also lived, on the occasion of his father's death, and has never left. It took him six years to find steady employment. Today he helps to manage a department of the ILO, and sings in a classical group. She joined him in 1985, and the two have no plans to leave Meyrin, at least as long as their daughters are attending school there. A dietician and nutritionist by training, Sharadha now devotes herself to her family and occasionally gives courses in Indian cooking....

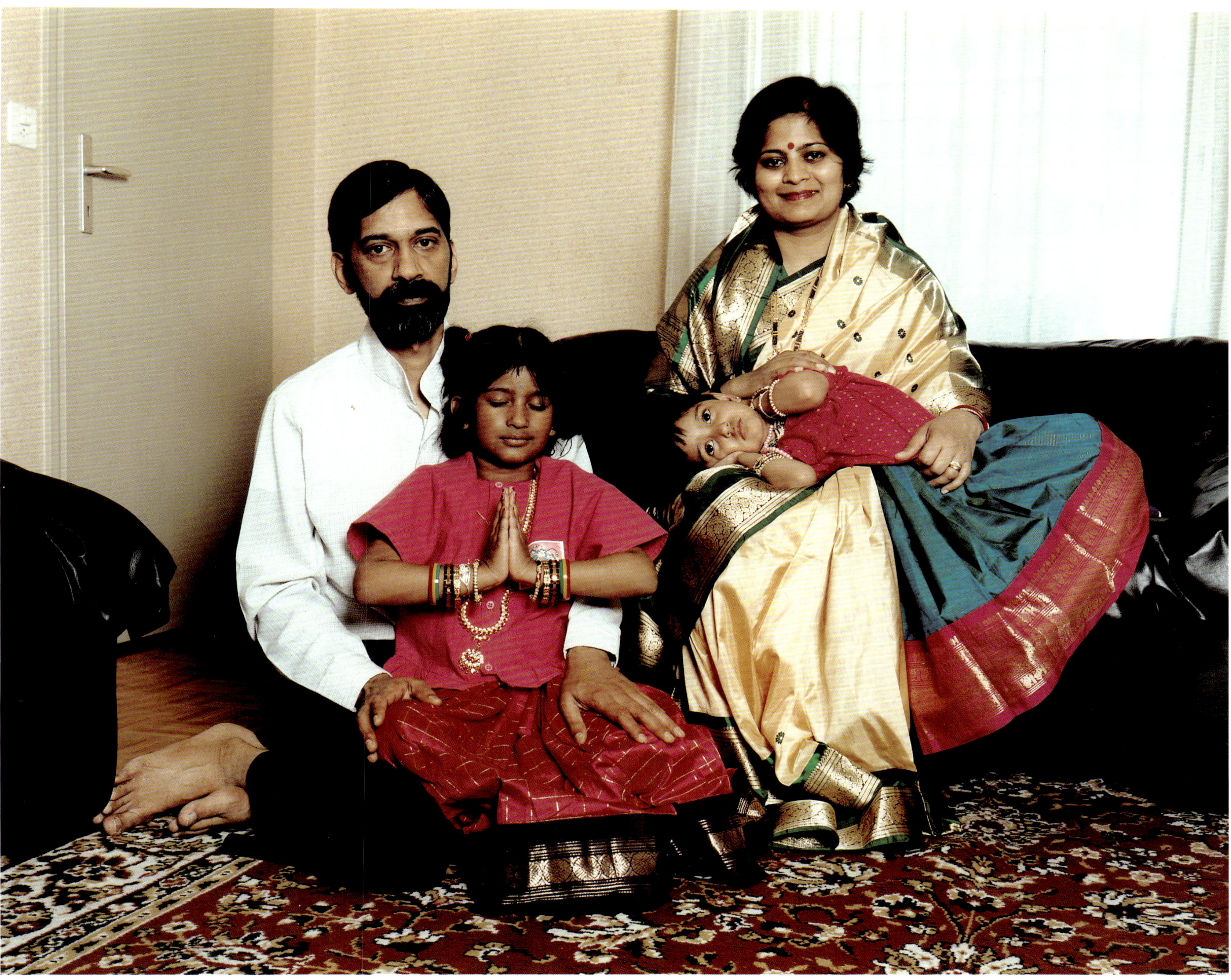

Martin and Rose Ngong Mbako, Cameroon

Seven.

Seven doors on the entrance landing.

Seven people, in the modestly sized room, eating.

The men are in chairs, facing a small table against the wall. Martin welcomes his brother, who is in the process of moving to Geneva like him. The former is an embassy chauffeur, the latter is joining an international organization.

Then there are the women—Rose and her daughters Regina, Brenda Lee and Esther—on a sofa, in front of a low table, with their two cousins. They have almost forgotten to eat, so hilarious is Esther.

The Ngong Mbako family has already been in Switzerland for seven years. At any moment their minister could transfer them somewhere else. The daughters speak English like their parents, and French like the people of Meyrin. Rose and Martin also communicate between themselves by using one of the two hundred fifty dialects of Cameroon, which the children do not understand.

When Martin first met Rose, he asked her straightaway: Will you marry me? She laughed and asked him to be patient.

He had seven bananas in a beautiful bunch when he returned a year later to see her again and give her this symbolic gift. She wasn't there. He persevered. And won her over. Her parents whimpered a little. They are in fact from the same province, but not the same village.

There are some Genevans who don't like blacks. There are others, perhaps sometimes the same people, who do not appreciate the dance of diplomatic cars. Hard luck, Martin. One day, a cashier put on one hell of an act to avoid physical contact: she made him lay his money down on the counter before taking it, then threw his change at him.

For seven weeks I drank the Cameroon coffee he gave to me, which he had brought back after a recent visit to his country. Because you came to my home, he said to me, smiling. And to think it was I who should have come with arms full.

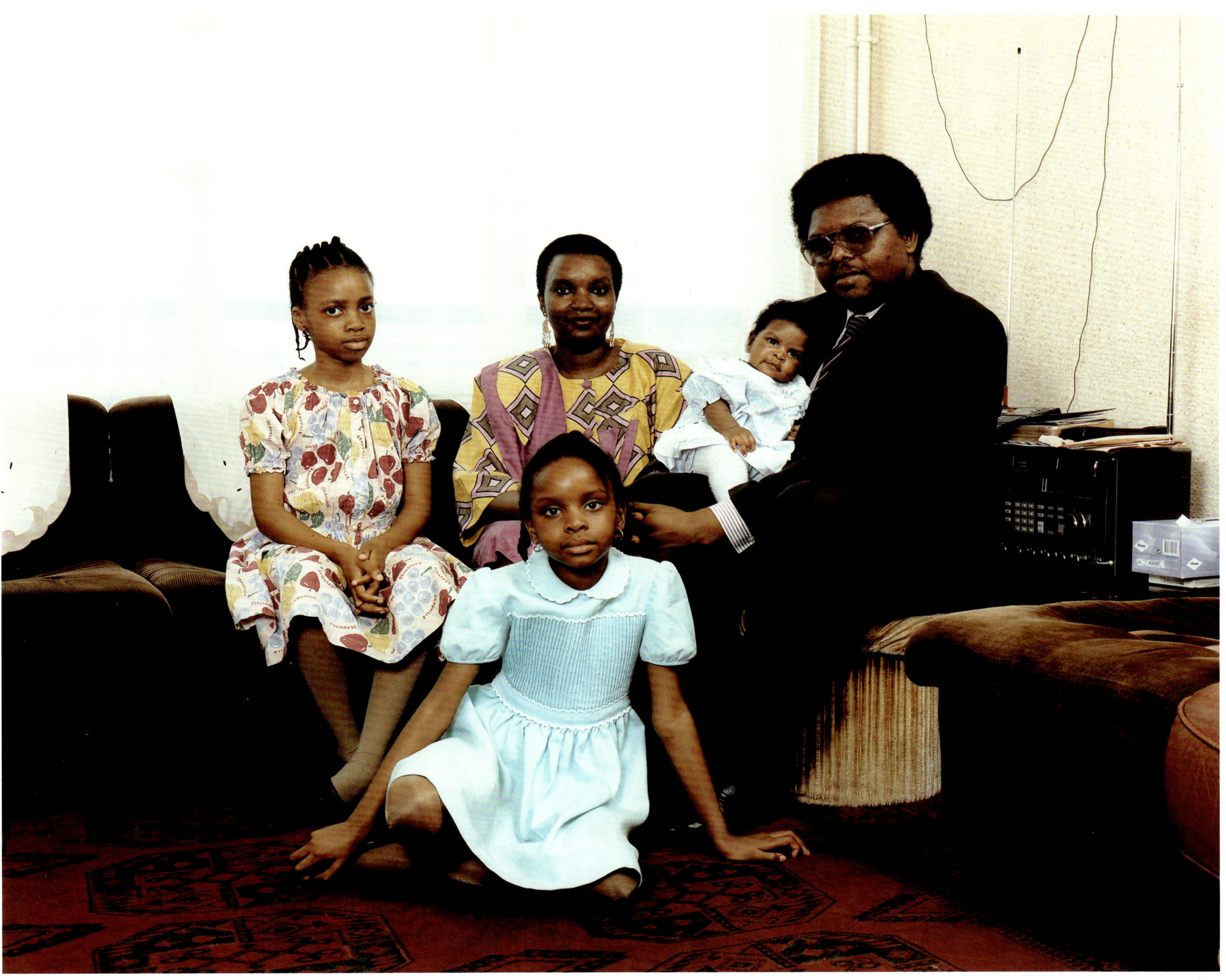

Saku and Jessie Ovaskainen, Finland—Taiwan

One look at the interior arrangement, one look under the cover of the wok, and it's clear: a man of the North, "turned to the East." It was in fact in Bali that he met his future wife. Like him she was there on holiday. She would later follow him wherever he was sent by the Finnair management, for Sakari, known as Saku, is director of stopovers for his national airline. Earlier stationed in Brussels, he now works at Geneva-Cointrin.

Every day he reads a Helsinki daily, while every day she receives, though with a few days' delay, her Taipei newspaper. They speak English to each other. Their son is learning the family tongues—Chinese ideograms as well as Finnish, which like Hungarian is something of a mystery as to its origins. He is a rare case of extreme biculturalism. Even his name was not chosen lightly: Seeta, an ancient Finnish name, actually corresponds phonetically with "Chita," a Chinese name no less ancient. A single surname serves to designate this child of the future in both worlds.

Curiosly, these two great travellers hardly ever leave Meyrin to go into Geneva proper. Once a month, perhaps. It's more towards France that they set their sights when they really need to leave the community. They have put down roots in Meyrin. Or else sometimes they'll take their camper and explore this Switzerland that they find so beautiful but whose languages they find so hard to master. No matter: equipped with survivors' French, they play the tourists in their adoptive country, as if, it seems, to approach it all the better with much affection and a little distance.

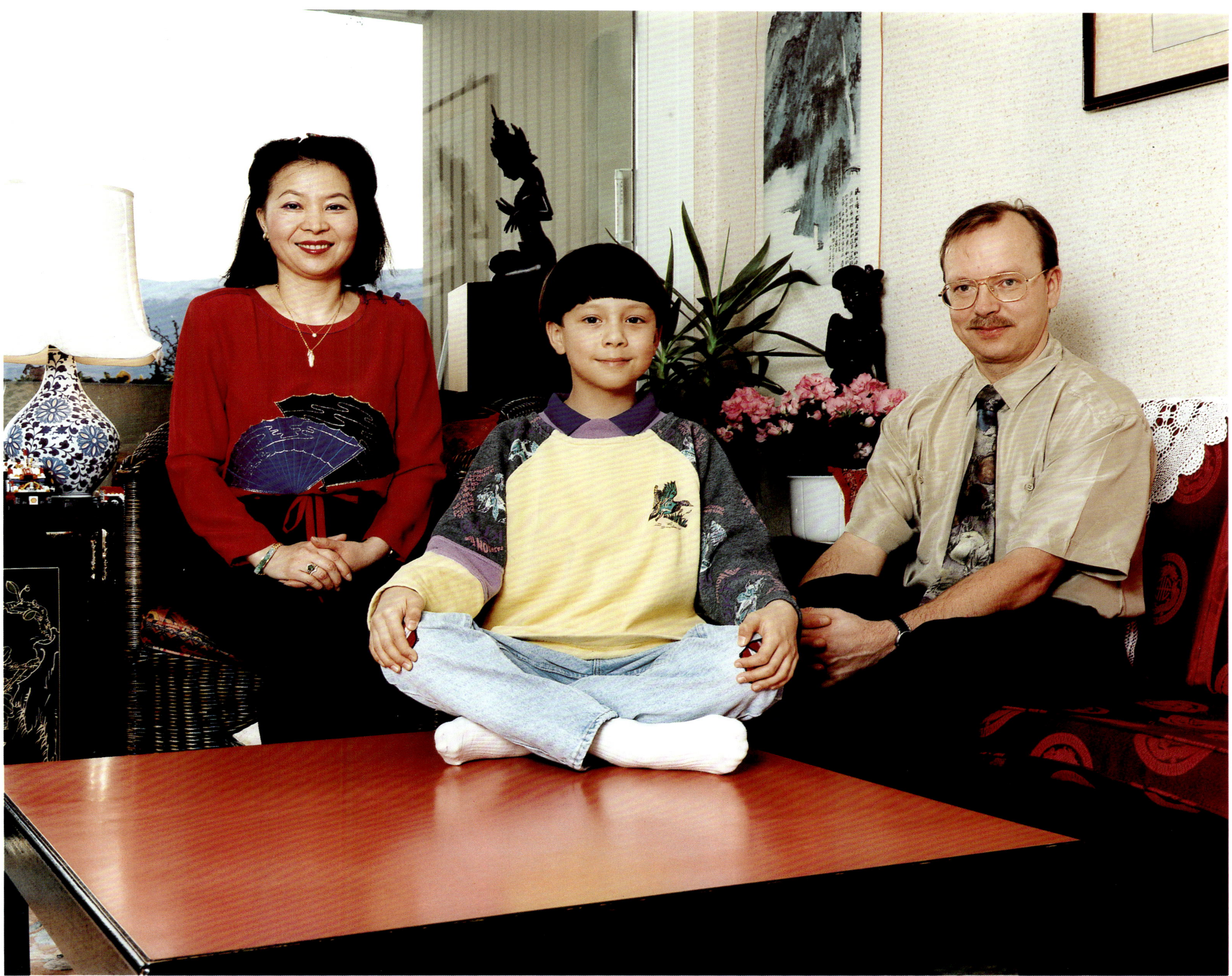

Thinley and Gayley Penjor, Buthan

The Detached Thoughts of a Buthanese:

Having spent six unforgettable months in Meyrin, I most gladly accept your invitation to write a few words to convey my impressions of our life in this magnificent city. I can only agree with Lord Byron that Switzerland is situated in the most romantic region in the world. My wife Gayley and my son Choyning have fallen in love with the splendid gardens of Geneva and Meyrin. We have devoured the hole-filled cheese and chocolates that have won your country an unequalled reputation. We have even bought watches, cuckoo clocks and Swiss Army knives. All the same, we have regretted our inability to speak French, a major handicap to our ability to make friends among the local population.

During our stay in Meyrin, we were told that the city numbered 120 different nationalities among its inhabitants. But this does not mean, to my mind, that the average Swiss is particularly open to foreigners. A little more tolerance wouldn't hurt....

In a world of instantaneous communication and supersonic travel, we are often called upon to live in communities whose habits and behavior might seem strange to us. It is said that culture is a universal form of expression; I believe that a better understanding of this particular culture would favor a more harmonious coexistence. We express our sincerest wishes that the Forum of Meyrin will meet this goal.

Sincerely,
Thinley Penjor
Buthan Embassy, Kuwait

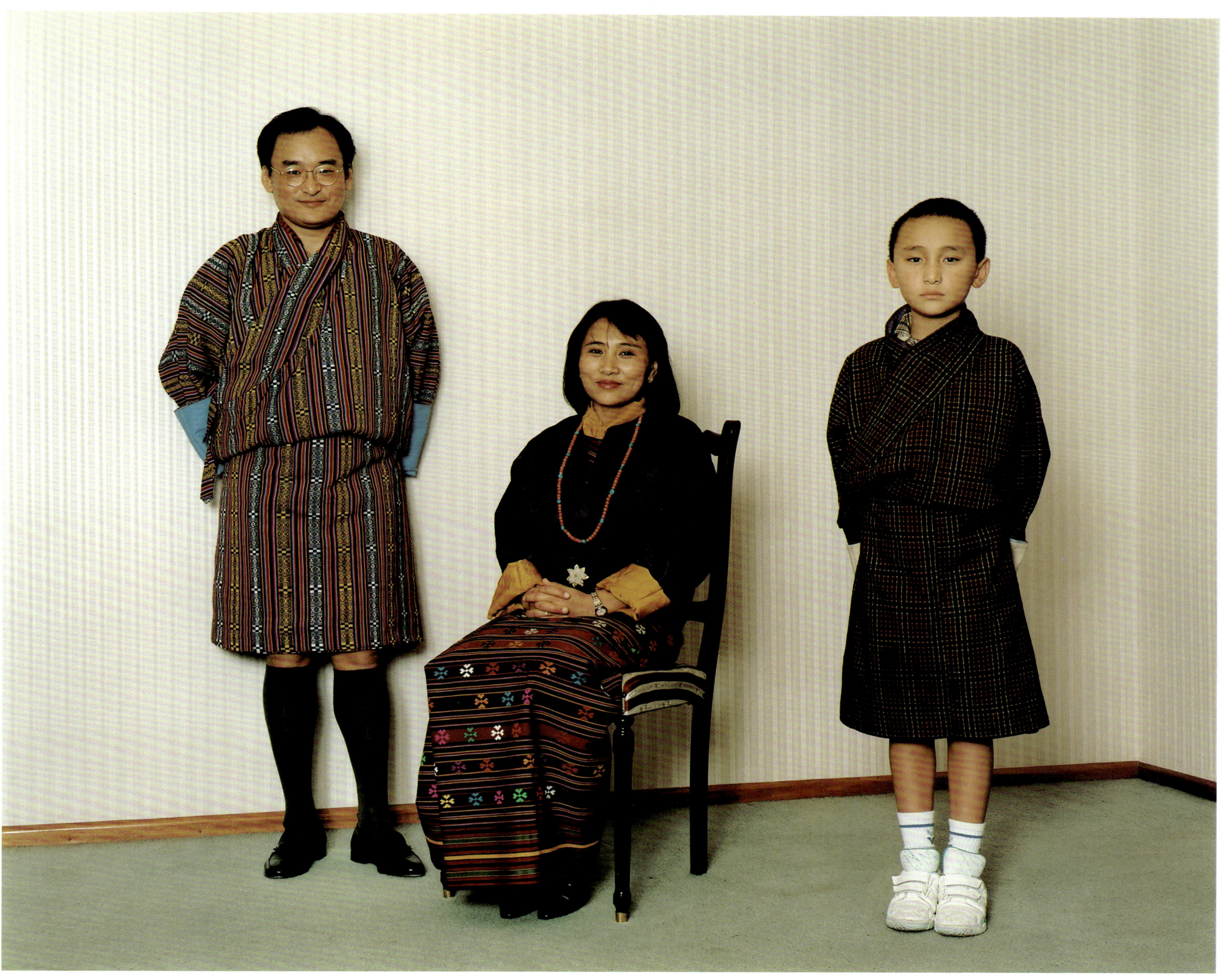

Claire and Noël Rabemanantsoa, Madagascar

The religious community in Madagascar of which pastor Rabemanantsoa used to be the secretary general numbers more than a million souls. It is only relatively recently, however, that Africa has opened up to Christianity. Various colonizations may at times have accelerated the process, but for the most part the continent remains associated with other religions.

In Geneva, the Ecumenical Council of Churches has an office devoted to African activities, where Noël was elected secretary general in 1985. Since then, he has been circulating and spreading out, coordinating the activities of the various churches growing there.

Unlike a number of his neighbors in Meyrin, Noël Rabemanantsoa had not really expected to move to Switzerland. When the possibility of being elected to the ECC presented itself, he prayed and left it up to God's will; his family did the same. It's a fine family. A real family. Five children, all close in age: "I was a student but, where I come from, when you have faith, you begin by starting a family." All are amateur musicians, and play and sing at the church. Only the eldest has taken the theological path.

Surnames do not exist in Madagascar. An event, a vow, the memory of a circumstance determine people's names. They are poems. And difficult to translate.

Noël Rabemanantsoa: the great one who has good things.

Claire Ravaoarisoa Andriantsoa: the new and beautiful creature.

Arintsoa Zafindriaka: the son of Tsoa and grandson of Driak who is mourned.

Vololontsoa Rano: the young sprout of Tsoa that comes from the water.

Andriantsoa Manga Vatomazava: the pillar of the family, precious as blue stone.

Aimanantsoa Mamimahafehy Masimanoro: the happy and voluntary life that presents happy circumstances.

Rabemanantsoa Toky: Toky means trust. Rabemanantsoa is his father's name. Toky's birth was registered in France.

The photo includes two friends, Theodore Zandriamalazarivo and Felana Rasolondraibe, whose beautiful last names will have to remain a secret.

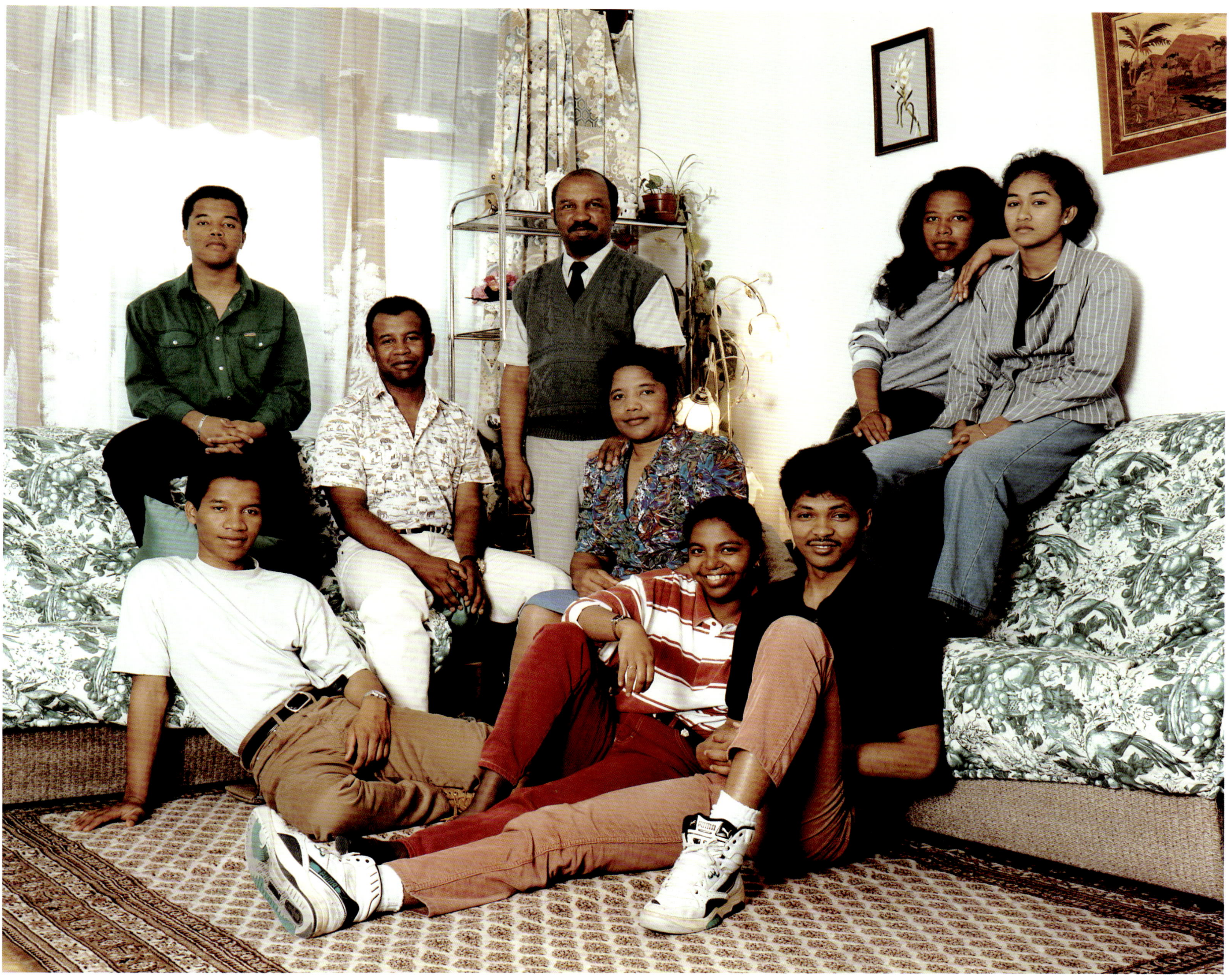

Chinnamah-Vasanthy Ragavan, Malaysia

There was a marriage which in 1980 brought Vasanthy to Geneva and ended in a divorce.
There is Malaysia, that distant land she still thinks about.
There is a family there, who would welcome her back at any time, but whom she wouldn't want to disturb.
There is the language, learned on site in this totally unknown city of Geneva.
There are Surane and Suresh, two Meyrinese boys, her sons, for whom she does everything she can.
There is this city, which she has come to know and love.

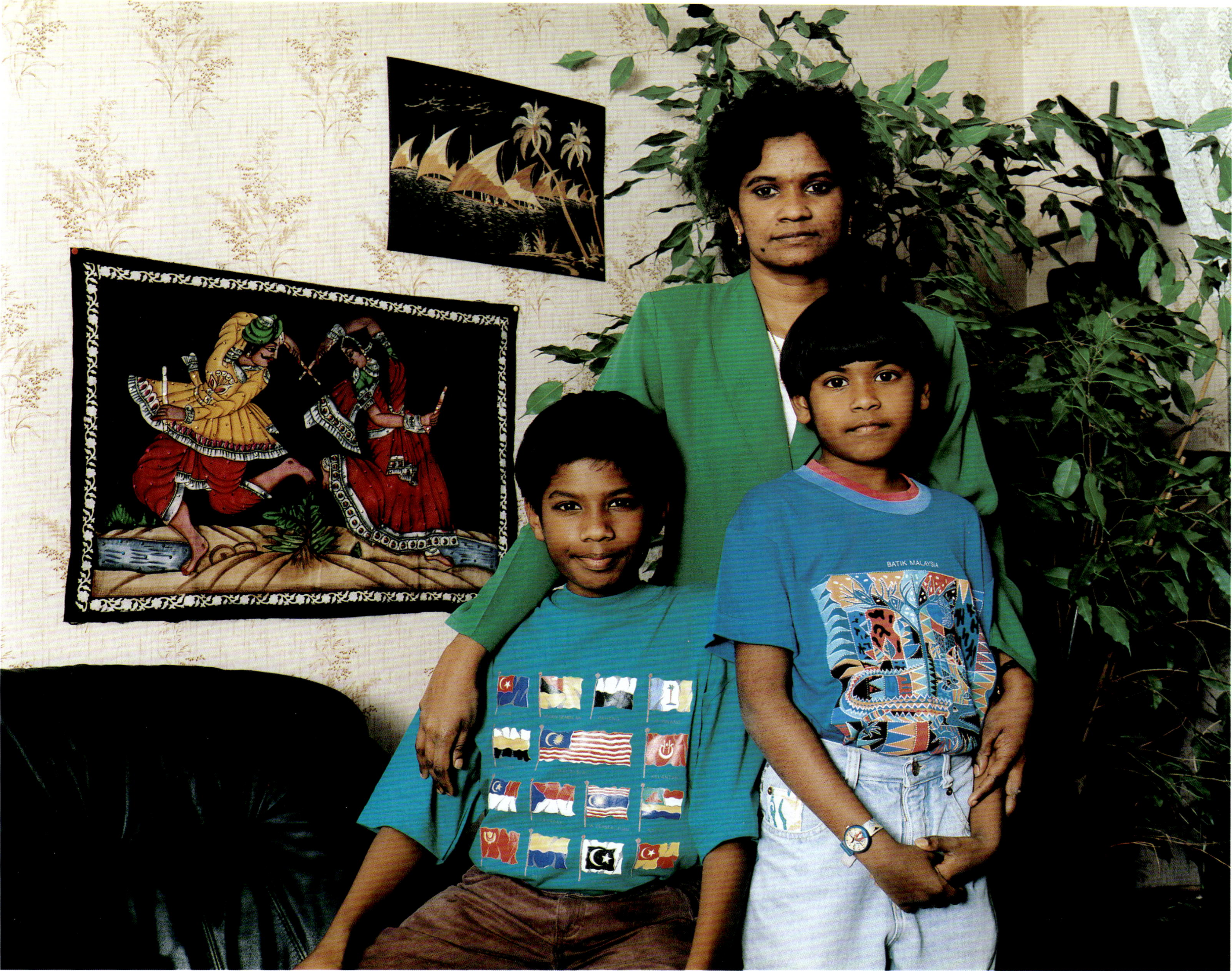
BATIK MALAYSIA

Baltazar and Mauricia Ramos, Portugal

It's a little like in a fairy tale.

Imagine them in grammar school. They are, let's say, seventeen or eighteen years old. They see each other, notice each other, like each other. They are beautiful. One is always beautiful at age seventeen. And more serious than Rimbaud said. "June night! Seventeen! You let yourself get drunk." I can hear Léo Ferré singing the poet's words, but it's Brassens the stereo is playing: "Sur un banc public, banc public, banc public...." Brassens rasps, but I forget him in my distraction with Rimbaud. In my head: "You're in love: your sonnets make her laugh...." Was it love at first sight? Actually, I have no idea. I only like to imagine it. What I know, since in fact it's what they've told me—with a loud laugh—is that they fell in love with each other at grammar school. Anyway, they proved Rimbaud wrong. Their month of June was stretched out, past August and into December, after which the years added up, one after another. In Portugal, she was a schoolteacher. He wanted to leave the country. To go out to sea, perhaps in a great boat from which he would see an albatross, a cod-fishing boat. But as an only son, it's hard to go too far away from one's parents: "They've taken care of me. How could I leave them at the moment when they in turn might need me?" Unthinkable. Geneva was a practical decision, a mere two-hour flight away from Portugal, and since a friend had recently moved there, he thought he would try his luck, like the others, just "to see." She followed him. Baltazar became a nurse. Mauricia has become a nurse's aide out of attachment, so as to work in Loëx like her husband. A beautiful love story, as I said, but I forgot: there are also two beautiful children born in Geneva.

A mature woman is embroidering in the bright living room, sitting against the light. Her features are dry, they are those of woman full of secrets, of self-abnegation and familial love. She is Mauricia's mother, and remains silent because she doesn't understand French. She smiles when we laugh, just because that confirms the cheerful atmosphere, showing that the children are happy in the company of the intruder. Oh my, a writer! Baltazar put on a tie for the occasion. When the tone becomes more serious, she feels it too and modestly turns her eyes to the fine white weave before her. In the iconic woman's hands, a tablecloth perhaps—it's too early to tell—begins to take form. It must be frustrating for her not to understand anything. In 1985, upon their arrival, the Ramoses themselves had to make an effort to learn French, at first picking up only schoolbook fragments. Grandmother's agile fingers are as fast as a 1930s Singer. She's an authentic grandmother, with white hair of course, coquettishly teased, passing through for a family visit in this strange country where "everything that is not prohibited is obligatory."

Now they're trapped. Should they move back home? Probably, yes. You never can tell. But the children are starting school. They will soon become true Meyrinese. We'll see later on. Perhaps the ways will part yet again.

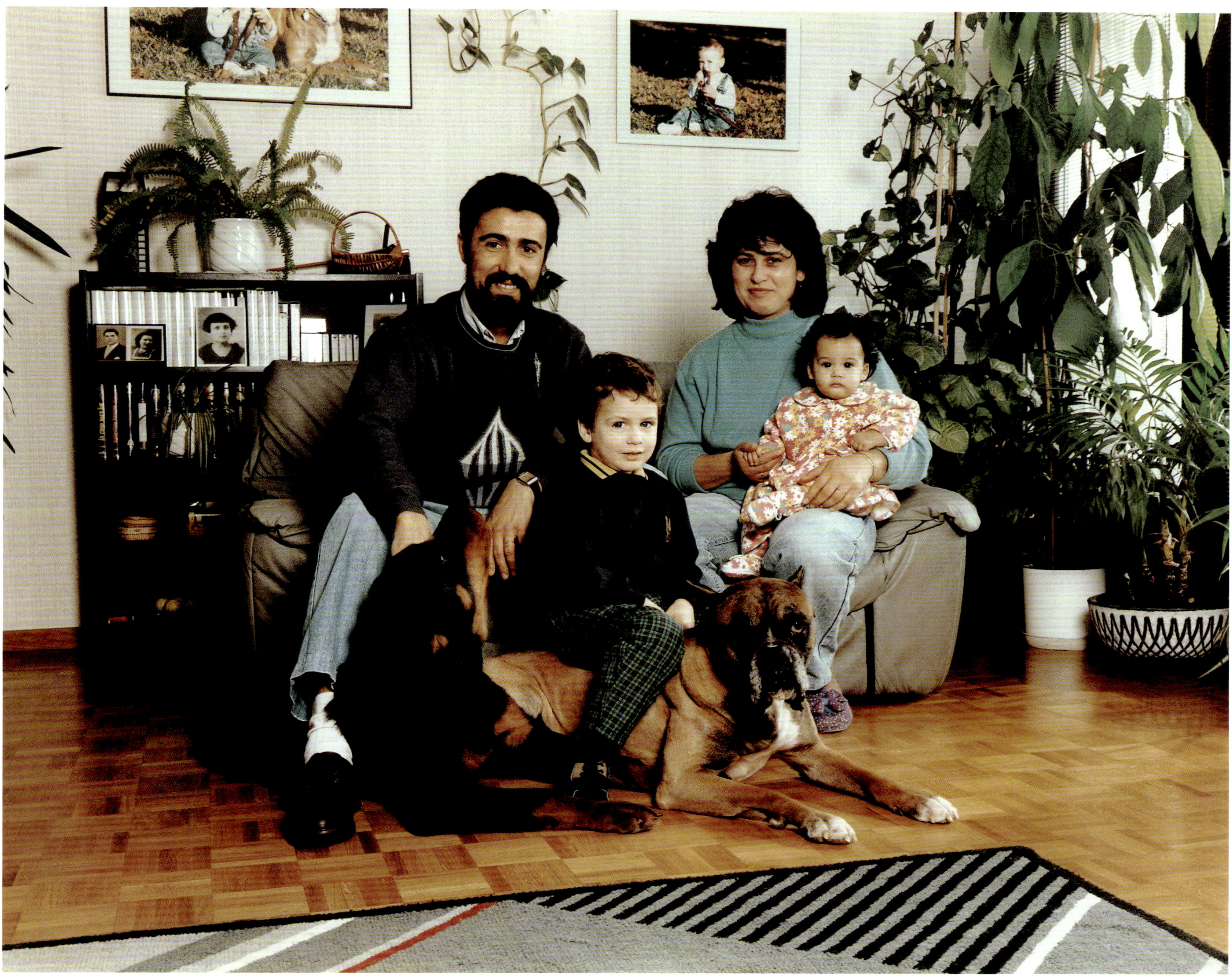

Michel Renia, Guadeloupe

Charles is fourteen. Of Michael, he says: He's like a father.

Miguel is eighteen. He goes further: He puts his trust in you. I've had my license for only six months, and he lent me his car!

Michel Renia shyly raises his eyes from the television screen, which is spitting out Servette-Young Boys.

The neighborhood teenagers have got into the habit of streaming into the back room of his print shop. To receive them properly, he has furnished it with a few armchairs, a refrigerator and some Gyger-style frescoes collected when a discotheque changed owners. Under the bar, a sizeable collection of music videos.

At first, certain adults—parents—raised a few eyebrows at him. Then they came to see for themselves. They saw the printing press, discovered the room where a facetious headline reads: "Basement apartments, life in darkness," and shed their fears. No violence, no drugs. No manipulation either. He gives advice, explains things: he's cool, he never forces, says Tony. In fact, Michel Renia has come to play an important social role for the young people of Meyrin. He knows everyone's personal history. He doesn't judge; he helps. He's a big brother.

Where he comes from, in Guadeloupe, the young always had someone older nearby to give them advice. Michel Renia has never forgotten that. "All I've done is reproduce, in a neighborly way, a Guadeloupan set-up: in my country, the grown-ups look after the kids. That way they can't turn out badly."

At age eighteen, the military authorities sent him to the Vendée. Having fulfilled his obligations, he went off to Paris in search of musician companions capable, like he, of living on love, fresh water, soul and funk. James Brown and Otis Redding were his inspirations. Sometimes he would rewrite their lyrics in Creole. It worked well. He first came to Geneva to play music. Old photos show him playing guitar next to some fine specimens of '68, lost in dreamland. It's amusing to see the respectable shopowner decked out in the garb of the time. That was a time of two and three week contracts to play in Genevan night-clubs. When his daughter was born in 1974, he put down his guitar. "I needed a steady job."

And so this great-grandson of both a Dutch pharmacist from the island of Dominica and an American Indian became a printer in Geneva, a small shop-owner in Meyrin.

A certain Nicolas, twenty years old, passes by the print shop. He too wants to become a printer. "Michel? He helped me to find myself", he says gratefully. Michel Renia did not want to train him himself, however. "One mustn't mix friendship and work." But Nicolas knows that after his four years of training, a place is waiting for him in Meyrin, the town of his childhood.

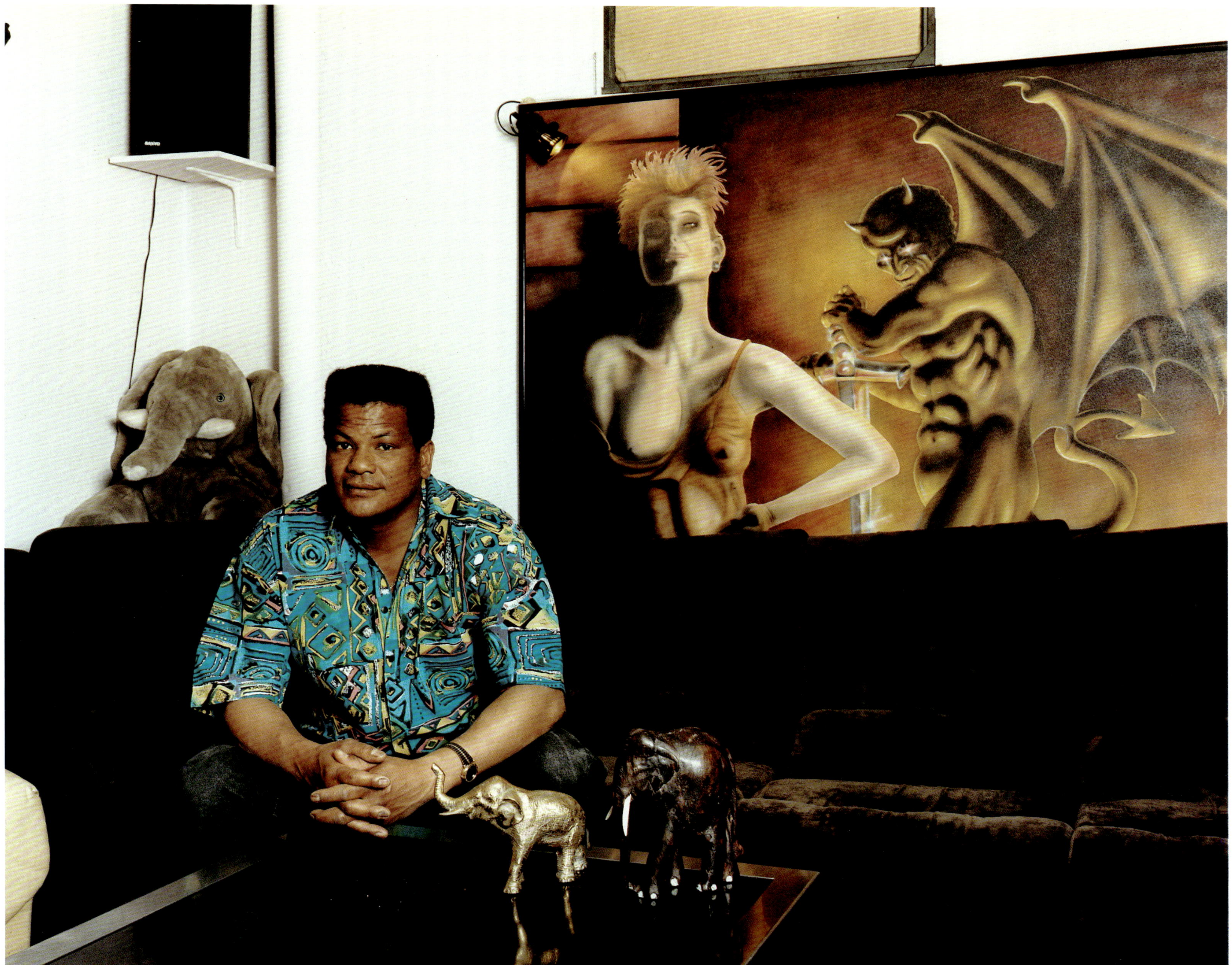

Sayed and Golalaï Reshtia, Afghanistan

Golalaï Reshtia does not like her given name. In itself, that's nothing out of the ordinary. What is perhaps a bit more unusual is that her mother didn't like it either. It's a Persian name that indicates—and is practically synonymous with—"beauty." Indeed, it took her mother twenty-four days to decide to register it with the legal authorities. Reason of state. Already.

You see, in Afghanistan, where the people spoke Pharsee as well as Pashto, the king preferred Pharsee. Now, the king was actually Golalaï's uncle. For this reason, it would have been difficult for the family not to set an example. To this day the princess Golalaï still rails against her name, to which has been added another, prestigious name, that of her husband: Sayed Reshtia, former minister of culture and information, former director of Afghani radio and an ambassador, journalist and historian.

Four objects link the past to the present. A photo, a silver platter, and a pair of plates. The latter come from Prague, souvenirs of the time when Sayed Reshtia represented his country there, extending his influence over Poland and Hungary as well (since Afghanistan has only a limited network of embassies). The platter is an homage to His Excellency and bears the signatures of the entire diplomatic corps accredited in Tokyo in 1973, when the fall of Prince Daoud heralded the institution of the Afghan republic and the end of Reshtia's career. Lastly, the photo shows Golalaï at age two. The image was saved by a miracle: shortly before the seizure of the Reshtia house by the Soviet authorities, a steward of the Ariana company snatched it up in order to bring it back to Golalaï Reshtia, his former boss....

"We had five or six domestics. I knew nothing about housekeeping matters. The cooking? I couldn't even boil an egg before coming here!" says Golalaï Reshtia, smiling. "But I adjusted very quickly!"

Show him some more photos, says her husband.

They address each other in the polite form. The coffee is steaming. The Afghani pine nuts are delicious.

Eat, eat!

What about you?

Oh you know, for us it's Ramadan....

I feel embarrassed.

Oh not at all....

Never depart from the laws of hospitality. Class is one of those possessions one takes with oneself everywhere in exile.

Now members of the Meyrin Club of Elders, they both live in a modest three-room apartment, furnished through the loans of charitable organizations which they pay off at a rate of fifty francs monthly. They will not leave this home until a "true democracy" is re-established in their country. Today Sayed Reshtia is reading his Memoirs, which Golalaï has typed out for him; he contributes to various publications and also helps out at the Afghan library of Liestal, near Basel. In Kabul, one of his properties has been made into a kindergarten and the other... the headquarters of the secret police. He's an optimist, she's a pessimist; they are both just back from a pilgrimage to Mecca. The view from the living room looks onto the shopping area: "We have found everything we need here to rebuild our lives."

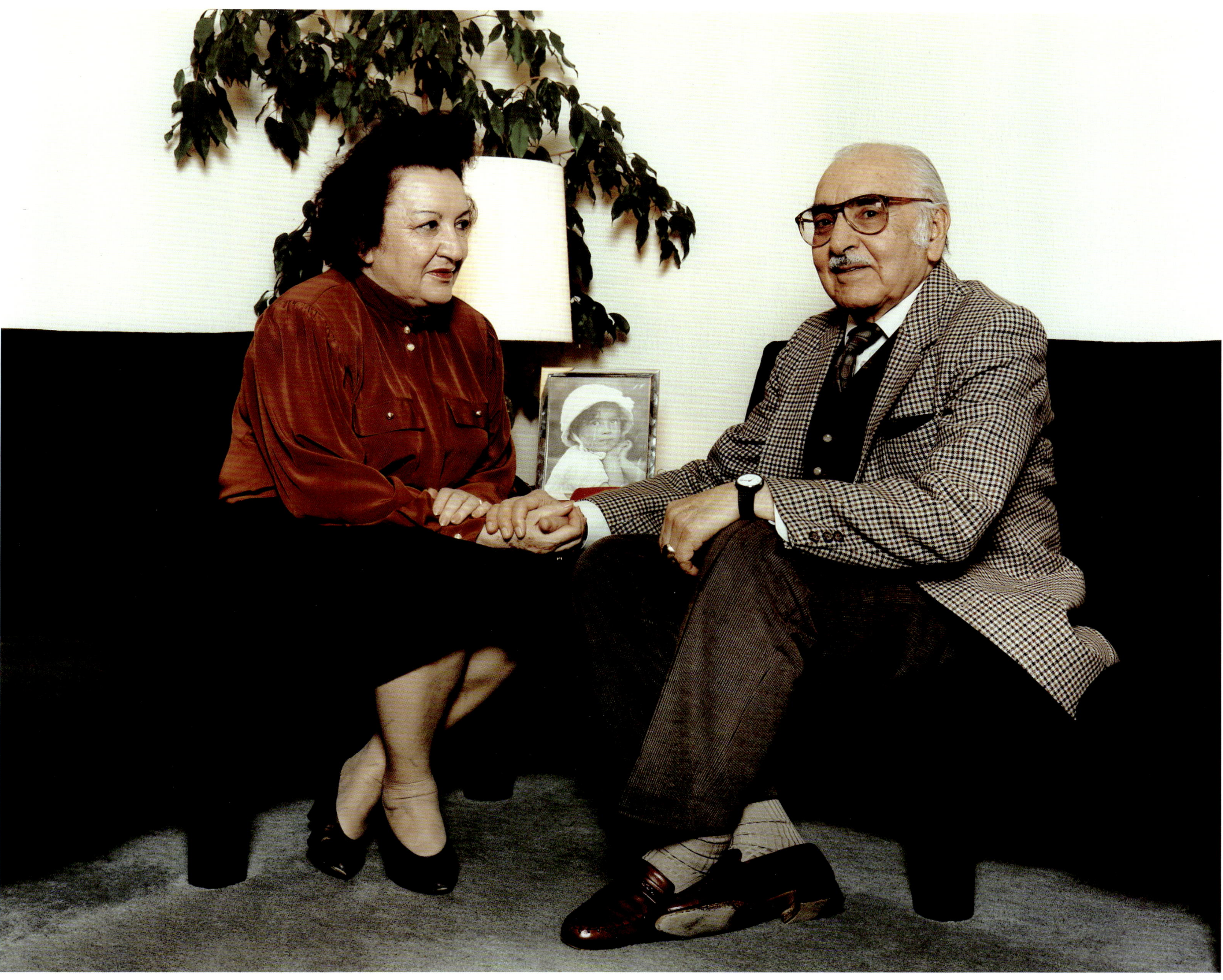

Samuel and Ethel Salazar, Argentina—Chile—Israel

Buenos Aires
Ethel was born in Argentina to parents originally from Belarus and the Ukraine, respectively. Under Peron, the family went to the USSR, where Ethel lived until she was twelve. It would take her mother seven years to obtain an emigration visa; they were communists upon entering, but not upon leaving.

Santiago, Chile
Samuel is the twelfth child, the youngest in a large family in whose veins flows a mix of Indian and European blood. The fall of Allende prompts him to go to Argentina, where he meets his wife, whom he marries in 1976.

Jerusalem
A Jewish militant of the Left, with Hashomer Hatzaïr leanings, she wants to fulfil her Aliyah: to "go up" to Israel. He becomes a graphic artist for the *Jerusalem Post.* He is happy there. She isn't. Political disappointments. Rejection of religious pressures. Dafna and Gabriela are born.

Tel Aviv
Fresh air on weekends. The city emptied of crowds. Comes 1982: Samuel is called up by the army. The war in Lebanon. They are against it, so they leave. When their son is later born in Switzerland, they will give him two first names: Simon, the Hebrew, and Omar, the Arab.

Annemasse
One of Samuel's sisters lives there. Destination: Europe. The daughters and their mother settle in near Geneva, trying to find their new bearings. Looking for work. In a few months, the Salazars burn up their savings while waiting to figure things out.

Milan
Samuel meanwhile has been scouring Italy. From Milan to Turin, by way of Venice and other cities, he casts his nets but snares no jobs. High and dry, he returns to Annemasse, where the family will have to work things out. She, meanwhile, has found work.

Geneva
Ethel works at GATT, where her ease with languages in general and Spanish in particular lead her to the secretariat. She had wanted to leave Israel; he hadn't. She found a job, he didn't. A difficult moment. Then he finds work as a typesetter.

Meyrin
No problem integrating. A question of getting used to it. The welcoming of new arrivals seems more typical of Israeli culture than Swiss.... Hebrew remains the "language of complicity" between the parents; the children are learning other tongues as well.

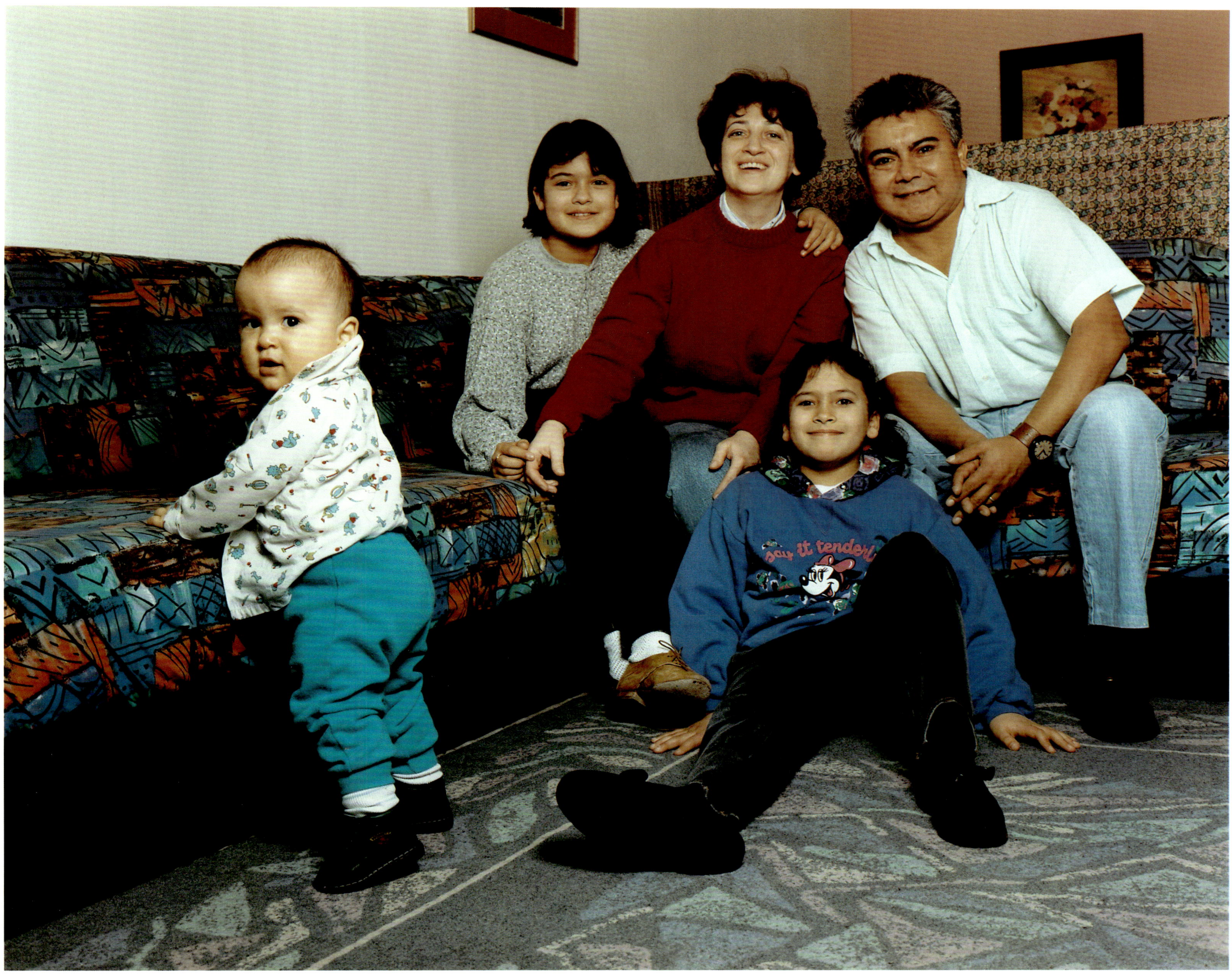

Marie-Paule and Raymond Sibailly, Ivory Coast

Before the Ivory Coast won independence in 1960, July 14 was celebrated in Abidjan. The greatness and aberrations of past colonies. What could the "Gallic" ancestors of these Africans have been thinking when they saw them take a holiday merely because one day in France some revolutionaries had stormed the Bastille? The French had upended the Crown in 1789; in 1842, they began installing trading posts that would spread progressively around the country for a century. In 1945, while Paris was celebrating the Liberation, Félix Houphouët-Boigny was in Abidjan taking over the management of the Rassemblement Démocratique Africain, which would lead his country to autonomy in 1958, then independence.

Marie-Paule was born on July 18. At the time Raymond, a distant relative, was spending his holiday in the company of a baby that had been temporarily placed in his care. With one eye rivited on the tiny little woman and the other on her feeding-bottles, he coddled her. To say that the Sibaillys have known each other since the cradle is not, for once, an exaggeration....

Raymond and Marie-Paule come from the higher strata of this country's society, where 85 percent of the inhabitants devote themselves to agriculture. In their families they have lost count of all the ministers, magistrates—Marie-Paule's father is a veteran of the Supreme Court—and high-level functionaries. Both have enjoyed the privilege of going to study in Paris, where they met again in 1976, now grown-up, and fell in love before returning to their country. Having obtained his doctorate in political science in Paris, Raymond taught at the university of Abidjan before going to Geneva to create a non-governmental organization, the Pan-African Institute of International Relations. Though the institution now has its headquarters in Brussels, the Sibaillys have not left Meyrin. She works at the embassy; he has opened an office of consultants specializing in the development of African resources. A middleman and adviser, he particularly directs investors from the North toward the South. And he is working hard to bring back to his country the many exiles trained in economics, technical sciences and administration who are currently living in Europe and the United States, a great loss of human resources for the Ivory Coast.

Their children, Ochelio, Guibet, Oné and Bauly, have African names. The two oldest ones lived there for a few years. But not the youngest. The latest arrival was actually born in Meyrin. The Ivory Coast, for them, is a place of origin, a cultural legacy, a concept.... But their home ground is henceforth Geneva. Where will they live when it comes time to take off? They are, deep down, more Swiss than African.

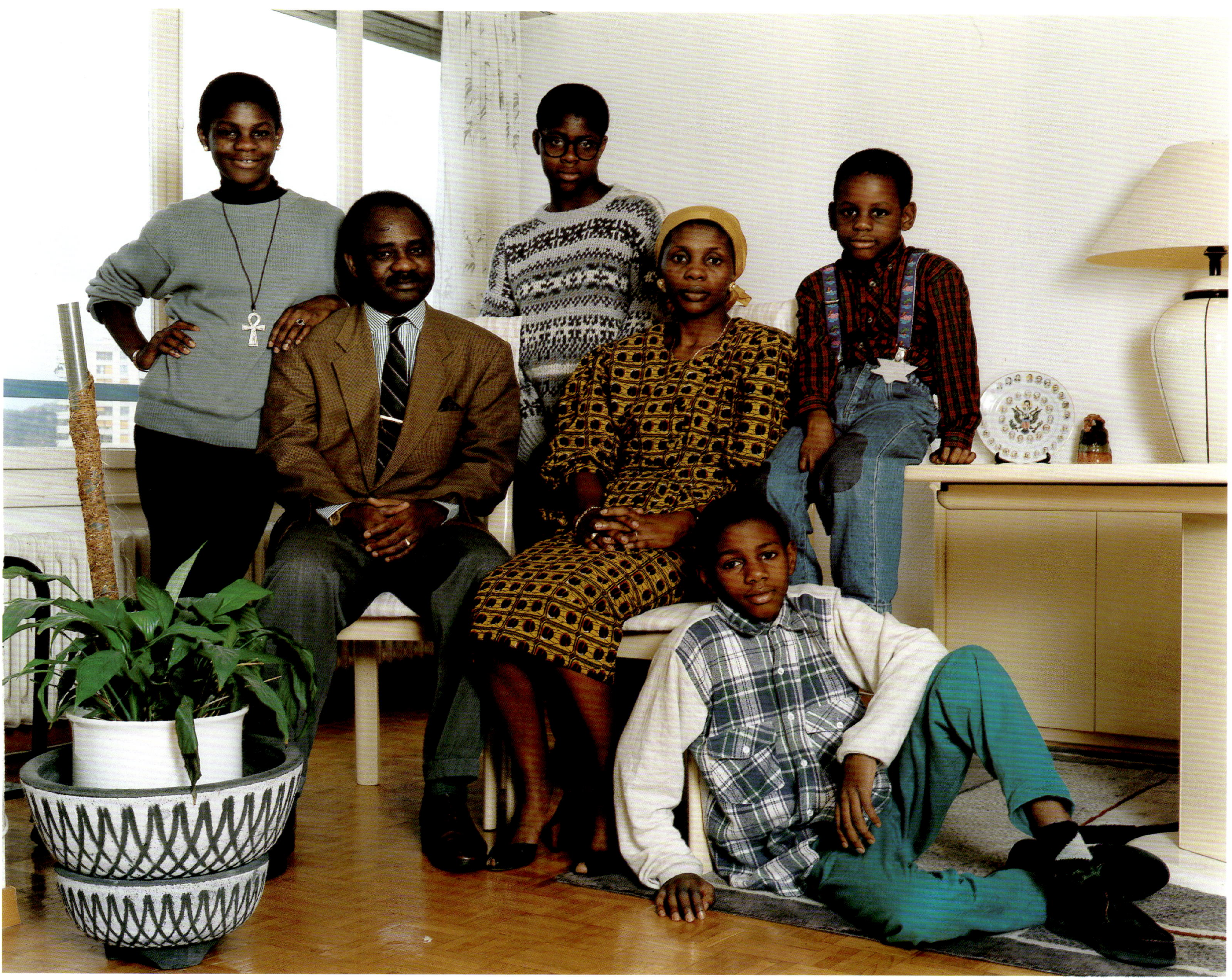

Muhammad and Rehana Sualeheen, Pakistan

First of all, they compliment their visitor who, as a native of the Léman, comes from a city that advertises "two mosques as a sign of openness."

Then, out of humility, Muhammad minimizes the story of his life, which I know to be thrilling because I know certain things he won't tell but which he tries very hard to make people believe without seeming to do so.

Then there is the discretion of the children. There are five of them, but they don't stay around for very long.

Finally, the table is divided because in their country, there is always someone dropping in unannounced, and thus there is always a plate that seems to be waiting.

A former official of the Pakistani government, Muhammad has since been in the employ of the United Nations, in a modest position, he says, "because it's pointless to earn a little more money if it only brings a lot more worries."

In her shop in the heart of Meyrin, Rehana sells books, clothes and food from India and Pakistan: there are at least twenty-two vegetables, which she talks about with great passion because on that land, nothing unpleasant can happen.

Muhammad plays chess because "it's all there: battle and strategy, nothing material, nothing but politics."

Their neighbors hardly notice them, if at all. It's such a silent game, chess. And a neighbor, in Switzerland, is so distant.

When it comes time to retire, the Sualeheen will return to Pakistan. Preferably to a rural area "because they are poorer there, and one could help others." Of their five children, two have already left home. When they've all completed their studies, they will be, God willing, respectively, a doctor, an accountant, a journalist, an engineer and a merchant.

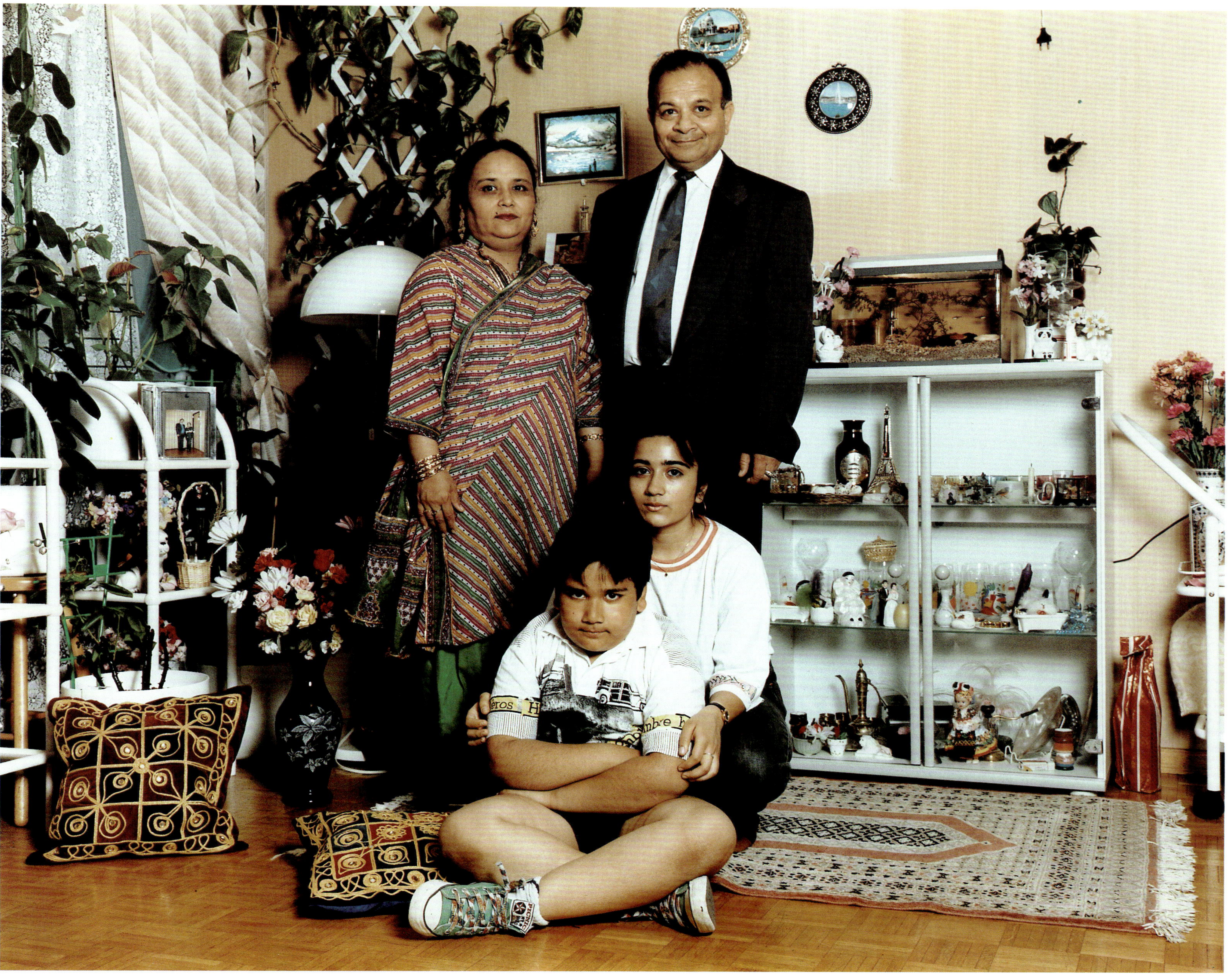

Silvio and Olga Taioli, Italy

Part of the history of Geneva could be told right here, around this table uniting three generations. And in the reconstruction of this history, which the Taioli embody, the full significance of the natural effects of an ordinary emigration would emerge.

Take the men, for example. Silvio knows the dialect of his home region, the Emilia Romagna. His son Angelo speaks Italian. And his son's son, David, who doesn't know the dialect, is uneasy in Italian, and has the strongest command of French, his mother tongue.

Then take the women. One will only get a furtive glimpse of the lovely smile of Olga Taioli, an old-fashioned wife who welcomes you then steps back. Her daughter-in-law Maria, on the other hand, sits down with the men, listens and speaks her mind.

Note the evolution of their professions. At first a mason, Silvio later managed to work in a factory, far from the harsh weather conditions his fragile health required him to avoid. His son Angelo did heavy work before moving into the company offices.... The grandson is a programmer-analyst, a trade very much of his time.

Silvio Taioli is one of those thousands of Italians who in the 1950s came to work in a Switzerland that believed itself to be open and generous whereas in fact it was only in desperate need of docile employees attracted by change and favorable salaries. This display of generosity had its limits, though: seasonal-worker status. You come and work, you get your pay and then you go back home for a few months a year, back home to where you left your children, just in case you should get the idea of digging yourself in somewhere between the Léman and Lake Constance....

Arriving in 1954 in Andermatt, where they lived before moving on to Geneva, Silvio and Olga, only allowed to stay a few months each year, worked at the bottom of the ladder in the building and hospitality industries. Back home in the village, Angelo lived with his grandparents, anxiously awaiting the Christmas holidays, which each year brought a different thrill when the parents returned with their arms full of gifts. The Swiss mirage. Later, abandoning their seasonal status, the parents made their home in Meyrin, being among the first, in 1962, to move into a building they have not left since. Better still, now their descendents have moved in too.

Riddle: which of the three men is Swiss, and which is not? The Swiss is Silvio, the grandfather whose speech is marked by a subtle accent. His was a crisis naturalization: In the 1970s, one part of Switzerland, suddenly tired of its manual laborers, or perhaps concerned about some imaginary damage of the sort that people are always quick to attribute to foreigners, was going through a crisis of xenophobia, with the vigorous support of a politician of the time, James Schwarzenbach. Later, however, neither Angelo nor David in fact felt the need to request naturalized citizenship of a country that had nevertheless become their own, and which they have no intention of leaving. One may read this choice as proof of the recovery of a certain social serenity. One hopes one is not mistaken.

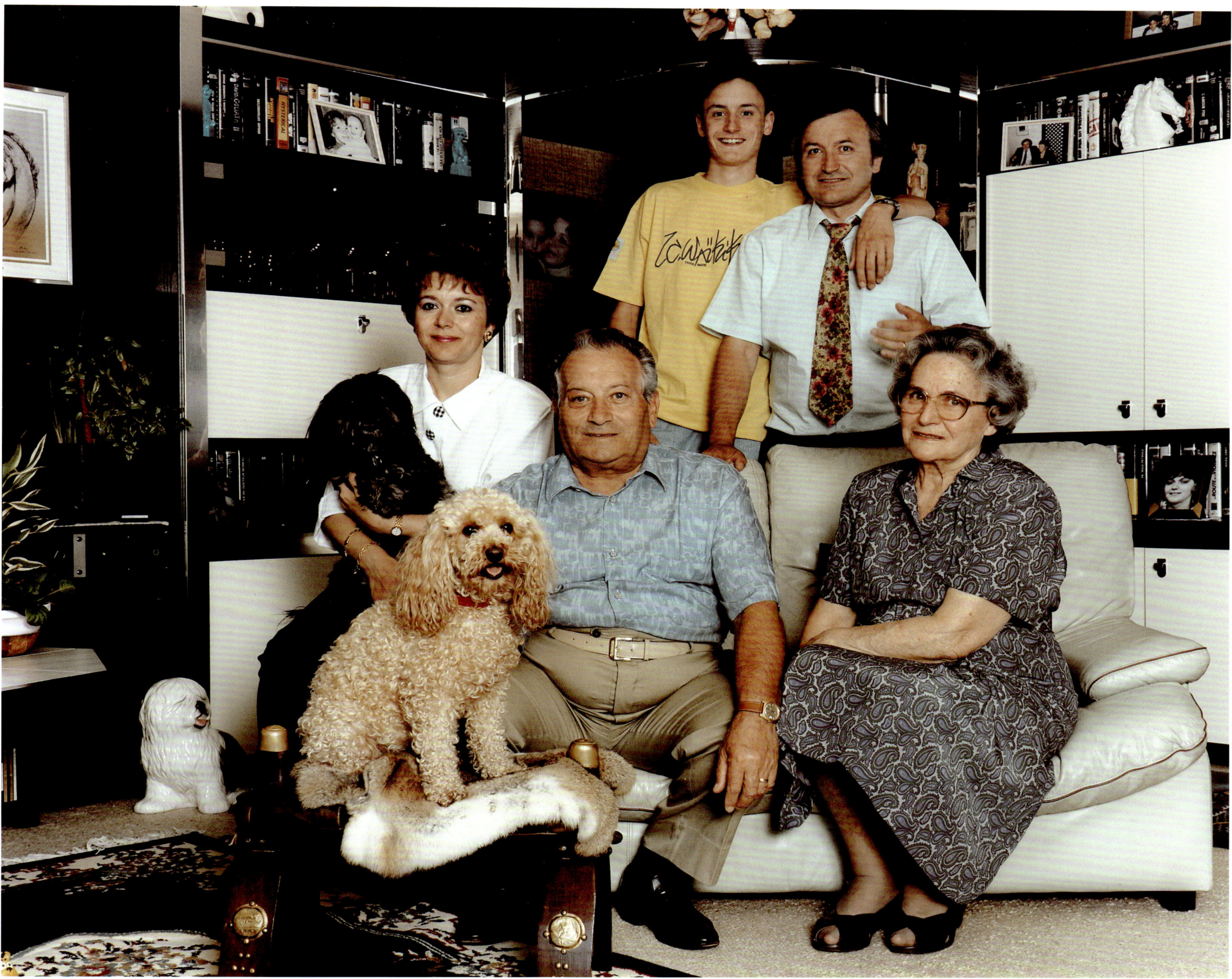

Mussie and Birikti Tesfaï, Eritrea

A total contrast between tradition and modernity: as soon as the photo session is over, Temerza, the eldest child, slips into her blue jeans with a sigh of relief while her mother goes back to making bread—a flat bread made of greyish-brown flour, corn and wheat that have soaked for three days in the bottom of a bucket. At the moment Birikti is spreading out her moist paste in a frying pan, where the fire then catches hold of it. She will then extract thin pancakes from it.

Traditionally, one spreads the bread paste over terracotta. In this tiny kitchen, a sort of round plate surmounted by a pointed hat, looking like a flying saucer on the counter, is an indication that industry has taken the trouble to create modern equivalents. But the mother prefers to work the paste in a frying pan. If the materials are not ideal, and the ingredients less than perfect, no matter: "necessity is the mother of invention." As we say in France: "necessity makes law." One must admit that, while meaning the same thing, the English expression better expresses creativity.

Civil War brought the Tesfaïs to Switzerland via Italy. Appalled by the massacres plunging northern Ethiopia into mourning, Mussie led a march of protesters—legally—and participated in other actions until the day when the Ethiopian embassy in Rome finally refused to renew his papers. Political refugees, the Tesfaïs then chose to go to Geneva, "because of its reputation," and ended up building a nest there.... Their daughters, born in Switzerland, are Meyrinese.

Mussie never became a doctor, though he did study for four years in university before leaving Italy. Today he handles miles and miles of statistics at the UN. An altruist, he participates from afar in an Eritrean children's aide project, for which the city of Meyrin has given him a little money as a gesture of confidence.

In the building's atrium—where the bolts and paint are falling off the walls—a signboard invites the residents to "drink to the health and happiness of all and to turning on the cable."

Six months later.

Back to the Tesfaï house. They've moved. To another place in Meyrin. Coffee. The long braids of another female visitor impress my daughter. They're never satisfied: black women love straight hair and white women love frizzy hair. My daughter will come away this afternoon with her hair tied in corn-rows.

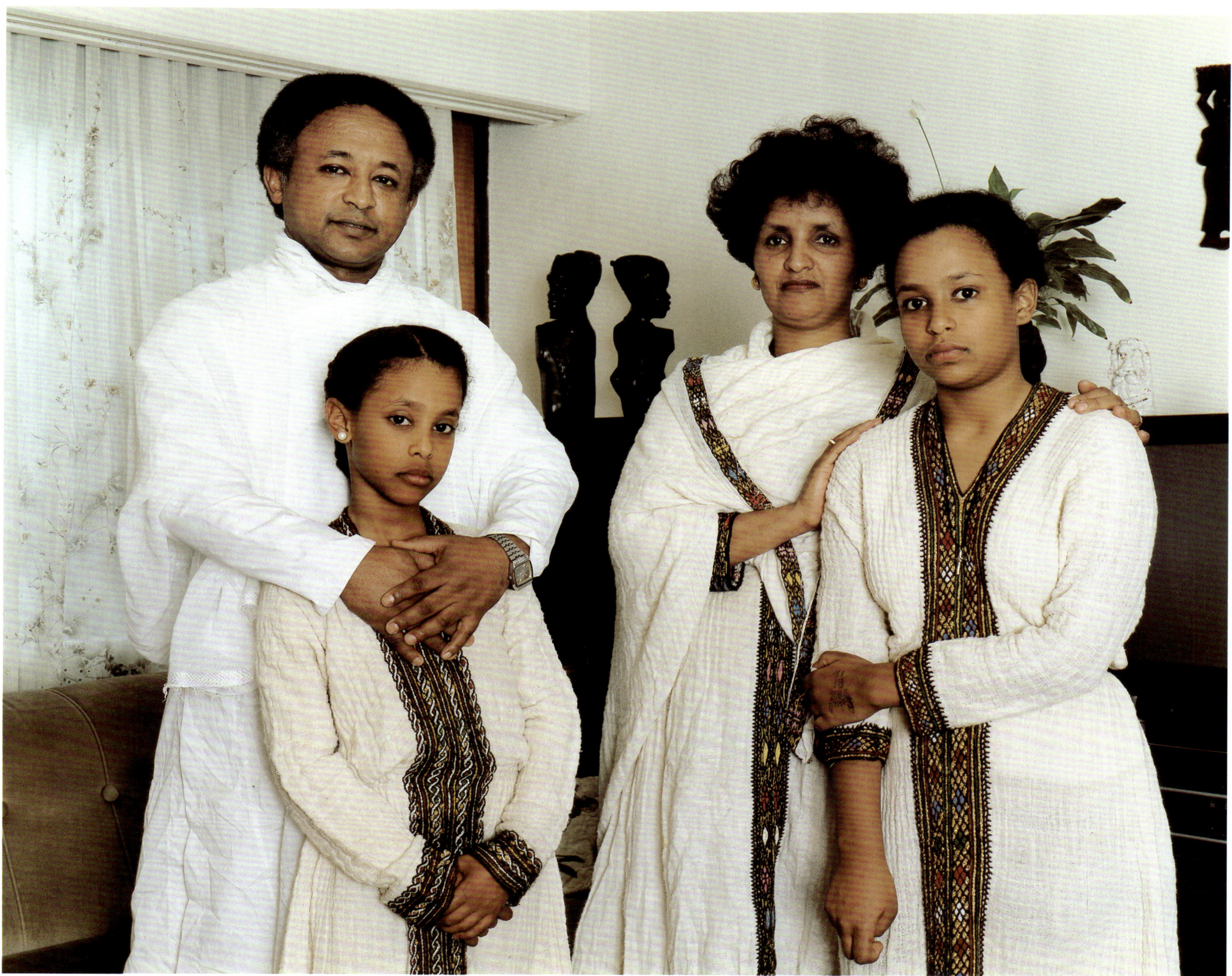

Igor and Olga Tkatchouk, Ukraine

Returning home from an afternoon stroll, a babushka enters with tiny steps, holding a little girl by the hand. I see snatches of the films of Paradjanov, horses of fire, dachas in the Ukraine, the flamboyant lyricism of the little people he portrayed. The old woman guest, like all old women, carries with her a history I'll never know. So I'll just have to imagine it. I see a rural folk bound to the land and to traditions, even superstitions, soon to be confronted with the constructive modernism of an egalitarian state—or a totalitarian one, depending on your point of view.

I see traces of other dreams in the books adorning the library, many of which refer to the cities of Western Europe and America. Paris, New York: elsewhere.

And that plaque.

A panel that the translator picked up from a United Nations desk when the world teetered: Soviet Union. These few letters today remind the world of a fallen empire. They were a sign of strength. The identity of a superpower. In the library, rather second-rate, the plaque remains puzzling.

There are many mysteries in this encounter. A professional reorientation with no details given. In the conversation, no hierarchy is imposed on past and present. What was, was, what will be, will be. It is too early to judge.

Just early enough to consider rebuilding one's life. The world changes and man adapts. Does he really hold the keys?

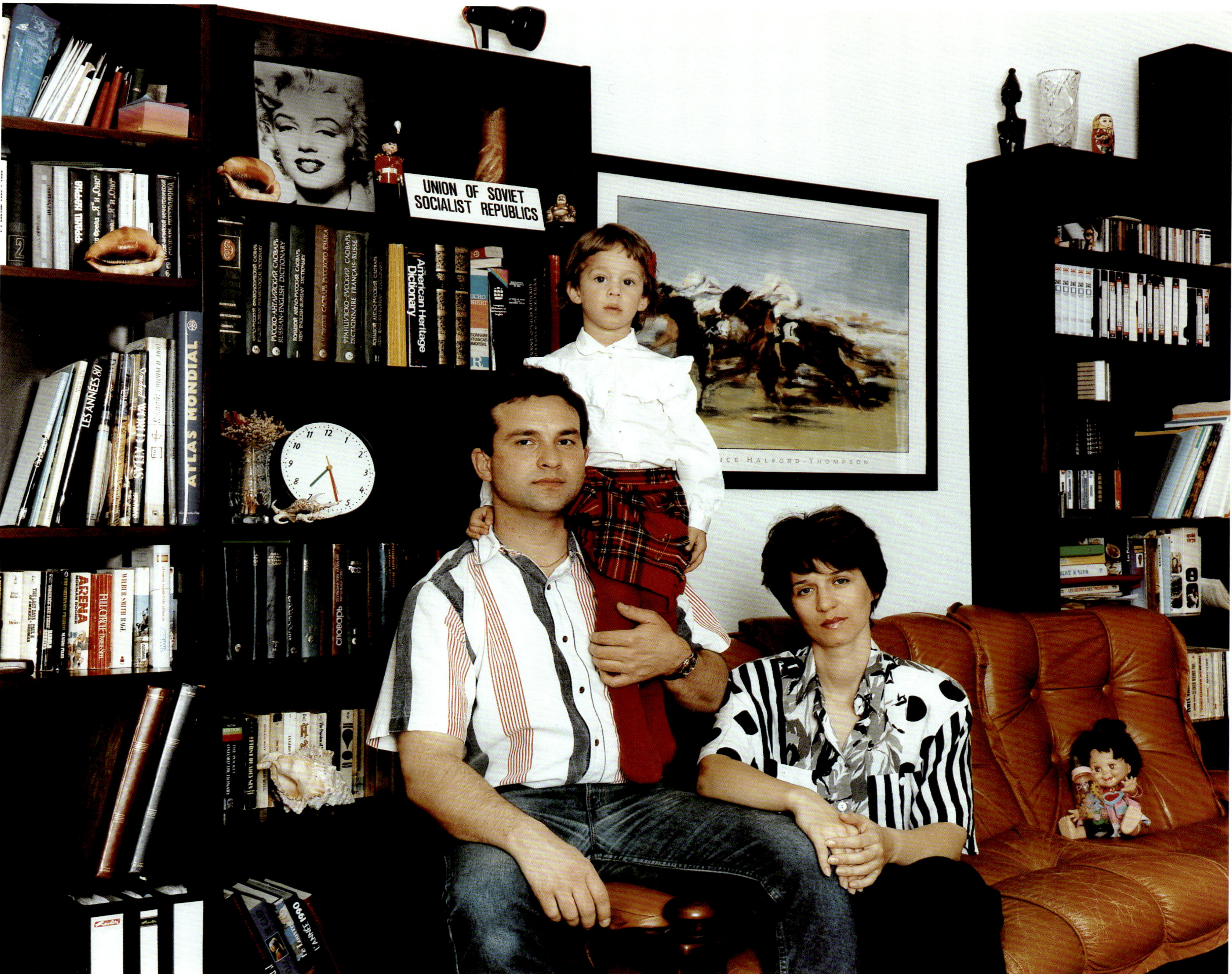
UNION OF SOVIET
SOCIALIST REPUBLICS
American Heritage
Dictionary
ATLAS MONDIAL
LES ANNÉES 80
ARENA
СЛОВАРЬ

Adrian and Maria Tunaru, Rumania

Rumania under the Ceaucescus has often been compared to Kafka's universe. Adrian's account only reconfirms this notion. Here is a man who, as son of a pastor, was subjected to surveillance and searches, and who, in adulthood, found himself blackmailed by the state. He was foreman in the open-cast state coal mines; he had about forty men working under him. It was when the bureaucrats demanded that he enroll in the Communist Party and report on the activities of his co-workers that everything started to go wrong.... He didn't want to become an informer; it would have gone against his Christian faith and his ethics. The Securitate could go to the devil. As of that moment, Adrian lost his job, was looked on with suspicion, made fun of and subjected to constant surveillance. To preserve both his honor and his freedom, he had no choice but to flee.

The point where he chose to cross over into Yugoslavia presented extreme risks, but he didn't know it at the time. Very tricky: it was in fact a sham border blocking the fields! Many an escapee, after crossing this phony line and beginning to relax, had run into an unexpected patrol. For his part Adrian, hiding out for fifteen days, took the time to study the terrain and anticipate the possible traps. Sleeping during the day and inspecting the land at night, thus avoiding soldiers and combines, he never stopped weighing his chances until the very moment when he took the plunge. His first attempt was successful. His brother, who had already fled the country, had had to make four tries and thus spent some very harrowing moments.

Having entered Yugoslavia illegally, without papers of course—a passport being at the time a privilege granted only to the "safest" citizens—Adrian spent some time in prison before being taken to Italy, from where he reached Switzerland. He would wait more than two years before being fully accepted there as a political refugee, a status that would finally enable him to see his wife and children again.

Five years later, the Tunarus followed on television the incredible revolution of December 25, 1989, which would put an end to the regime and to the lives of the Ceaucescu couple. Since then, still a little shocked, suspicious, and subjected to exclusion when visiting Rumania, they have chosen not to return to the land of the Carpathians. Their children, currently stateless, are steeped in Swiss culture. Caroline was even born in Geneva. They are Meyrinese. While Adrian trades in import-export, Maria crosses paths with a whole world in town: she is a cashier at the shopping center.

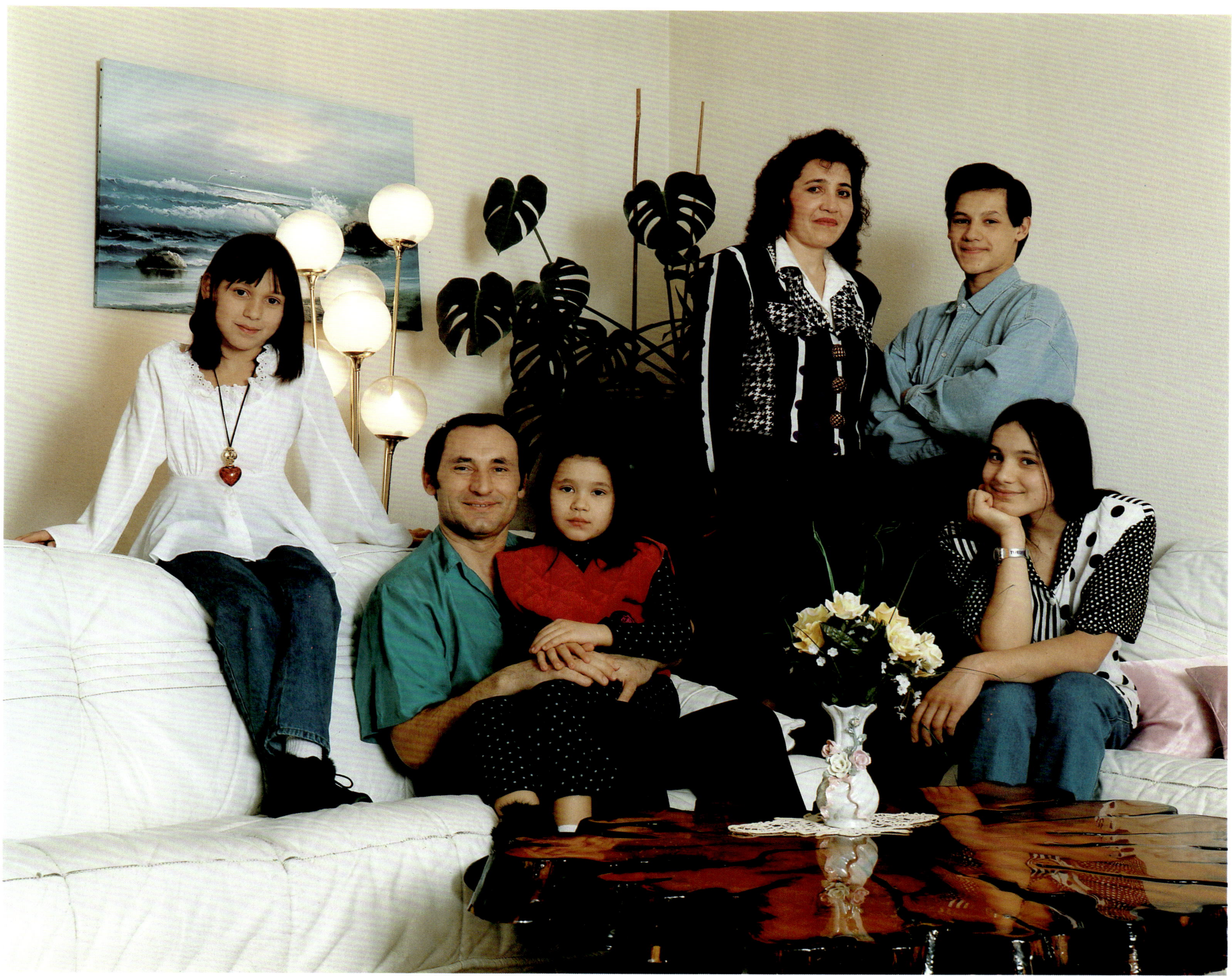

Pyset and Nady Ung, Cambodia

It was the time of Pol Pot. One only had the right to work, not to speak—and there was nothing to eat.

It was the time of large families. Of Nady's four children scattered by the war, none survived.

It was the time when, like so many Cambodian children, Vuthy, at age five, was already working hard. Somewhere, his parents were dead.

It was the time when Cambodia had ceased to be beautiful. Terror can transform the features of cities as well as people.

It was the time when the family and friends of the Ung, with their children, disappeared into the shadows. When the Vietnamese overthrew Pol Pot, there was nothing left; they had no possessions, no friends, no parents, no relatives.

It was the time when, upon meeting Vuthy, the Ungs, like him looking for a family to rebuild, adopted the child, who barely spoke and could only remember his own name but not those of his vanished parents. He was a frightened young bird.

Then came the time of the mined roads that one had to cross without blowing up, the uncertain hell of the Khmer Rouge who, clinging by force and constraint to a lost power, would fire on frightened fugitives, the time of the internment camp in Thailand and temporary emigration to the Philippines.

Then at last came the time of the vain attempts to regain country and serenity, so as to start over again. Before this glimmer of hope, it was Switzerland that responded to the efforts of the Ungs and the Red Cross. Already once burned, the trio didn't feel ready to go on living until the airplane finally landed at Cointrin in June 1982. Three months later, the Ungs were working for an American family before moving into a furnished studio at Carouge, then into a three-room apartment at Châtelaine, just long enough to allow them to understand the Genevan way of life.

Today the hours are punctuated by the laughter of Samaly, born in Meyrin, where the Ungs have begun to live again. In an apartment that runs along on old wall comfortably covered by ivy—a sign of longevity—a few paintings recall the distant country they have never seen since. They have learned the language and way of life of this part of Switzerland. Pyset works in a garage and Nady, a day-nanny, receives children whom she feeds, amuses and educates, fully aware that nothing is more precious than a child's expression of wonder and happiness at a life he finds so beautiful.

Samaly dreams of Cambodia.

Once he has become Swiss, he will surely go there the way one visits the land of one's ancestors: as a foreigner.

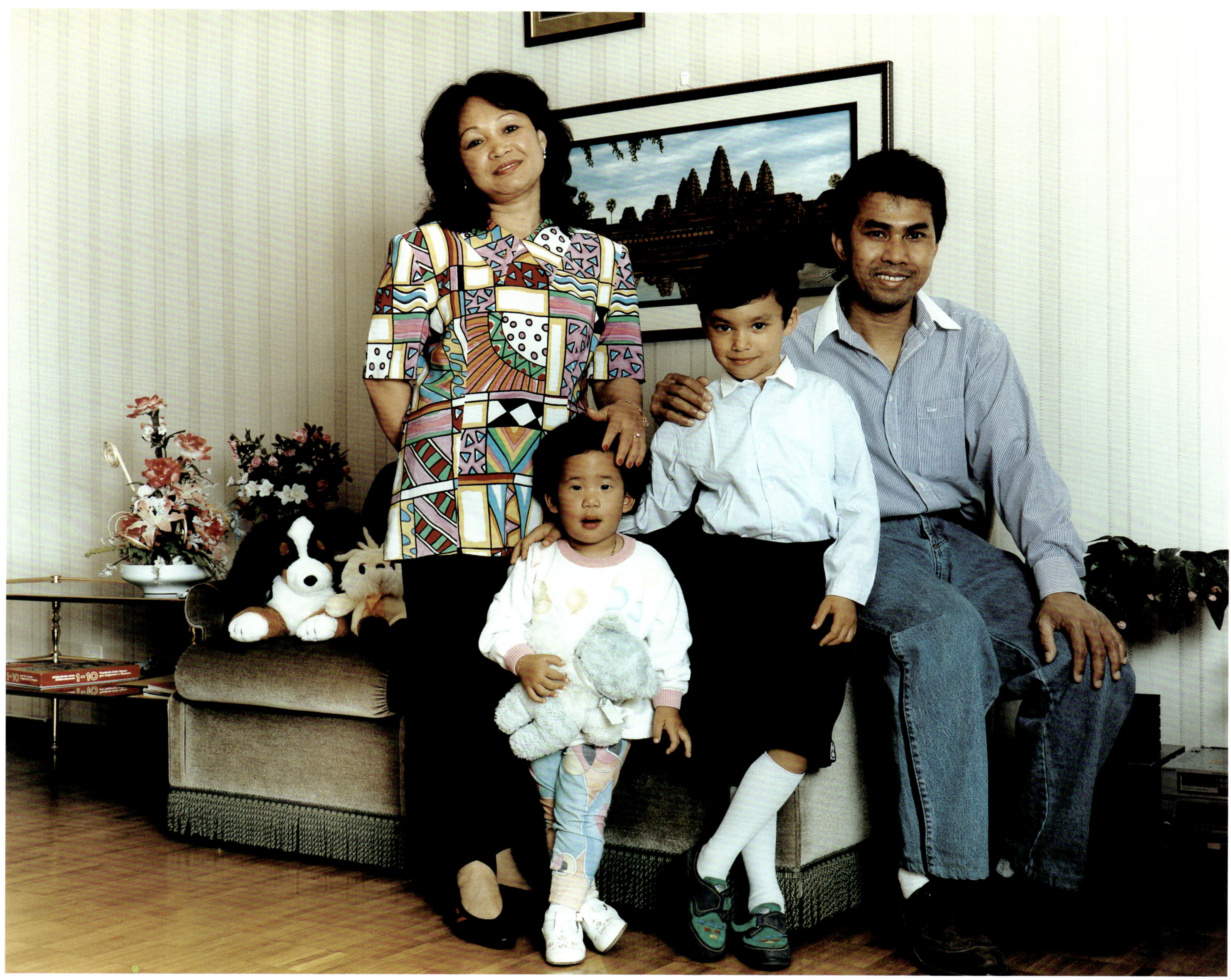

Johann and Mona Van Boetzelaer, Netherlands—Egypt

A line dividing North and South. A symbol par excellence of the international character of Switzerland: he, son of an old Dutch family, came to Zoug to round out his education; she, daughter of a high-level Egyptian economist, moved in with her family in Geneva, where there are many international organizations. Today, loyal to the right bank where their three children are flourishing, Johann and Mona are, respectively, a specialist in maritime trade and transport and a manager of fashion boutiques.

Solid business experience. They chose to live together in Geneva after having traveled about for while: he in Latin America, especially Costa Rica, she in Egypt, where she guided French businesses through the complex administration when the country was opening up to foreign investors. Her punctuality and the precise habits she formed in Geneva have earned her, in Cairo, the nickname of "the Swiss lady," which is intended as a compliment.

Two reformed agitators. Ex-students of the hot years (well, in Switzerland, the warm years). Once in jeans and old sweaters, now it's more like silk and cashmere. The meeting of two cultures: he went to live a while in Egypt "to deepen his understanding of the country"—she, in exchange, knows the Netherlands well. Need for mixing, movement.

Shuttling between Italy and Brazil, their neighbors are also their close friends. One sign is unmistakeable: in the hall of the house that they share, a (huge) single piece of furniture holds the shoes of both families. "It's impossible to live without coming into contact with your neighbors". Children's cries. Balls and bicycles in the courtyard. Fragrance of life. "There are people better off here than in Egypt who never smile, whereas in Cairo, even the poor—who often are very poor—take pleasure in smiling!" It's a bit uptight, though, Geneva. "I've lived in luxury. In beautiful neighborhoods. It was terrible: people didn't speak to one another." Long live Meyrin, as it were.

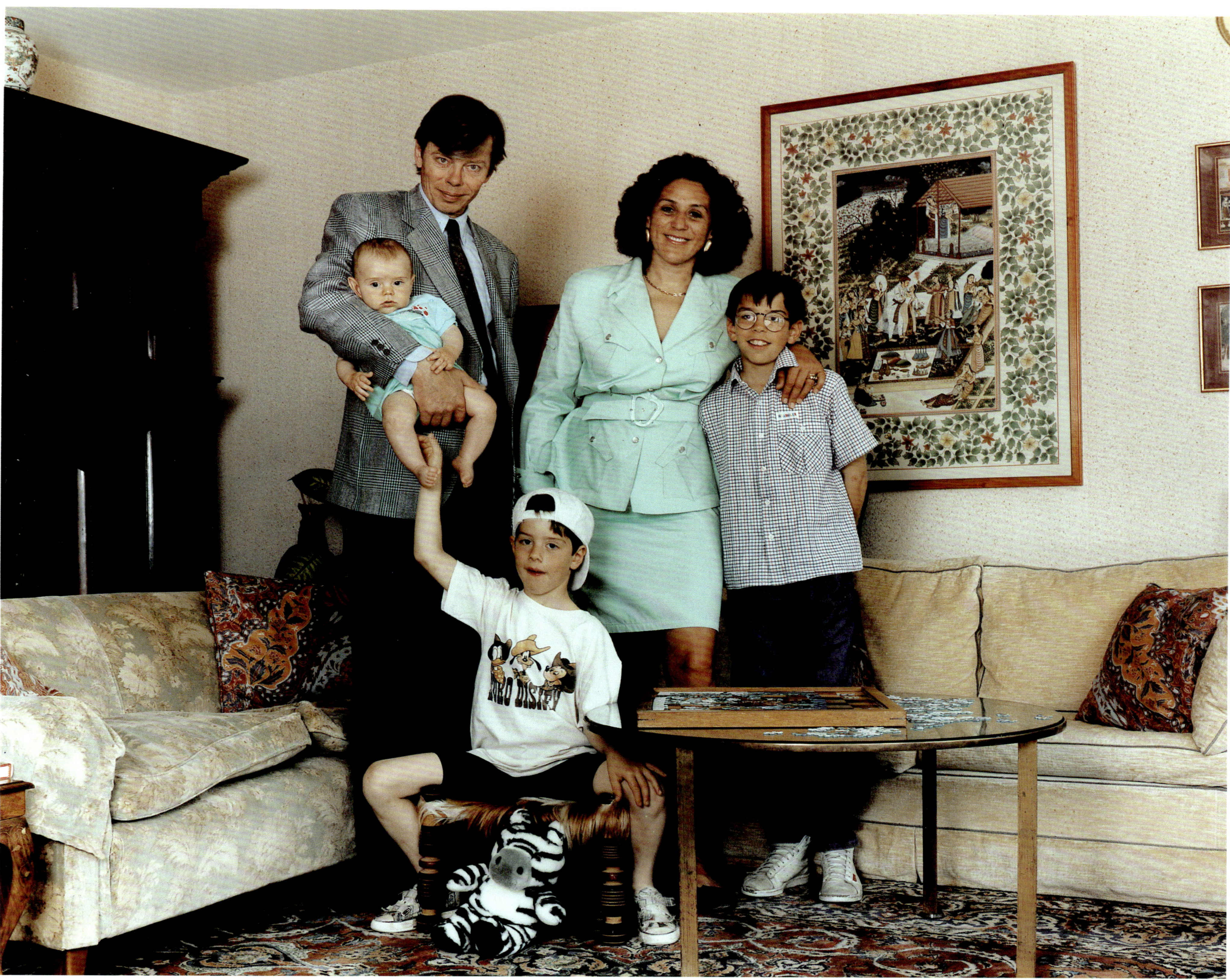

Jos and Hilda Vlogaert, Belgium

It could be a Flemish painting. But it's the inhabitants of the house that are Flemish. The painting is Meyrinese. A good story: the portrait is of the mother of the abbot du Mont, a popular curé who celebrated the Mass for twenty-eight years at Meyrin-Village. What is that painting doing here, and what is its history? Initially, a loving painter immortalised his wife. Their son, having become a priest, obviously did not provide for any descendants, and so he gave a few paintings away as gifts to his friends in the parish. The Vlogaerts figured among these friends. And that's how the mother of Monsieur l'abbé ended up in this living room.... A house of God: the crucifix is one sign. On the table, near an edition of *Le Monde*, the Catholic daily *Le Courrier* discreetly confirms a family commitment which Jos and Hilda speak of rather sparingly. The only healthy commitment is that which is untainted by pride.

Christ had stones thrown at him along the Way of the Cross. The Vlogaerts confess with a smile that they too, in their youth, became experts at heaving paving stones. A few Belgian gendarmes may still resent them for it. Louvain was demonstrating; Louvain la Flamande—the "real" Louvain—wanted to "drive the Walloons out." To this day the Vlogaerts, should they return to their now federalized Belgium, cannot imagine not fighting for a strong Flanders, a Flanders that would no longer drag Wallonia along like a ball-and-chain but would live alone with her industries and her loves with the nearby Ruhr.

Jos Vlogaert was working at the Catholic university of Louvain when the chance for an apprenticeship at the IAEA presented itself. A three-year contract to work on an accelerator project. The magnetism typical of this nest of researchers has bound him to them ad aeternum. Thus, once he was convinced, he spent days at the land registry actively searching for a suitable plot of land, in Meyrin, so as to build a house there. Piter and Joris, his sons, were born in Switzerland but remain Belgian. Unlike many Meyrinese children of foreign parents, they do not necessarily plan to live their adult lives in Switzerland. Piter will perhaps become a historian, preferably a researcher at—guess where, and why not?—Louvain-la-Neuve.

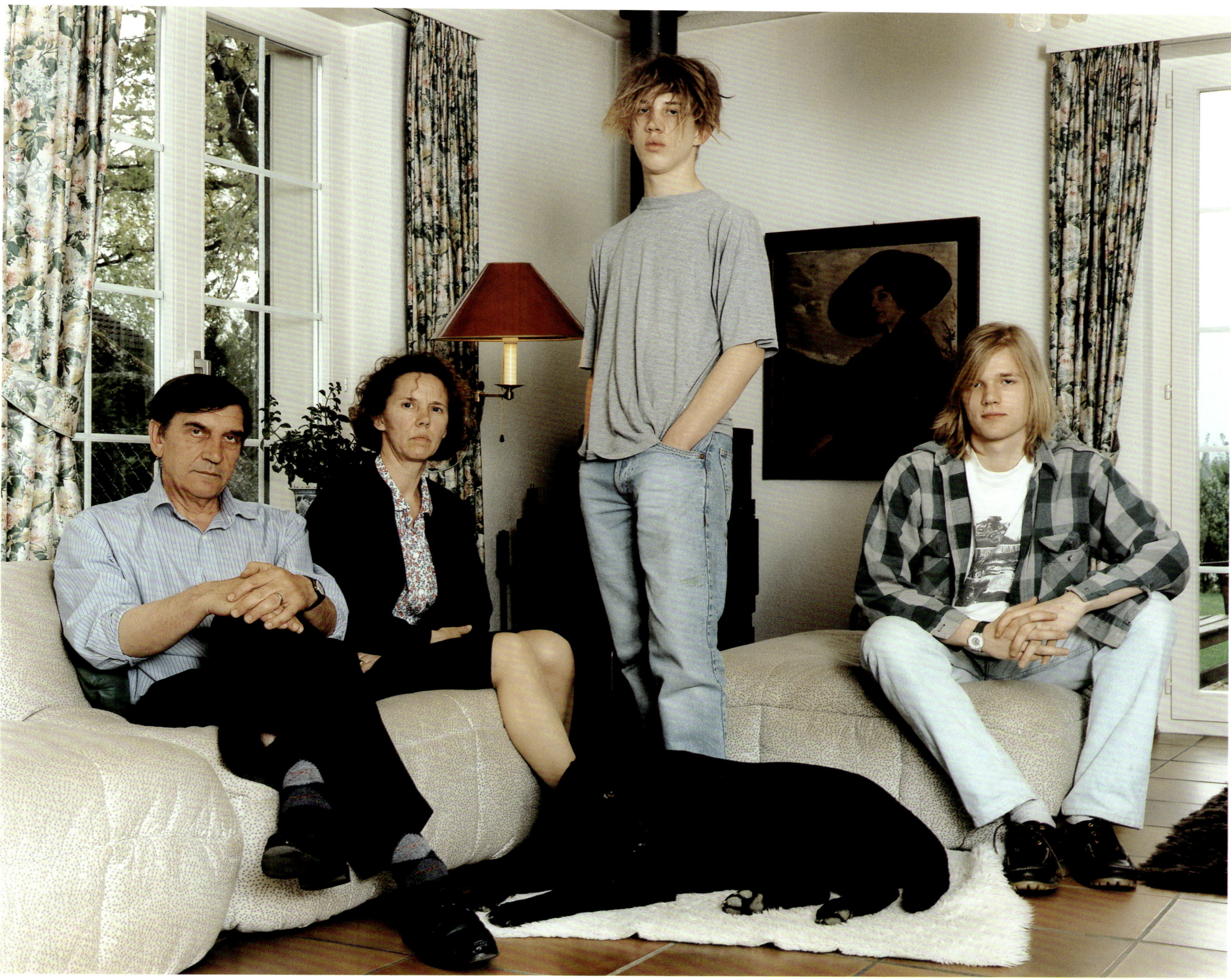

Palitha Wieckramasinghe, Sri Lanka

His parents had four daughters.
He was the son.

His sisters each have five children.
He has none.

His father was an important tea merchant.
He was not drawn to business.

His sisters married countrymen.
He fell for a Swiss woman.

That was in Paris.
Then they came to Meyrin.

She left.
He stayed.

With his reveries.
With his painting.

A lab assistant by day,
A painter by night.

Bunches of orchids.
Smoking his pipe.

He knows the secret to integration:
"Respect the culture and the laws."

Citizen of the world
With a passion for the mountains.

Radiant.

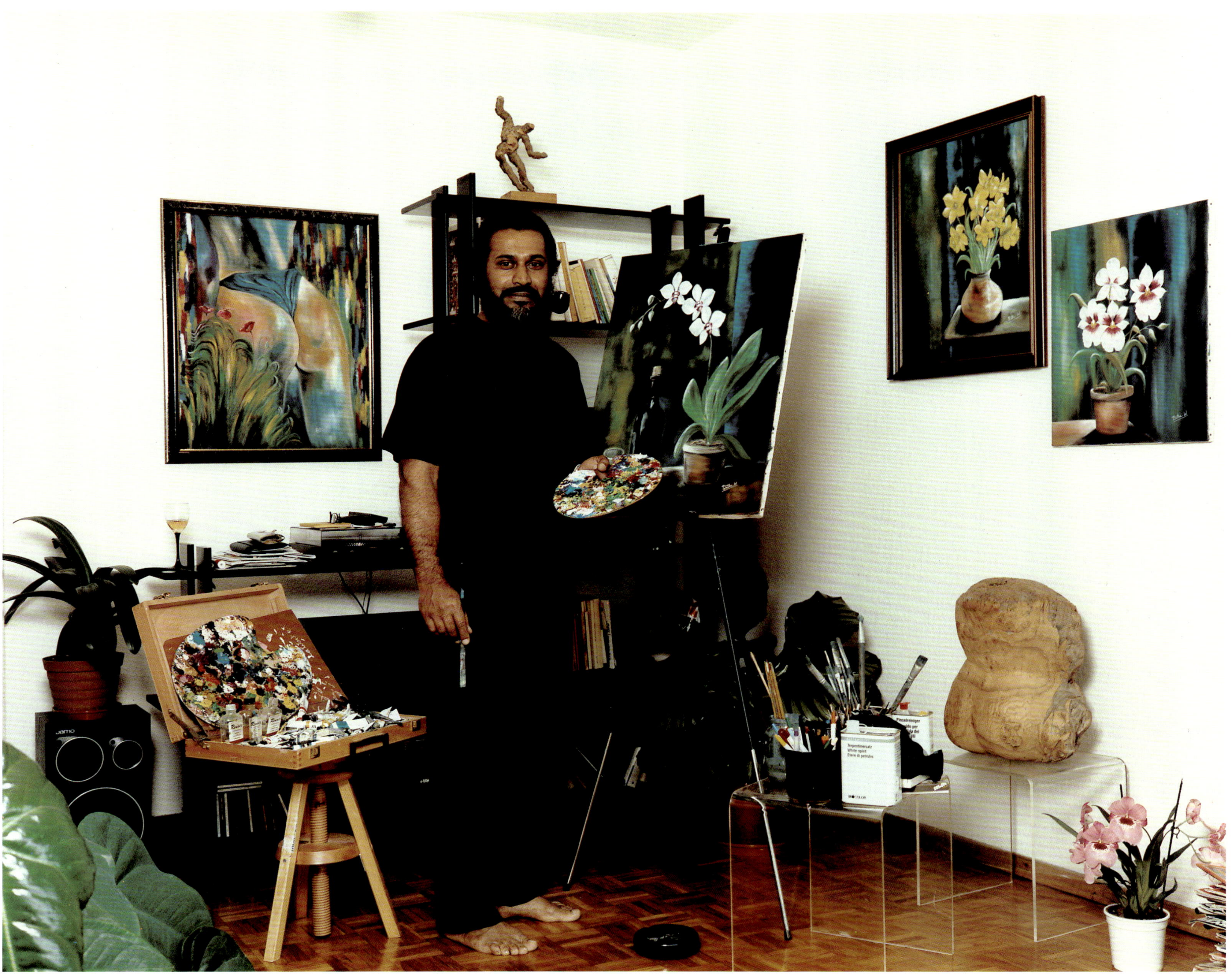
jamo
Pinselreiniger
Terpentinersatz
White-spirit
Etere di petrolio

Jaroslava and Milan Zoubek, (former) Czechoslovakia

In 1968, the Soviet tanks took up positions in the streets of Prague and put an end to the mad hope of liberalizing the regime. The repression began and the controls tightened. The prophecy uttered by Churchill as soon as the Yalta accords were signed came true, while an insuperable wall in Berlin already separated the two worlds. An "iron curtain" had fallen over Europe, and Soviet power, that big brother whose model was forced upon the countries under its influence, tightened the screws as far west as the St. Charles bridge, where the sight of Soviet officers visiting a surrounded city was to become commonplace. The playwright Vaclav Havel would go to prison for crimes of opinion. Later, when the regime was teetering, the same man would rise to the office of President of a Czechoslovak Republic finally rid of her red stars, then would bear witness to the country's split, desired by Parliament, into the Czech Republic (with Prague as capital) and Slovakia (with Bratislava as capital).

Milan's mother, sisters and brother fled Czechoslovakia in 1968 and went to Switzerland. In the days of the dictatorship, rebellion in the family was a bad mark in a citizen's dossier. As the authorities had taken away his passport, Milan's hands were tied. When, in 1980, the precious document was returned to him, he slipped off to Switzerland in search of political refugee status. Jaroslava, his wife, would remain in place for another year before joining him in Meyrin with their son Daniel, not yet eleven years old. There they discovered color television and exotic fruits as well as the most precious possession of all: personal freedom.

A harsh immersion in another universe whose language was in no way similar to their own. At school, placed straight into fifth grade without even passing the reception classes specifically geared to facilitate the integration of foreigners in trouble, Daniel was subject to all sorts of bullying, which he wouldn't even talk about until much later: when he didn't understand the nasty remarks made in French, they thought he was faking it. This experience would leave its mark.

An electrical engineer, Milan found work at the Sécheron works. Jaroslava, a seamstress, retrained herself in Meyrin to work in electro-acoustics until the company employing her left one day for Singapore, after which Chopard would hire her golden fingers for the production of delicate watchbands. The Zoubeks now only leave their adoptive community on weekends, when they go to a camp site in France, where they have a caravan. They dream of a peaceful life and savor the success of their gamble with destiny. Outside the factory, their life is divided between the countryside and their apartment. Still an inveterate romantic by his own admission, Milan, who once wanted to be a forest ranger, devotes himself religiously to his two great passions, nature and DIY.

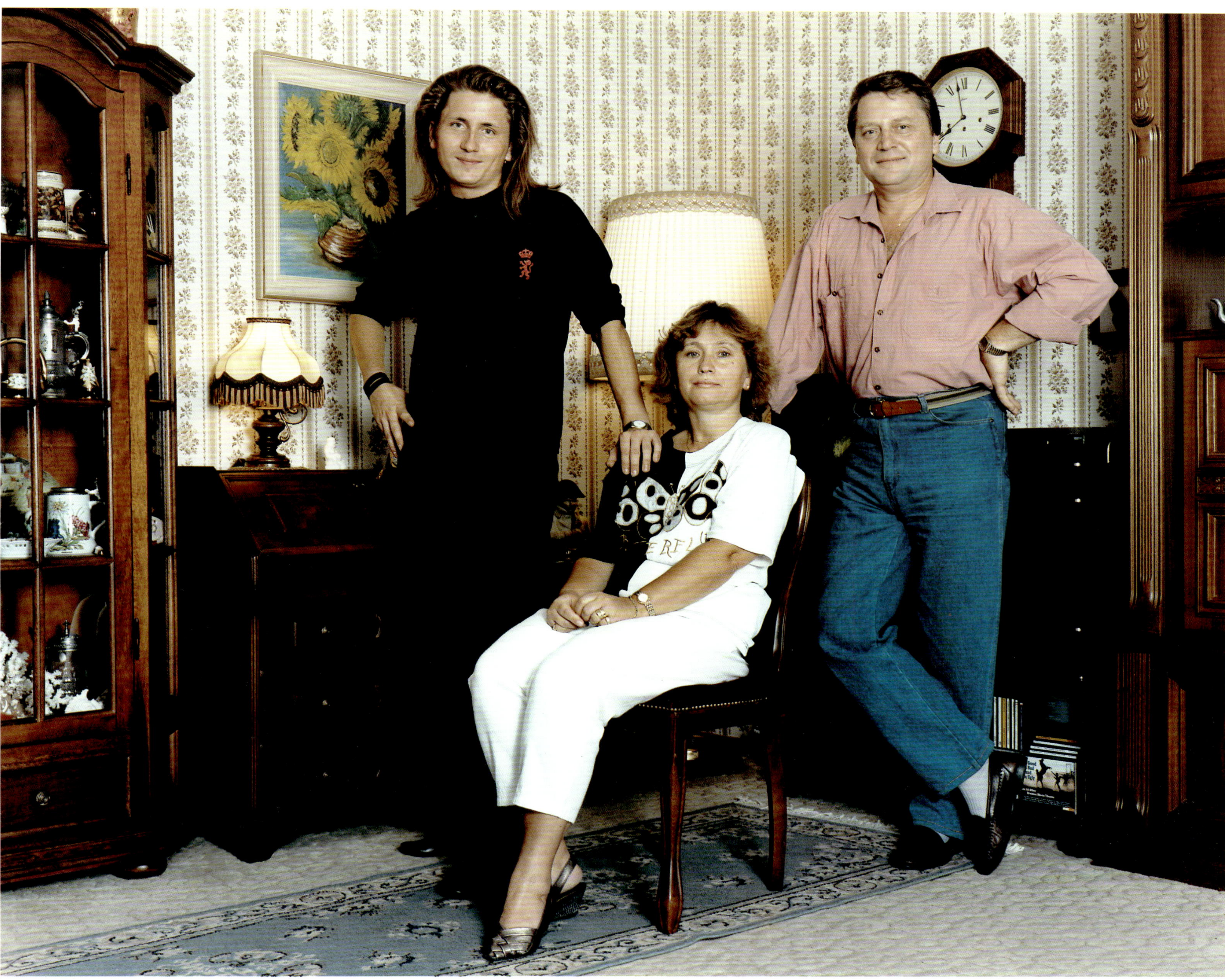

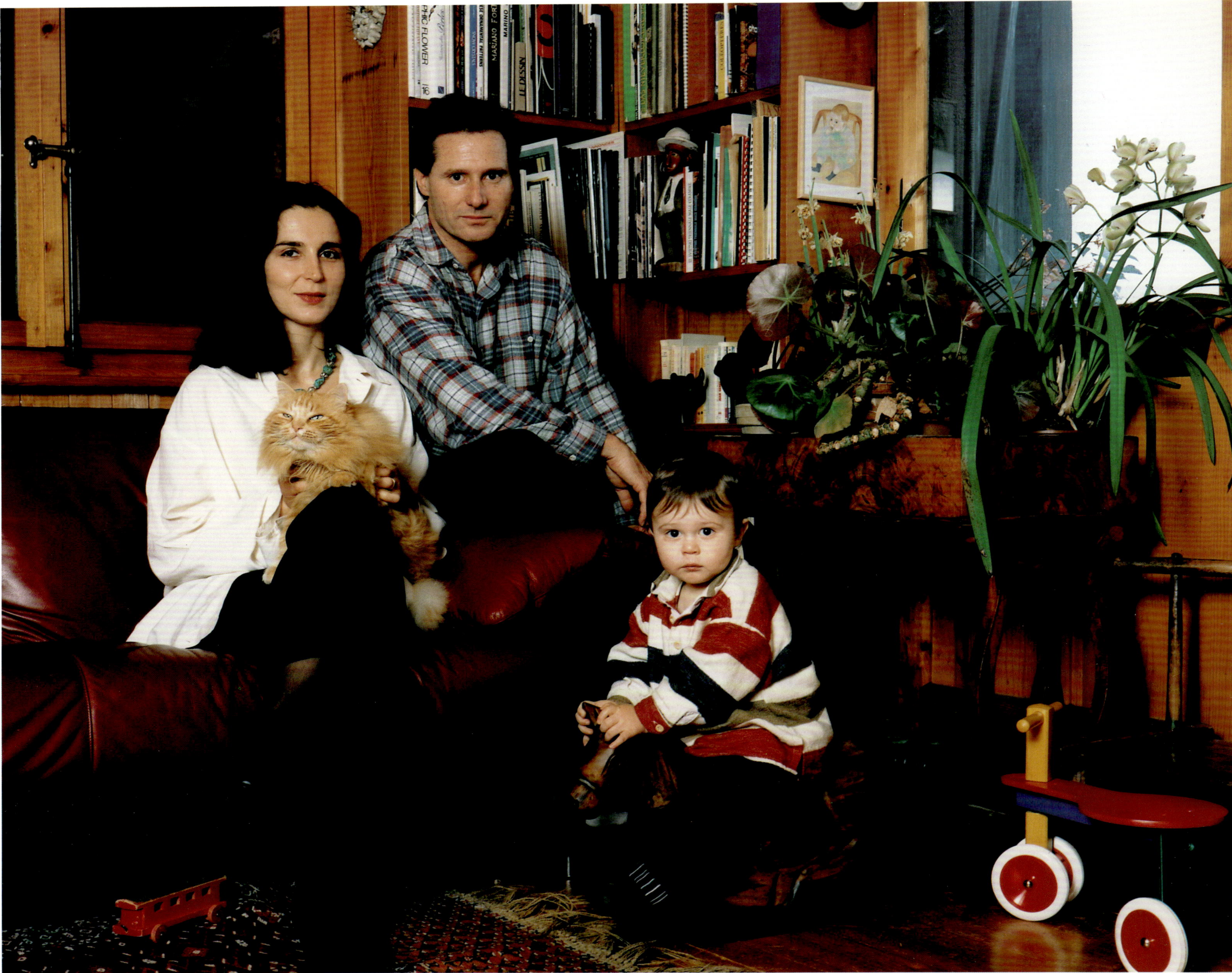
FLOWER
16
ORNAMENTAL PATTERNS
MARINO
LE DESSN

Nicolas Faure, Sophie and Mathias

The Photographer

He was an excellent jeweller. But when his apprentice gave notice to devote himself to other passions, Gilbert Albert must have said to himself: "That's it." But Nicolas is not the sedentary type. He needs to move, to know the world. May 1968 was not long past. The heady atmosphere of the student revolt was still hovering over an entire generation. Long-haired hippies took to the road dreaming of music and brotherhood. Nicolas, who played the guitar himself, was to follow them and roam the world for four years, heading for Asia. With a long stop in Beirut, where he settled just a stone's throw away from the rue Biblos, so famous for its night clubs (there is hardly a country in the world without its nighttime "Biblos"), the jeweller plied his trade. Until the day when he resumed his travels, and came to know by turns hospitality and contempt. There was a stop in Saudi Arabia, then the crossing of the Iran-Iraq border, already bristling with half-buried cannons in the Shah's day, then an attempt at settling down temporarily in Japan.... It was there, perhaps, that his life began to teeter.

If he had not then returned briefly to Geneva, would he have let himself drift from meeting to meeting towards New York before moving there for seven years? It was in the Merce Cunningham circle that he discovered the thrill of the Big Apple, at the heart of a Factory filled with names like Patti Smith and Andy Warhol. He made his first attempts at photography, classics of the gifted beginner: spots of color, onlookers, Manhattan. Taken on by *Geo* magazine to do a report on the dregs of society over a two-year period—the piece was never published because it was deemed too subversive—he searched through garbage cans, discovered a cemetery of airplanes, studied his fellow humans, observed their way of life.

Sophie Honegger also searches through garbage cans. There are treasures to be found there, like the ravioli mould she has recycled to work the soil. The soil is an important thing in the Faure household. First of all, there is a splendid garden, at the entrance to which sits a hieratic block put there by Francis Traunig, in homage to an exhibition of photos of glacial stones realized by Nicolas. That was where we first met. I had gone to see the show; we spoke; I didn't know he was the photographer. Then there is the studio: the cauldron of an alchemist who turns soil into ceramics. It ranges from zen to baroque: sculptures, utilitarian objects, jewelry. A very beautiful place, very secret too. I had to insist before being allowed inside. A creator's jewel-box is a very intimate thing. Upstairs, behind the wood living room serving as playground for a fox-colored tomcat and Mathias, who wasn't even born when we first started our survey of Meyrin, Nicolas takes me back into the office where the large-format prints of the book are sitting. Everything is picture-perfect. Contrast.

Everything falls into place: it was while photographing Meyrin for a competition that he got the idea to go and meet the people, at home. Since then, Sophie has brought him into this family home, and five years later, it is as a fellow-citizen that Nicolas has immortalized the people of Meyrin. It's still the world, but concentrated now. He blends in with it in order to work, and soars above it in order to relax. He's a poet, a bird, a deltaplane madman, a solitary dreamer who takes to the skies. Fire, earth, air.

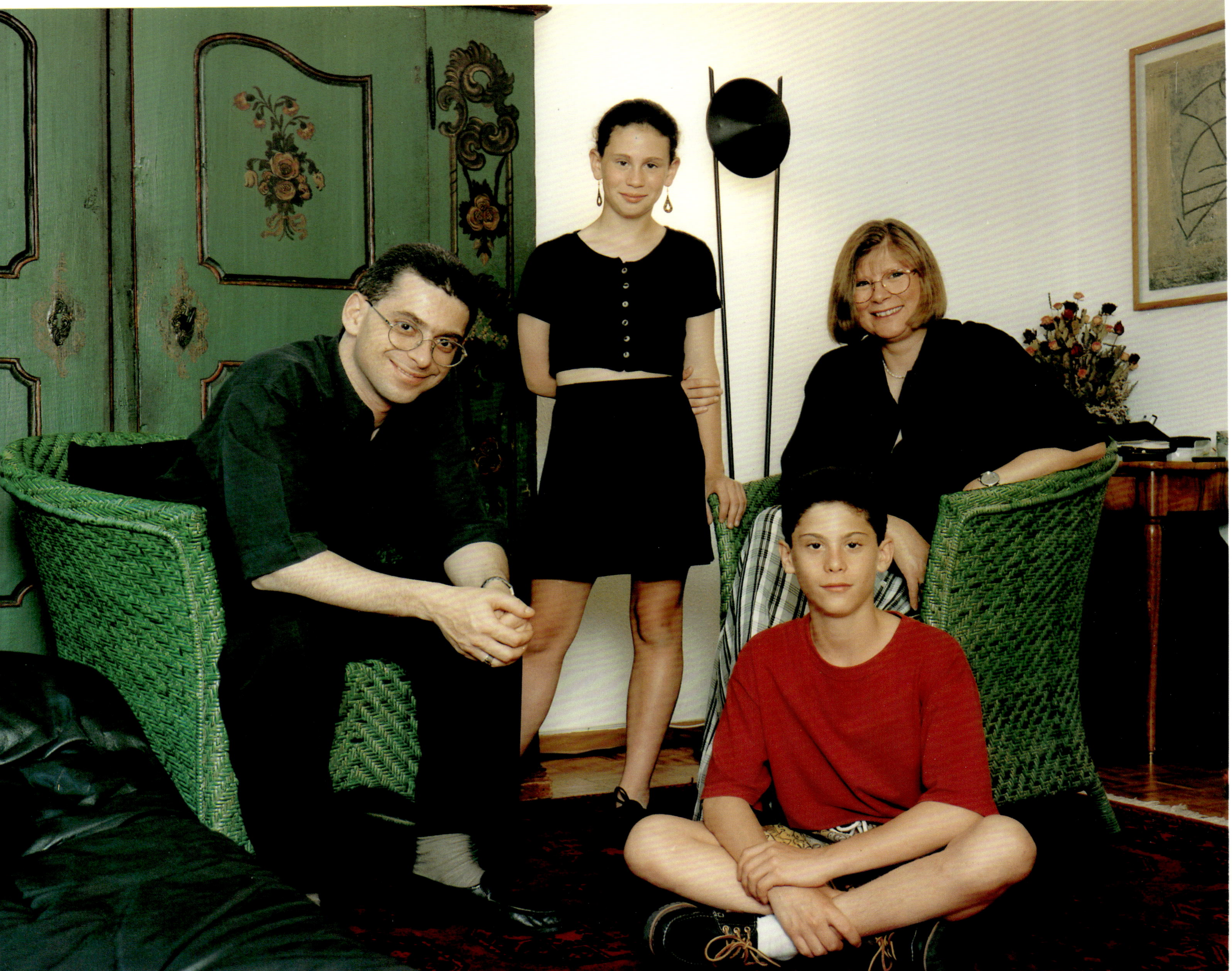

André Klopmann, Nicole, Sarah and Dimitri

The Author

At age ten I was very proud of a sort of floppy jacket I used to wear on rainy days: it was my "reporter's coat." I used to read the adventures of Jacques Rogy unaware that the character was inspired by a real-life journalist, Jacques Derogy. I was later to become an admirer. I would have to meet him. At age ten I also discovered the theatre. Maurice Aufair was starring in Molière's *Le Malade imaginaire* in the courtyard of l'Ecolint. It was a shock to me, and I was to become an admirer of his as well. He sometimes performed on Monday evenings on the radio, in detective plays that I would listen to with the sound turned down low. André Faure often played the heavy: as I was to learn twenty years later, he was Nicolas's father. I love it when paths cross like that.

Was it going to be theatre or journalism? My only diploma is from the Geneva conservatory. On the theatre side, I learned, acted, and still write. In the way of journalism, I had a trick. If I wanted to meet someone, it was very simple: I would phone them and tell them my age—about fifteen—and I would offer to interview them. Often, out of curiosity no doubt, they would accept. Albert Cohen was one such person. I remember the encouragement he gave me at his home, dressed up in his "national costume," his dressing gown, in front of a mantelpiece dominated by the photo of an academician bearing the dedication: "I am happy, my dear Albert, that you have picked up your golden pen again." It was signed Marcel Pagnol. I was very impressed. One day Cohen even introduced me to François Mitterrand, who hadn't yet become president of France. I put into practice the advice this fine author gave me—"always do what you have to do"—and went around with my pages, prying open the doors, windows and chimneys of editorial offices. And they began to publish my writings, perhaps out of curiosity as well.

Was it going to be theatre or journalism? I was seventeen and acting in *The Diary of Anne Frank*. I had just met her father, Otto Frank. No sooner had the interview appeared in print than Claude Richoz, editor-in-chief of *La Suisse*, invited my parents and me to meet with him: I was given a job. That decided me. I was hungry to meet people, to make new discoveries. When Yves Montand, with a dreamy, envious expression, put his hands on the blossoming, pregnant belly of Nicole—my wife and accomplice, who would abandon film-editing to raise children—I realized how privileged I was. Except for Bob Dylan, whom I only caught a glimpse of in a bar one evening, I've shot the breeze with just about everyone I've been interested in or passionate about. Preferably in their homes. Lino Ventura, Miles Davis, Charles Trenet, Woody Allen, Jean Piaget have all enriched my life, each in his own way, although no more than the farmers of Lavaux or Kosovo have done—and no more than the foreign residents of Meyrin.

I am always on the move. Radio, TV, paper: I think, I speak, I write. And I see my children grow: she's a math freak, he's an artist—pure-bred Genevans whose great grandparents, from Poland, German, Belgium and Serbia, were also immigrants.

Acknowledgements

I would like to express my heartfelt gratitude to the people who so kindly agreed to be photographed. Without their trust and spontaneity, these photographs would not exist.

I would also like to extend my special thanks to those people of Meyrin who supported this project with their encouragement. Thanks as well to the Commune of Meyrin for their generosity and understanding. I am particularly grateful to Messrs Michel Aebischer and Roger Portier. To all I am indebted for the trust they accorded me.

Thanks also to Mme Sasà Hayes for her invaluable collaboration at the start of this work, and to Messrs. Philippe Donzé and Jean-Jacques Maspero.

It is thanks to the City of Meyrin, the Office fédéral de la culture (OFC, Berne), and the Fonds Rapin (Geneva), that this project could be realized.

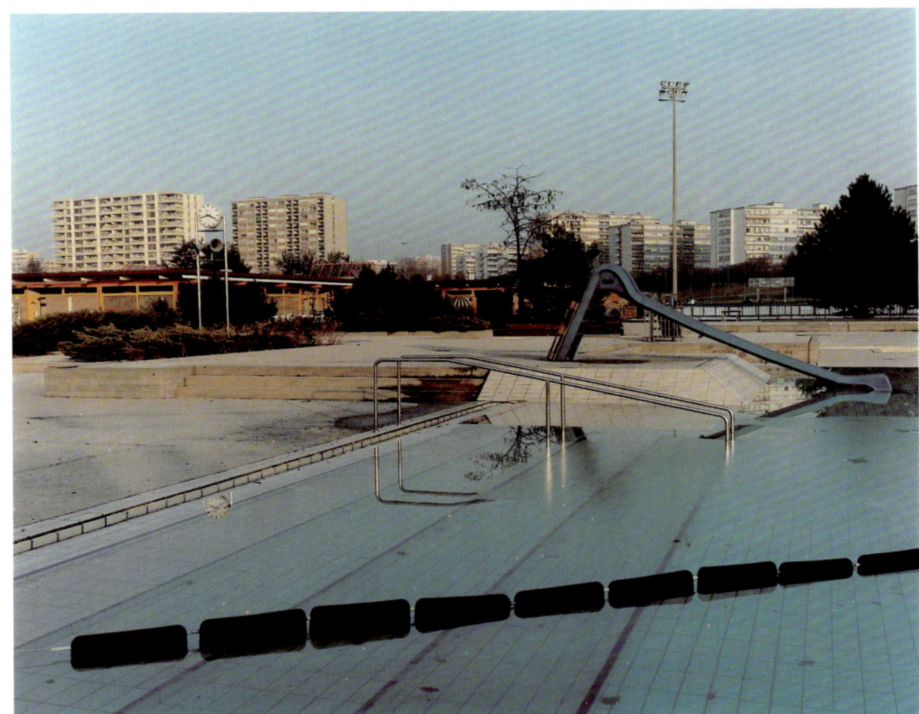

Without the written participation of André Klopmann, these photographs would have remained "mute." He has all my thanks for the added dimension his testimonies have given to this work.

Also heartfelt thanks to Mr Maurice Vouga who, with the quality of his prints, was able to give this work its necessary brilliance.

Lastly, many thanks to Mr. Joseph Julmy from Diaprint and to Swissair for their helpful collaboration.

Nicolas Faure